HEGEMONY OR EMPIR

Hegemony or Empire?
The Redefinition of US Power under George W. Bush

Edited by

CHARLES-PHILIPPE DAVID
University of Québec at Montréal, Canada

and

DAVID GRONDIN
University of Ottawa, Canada

ASHGATE

Published by
Ashgate Publishing Limited
Gower House
Croft Road
Aldershot
Hampshire GU11 3HR
England

Ashgate Publishing Company
Suite 420
101 Cherry Street
Burlington, VT 05401-4405
USA

Ashgate website: http://www.ashgate.com

British Library Cataloguing in Publication Data
Hegemony or empire? : the redefinition of US power under
    George W. Bush
    1.National security - United States 2.World politics - 21st
    century 3.United States - Foreign relations - 21st century
    4.United States - Foreign public opinion
    I.David, Charles Philippe II. Grondin, David
    327.7'3'0090511

Library of Congress Cataloging-in-Publication Data
Hegemony or empire? : the redefinition of US power under George W. Bush / edited by
Charles-Philippe David and David Grondin.
        p. cm.
    Includes index.
    ISBN 0-7546-4774-9
    1. United States--Foreign relations--2001- 2. Imperialism. 3. Hegemony--United
States. 4. World politics--1995-2005. 5. Balance of power. 6. Bush, George W.
(George Walker), 1946- I. David, Charles-Philippe. II. Grondin, David.

    JZ1480.H45 2006
    327.73--dc22

    ISBN-10: 0 7546 4774 9
    ISBN-13: 978-0-7546-4774-4

2006007251

Printed and bound in Great Britain by Antony Rowe Ltd, Chippenham, Wiltshire.

Contents

List of Figures

List of Contributors

Onnig Beylerian   Onnig Beylerian teaches international security and US foreign policy in the Department of Political Science at the Université du Québec à Montréal. He has co-edited in 2004 a book on great powers and international security institutions in the aftermath of the Cold War.

Stephen Clarkson   Over a career in which he worked in a number of fields, Stephen Clarkson's main expertise remains the dynamics of the Canadian-American relationship, so that North America's challenges in the wake of the crisis provoked by the terrorist attacks on September 11th remain central to his interests. Following graduate studies at Oxford (as a Rhodes scholar) and the Sorbonne in Paris (where he did his doctorate), Clarkson began teaching political economy at the University of Toronto. After publishing the fruit of his first research focus, the Soviet model of development, Clarkson also taught and wrote on Canadian foreign policy, federal party politics, and, following an unsuccessful campaign for the mayoralty of Toronto in 1969, municipal politics. He then developed an interest in the relationship of the other superpower with its large, strategically located, but weaker neighbour, Canada, writing *Canada and the Reagan Challenge: Crisis and Adjustment 1981–85* (Canadian Institute for Economic Policy, 1982; 2nd ed., Lorimer, 1985), which won the John Porter prize.

After Pierre Trudeau's retirement from active politics in 1984, he spent a decade co-authoring with his wife, Christina McCall, a two-volume biography of Canada's most charismatic prime minister, which won the Governor-General's award for non-fiction and the John Dafoe prize. More recently, he spent a year in Italy studying the European Union's alternative model to NAFTA for continental governance, and then, thanks to a Killam fellowship and a fellowship at the Woodrow Wilson Center in Washington, he was able to research and write his last book – *Uncle Sam and Us* – that assessed the impact of globalization and neoconservatism on the Canadian state. Stephen Clarkson is now working on the nature of North American governance under NAFTA. He was inducted in the Royal Society of Canada in 2004. In 2004–2005, he was Virtual Scholar in Residence for the Law Commission of Canada.

Simon Dalby   Simon Dalby is Professor in, and Chair of, the Department of Geography and Environmental Studies at Carleton University in Ottawa where he teaches courses on environment and geopolitics. He holds a PhD from Simon Fraser University in Vancouver and is author of *Creating the Second Cold War* (Pinter and Guilford, 1990) and *Environmental Security* (University of Minnesota Press, 2002) and co-editor of *The Geopolitics Reader and Rethinking Geopolitics* (both published by Routledge in 1998). A second edition of *The Geopolitics Reader* was published in 2005.

Charles-Philippe David Dr. Charles-Philippe David is, since 1996, Full Professor of Political Science, Director of the Centre for United States Studies, and Raoul Dandurand Chair of Strategic and Diplomatic Studies at the University of Québec at Montréal. He was elected member of the Royal Society of Canada in 2001 and was recipient of the Jean Finot Award of the Institute of France in 2003. He was Professor of Strategic Studies at former Canadian Military College, Saint-Jean sur Richelieu, from 1985 to 1995.

Professor David is a specialist in strategy, defense, conflict and peace missions. He has published a dozen books in French, including *Au sein de la Maison-Blanche : La formulation de la politique étrangère américaine* (Presses de l'Université Laval, 2004), *La politique étrangère des États-Unis. Fondements, acteurs, formulation* (Presses de sciences po, 2003), *La guerre et la paix* (Presses de sciences po, 2000), *Repenser la sécurité* (Fidès, 2002), *Théories de la sécurité* (Montchrestien, 2002), and in English, including *Foreign Policy Failure in the White House* (University Press of America, 1993) and *The Future of NATO* (McGill-Queen's University Press, 1999). He has also published articles in *Études internationales, la Revue internationale et stratégique, Politique étrangère, la Revue française de science politique, Security Dialogue, The Journal of Crisis Management, International Journal, Diplomacy & Statecraft, The American Journal of Canadian Studies, European Security* and *Contemporary Security Policy*, among others. Dr. David is a frequent television commentator on Radio-Canada, on crises, conflicts, defense and peacekeeping issues. He has also delivered many lectures and conferences to a variety of audiences in Canada, the US and Europe.

Frédérick Gagnon Frédérick Gagnon is Junior Research Fellow at the Center for United States Studies of the Raoul Dandurand Chair. He is a PhD candidate in Political Science at the Université du Québec à Montréal, where he also teaches undergraduate classes on US foreign policy. He is the author of a chapter on the influence of foreign policy factors in presidential elections, and co-author of a chapter on the domestic factors at play in the 2004 election (with Anne-Marie D'Aoust), in the book *Les élections présidentielles américaines*, published in 2004 by the Presses de l'Université du Québec. He also is the author of 'Toward a Theoretical Explanation of US Congressional-Executive Relations Concerning National Security Policy After 9/11', published as an Occasionnal Paper by the Center for United States Studies in 2004.

David Grondin David Grondin is Assistant Professor in International Relations and American Studies at the School of Political Studies at the University of Ottawa. He will be completing his PhD in Political Science in 2006 at the University of Québec at Montréal under the supervision of Professor Alex Macleod, after having received a BA in History from the University of Québec at Montréal (with a specialization in the history of International Relations) and a MA in Political Science from the University of Toronto. His research interests cover theories of International Relations; critical security studies and political geography (critical geopolitics); US foreign and security policy discourse as well as American Studies; and US strategic discourse on the securitization and weaponization of Outer Space. He has recently co-edited with Charles-Philippe David a special issue on the redefinition of American power in the journal *Études internationales*. He has also co-edited (with Élisabeth Vallet) a book on US presidential elections (Les Presses Universitaires du Québec, 2004), and is author of the article 'Mistaking Hegemony for Empire: Neoconservatives, the Bush Doctrine, and the Democratic Empire' in *International Journal*.

Aida A. Hozic Aida A. Hozic is an Assistant Professor of International Relations at the University of Florida. Her research is situated at the intersection of political economy, cultural studies and international security. Her work has mostly focused on American media industries and their relation to power and warfare. A recipient of numerous research awards and fellowships, including a Mac Arthur Fellowship in Global Security, she is, most notably, the author of *Hollyworld: Space, Power, and Fantasy in the American Economy*, published by Cornell University Press in 2001.

Cédric Jourde Cédric Jourde is Assistant Professor at the School of Political Studies, University of Ottawa. His research concentrates on the restoration of authoritarianism in West Africa and on the international relations of African states. He also studies ethnic and religious politics, as well as the interplay between culture and politics in Africa. One of his articles, on the hijacking of democratization in the Islamic Republic of Mauritania, was published in *Comparative Politics* in 2005. He is currently contributing to a book project on Islamism in West Africa, to a Freedom House study ('Democracy at the Crossroads'), and to a special issue of the journal *Politique et société*.

André Laliberté André Laliberté teaches courses on Chinese politics and on political transitions in East Asia at the Université du Québec à Montréal. He has published articles on cross-strait relations and on civilian-military relations in Taiwan and South Korea for the *European Journal for East Asian Studies*, the *American Asian Review*, *Études internationales*, *Pacific Affairs* and *Perspectives chinoises*.

Shirley V. Scott Shirley Scott is Associate Professor in International Relations and Co-ordinator of Postgraduate Coursework Programs at the School of Politics and International Relations of the University of New South Wales, in Sydney, Australia. Over the last decade she has published on aspects of the relationship between international law and international politics in key journals in both International Law and International Relations. She is the author of *International Law in World Politics: An Introduction* (Lynne Rienner, 2004) and of *The Political Interpretation of Multilateral Treaties* (Martinus Nijhoff, 2004).

Julien Tourreille   Julien Tourreille is a PhD candidate in Political Science at Université du Québec à Montréal. His main research interests are the effects of US hegemony in the international arena and the idea of empire in international relations. His recent publications include, with Charles-Philippe David, 'La consolidation de la paix, un concept à consolider', in Yvan Conoir (ed.), *Faire la paix, concepts et pratiques de la consolidation de la paix* (Presses Universitaires de Laval, 2005); and 'Les symboles de la présidence', in Élisabeth Vallet (ed.), *Le Président des États-Unis* (Presses de l'Université du Québec, 2005).

Élisabeth Vallet   Élisabeth Vallet holds a PhD in public law. Before joining the Raoul Dandurand Chair of Strategic and Diplomatic Studies at Université du Québec à Montréal, she completed a post-doctorate at the Public Law Research Centre at Université de Montréal. In 2002–2003, she was a visiting scholar in the US at Duke University and then a researcher at the Canada Research Chair in International Relations at Université du Québec à Montréal. Her publications include *Les correspondants du Trésor* (L'Harmattan, 2002), *Les élections présidentielles américaines* (co-editor, Presses de l'Université du Québec, 2004), *La présidence américaine* (editor, Presses de l'Université du Québec, 2005), as well as chapters in books and scholarly articles.

Robert Vitalis   Robert Vitalis is Associate Professor of Political Science at University of Pennsylvania and Director of Penn's Middle East Center. He is author of *When Capitalists Collide: Business Conflict and the End of Empire in Egypt* (1995) and co-editor with Madawi al-Rasheed of *Counternarratives: History, Society and Politics in Saudi Arabia and Yemen* (2004). Recent articles include 'Birth of a Discipline' in *Imperialism and Internationalism in the Discipline of International Relations*, (2005), and 'Black Gold, White Crude: An Essay on American Exceptionalism, Hierarchy, and Hegemony in the Gulf', *Diplomatic History* (Spring 2002).

Preface

Charles-Philippe David and David Grondin

The Bush administration's unilateralist assertion of American power compels a reassessment of the role of the US in the new, post–Cold War environment and raises questions about the future shape of the 'new world order'. At a time of growing international resentment of American policy, scholarly investigation of the nature of US dominance in a one-superpower world, the domestic and international facets of American hegemony (or perhaps empire), how it is perceived abroad and the implications for international security is called for.

The Center for United States Studies of the Raoul-Dandurand Chair of Strategic and Diplomatic Studies at the University of Québec at Montréal (where the editors of this volume serve as director and researcher respectively) has been engaged in a reflection on American power as part of a long-standing research project on the political implications of the Bush administration's conduct of US foreign policy. This book grew out of an academic conference on the topic that brought together scholars from different disciplines and different continents for a productive exchange of views on US power. Their articles make a timely contribution to our understanding of American ambitions as the US makes an unprecedented bid for 'full-spectrum' supremacy.

Outline: American Empire/Imperialism/Hegemony

The Introduction to this collection of essays sets out the general theme that runs through the articles: How are we to understand US hegemony or empire, and indeed which is it? The essays are divided into two groups. The first set looks at US hegemony and rumblings of empire in the present world order by examining the geopolitical/strategic, social-cultural, economic and theoretical dimensions of the management of US hegemony/empire as well as the legal aspects and the domestic political implications, addressing the domestic front from the ideological, political and institutional points of view. The second group of essays analyzes the regional and international dimensions of US hegemony, particularly perceptions of American power in Europe, Africa, Asia, the Middle East and Canada. The conclusion reconnects with the thematic framework laid out in the introduction and builds on some of the arguments made in the book to provide critical perspectives.

These essays critically interpret US hegemony/imperialism and American power from a range of topical perspectives and incorporate a variety of historical, theoretical and political viewpoints. Since they are the work of many hands, they are (intentionally) not uniform in their treatment of the question. While the contributors

xiv   *Hegemony or Empire?*

do not share the same assumptions or arrive at the same conclusions, they all agree that the extent of American power today is a critical issue, albeit to different degrees and for different reasons. They all consider it important to understand how Americans perceive their place in the world, and how these representations are perceived outside the US.

As political geographers John Agnew and Jonathan Smith have noted, 'Just as Americans are coming to a new understanding of American space, so they are coming to a new understanding of what it means to be an American place.'[1] This volume presents a wide-ranging survey of the various loci of American power and the places it inhabits.

Part I

Part I assesses some prominent representations of US hegemony or empire, while addressing the global and domestic implications of the redefinition of American power. US hegemony is discussed primarily from the American point of view.

Robert Vitalis probes the confusion and conceptual problems that lie behind the debate about whether the US is a hegemonic power or an empire. He suggests that there are at least two kinds of analytical errors in contemporary commentaries on American power. One is the use of 'hegemony' and 'empire' as though they were twin concepts. Many analysts use the terminology without attending to the literature on the distinction between the two modes of domination. The other common mistake Vitalis points to involves a misunderstanding of simultaneously operating hierarchical processes. Some observers seem eager to claim exclusivity for one or another, but Vitalis argues that these are in fact co-existing forces, and that divergent world orders can overlap.

Simon Dalby looks at the geopolitical-strategic context of the recasting of American power in the age of 'imperial hegemony'. After tracing the rising influence of neoconservative intellectuals over national security strategy and how discussion of US foreign policy is subsumed under an imperial discourse, he proceeds to a broad analysis of the neoconservative hold on the Bush administration's national security policy documents, highlighting the close similarities between policy documents produced by influential think tanks identified with the neoconservative movement (notably the Project for a New American Century) and the leaked 1992 Pentagon Defense Planning Document written under the George H.W. Bush administration by Paul Wolfowitz and Lewis Libby, at the request of then-Secretary of Defense Dick Cheney. Dalby considers the neoconservatives' imperial discourse inappropriate and criticizes the Cold War attitude among national security elites, which reproduces the

---

1   John A. Agnew and Jonathan M. Smith, 'Preface', in John A. Agnew and Jonathan M. Smith (eds), *American Space/American Place: Geographies of the Contemporary United States* (New York: Routledge, 2002), p. x.

logic of insecurity they sought to counter in the first place. He investigates a series of questions related to the neoconservative influence in the Bush administration, especially since 9/11, such as whether the National Security Strategy (NSS) is a guide to dealing with future conflicts or a strategy suitable only for Iraq, and how the Defense Planning Guidance of 1992 and the Project for a New American Century's *Rebuilding of America's Defense* of 2000 stack up in relation to the NSS of 2002.

Aida Hozic addresses the cultural dimension of US hegemony in the age of hypersecurity, discussing the Bush administration's rhetoric in the novel 'war against terrorism'. Using Žižekian insights, she studies the representation of truth and the media politics of the Bush administration's discourse in its war on terrorism, focusing on the relationship between public complicity and propaganda. She argues that under Bush we have seen a shift from a 'national entertainment state' to a renewed Cold War–type 'national security state' as the President seeks strengthened sovereign power for the US. In her view, the Bush administration has cast itself as an Empire and attempted to rhetorically act as such. Hozic suggests that the making and unmaking of the White House's authority, domestically and internationally, calls for consideration of sovereignty, imperialism and hegemony not just as political, economic or military practices but also as representational ones. We need to think about the Emperor's new clothes as much as about empire itself.

International law scholar **Shirley V. Scott** discusses whether the Bush administration has adopted an attitude towards international law fundamentally different from that of previous administrations. She contends that the basic point to consider is the degree to which rhetoric matters, and argues that justifying the same policy in different terms does make a difference. Scott goes on to suggest a measure by which to gauge whether US presidential rhetoric and actions are undermining the authority of international law. She compares the policies of the Bush and Clinton administrations and discusses the new elements in the Bush administration's attitude towards international law. Scott examines the sources from which the authority of international law springs, how US rhetoric and actions can weaken or strengthen that authority, and how the US can and does benefit from the rule of international law.

Frédérick Gagnon looks at how Congress deals with US hegemony at home. Arguing that Congress plays an important role domestically in the foreign policy debate, he focuses on congressional compliance with George W. Bush's national security policy between 2001 and 2005. While Congress has less power over foreign policy than the White House, members of Congress do use many tools to influence US foreign policy: they appear in the media, write letters to the President and, most importantly, debate, make speeches and cast votes on Capitol Hill. Gagnon notes that many US legislators are foreign policy experts and have a say in the domestic management of US hegemony. These experts sit on key congressional committees such as the House and Senate Armed Services committees, the House Committee on International Relations and the Senate Committee on Foreign Relations. They deal with issues such as US policy in the Middle East, protecting Americans against terrorism and diversifying US supplies of oil and natural gas, just as do the President and the members of the National Security Council. Gagnon sheds light on the role Congress plays in shaping US foreign policy and argues that scholars of American foreign policy and international relations must attend to congressional influence over the War on Terror and the way the US manages its hegemonic position in the world, particularly in view of Congress's still-important foreign policy powers.

Part II

Part II deals with perceptions of American hegemony abroad and examines the regional implications of the redeployment of US power.

Onnig Beylerian argues that despite the Bush administration's apparent resolve to prosecute the war against global terrorism, the United States remains ambivalent in articulating the nature of the adversary it seeks to defeat. He examines and evaluates the strategic goals of this war and concludes that the administration's objectives are still in flux and beset by problems in identifying and articulating the nature of the adversary, rehabilitating Iraq and promoting ambitious political reforms in the Middle East.

Stephen Clarkson examines the significant, if under-analyzed, role of the North American periphery in constituting and/or constraining both the United States' hard, material assets and its soft power. For instance, during World War II, Canada cooperated in Washington's strategic military planning and production in order to harness the continent's resources, defend its shores, and defeat the common enemies across the Atlantic and Pacific oceans, while Mexico gave the negative assurance that it would not be used as an enemy staging area. Building on the economic integration established in the first half of the 20th century, Canada provided the US with a rich consumer market for its products, access to resources and resource income for US transnational corporations, and also a flow of highly trained human resources. Although Mexico adopted a defiantly resistant attitude and tried to preserve the autarchy of its economy, US investment also flowed south, US products were sold in Mexican markets, Mexico supplied low-cost labour through the *bracero* program and sold the US larger quantities of oil. Through the North American Free Trade Agreement, the United States established an external constitution that binds both of its neighbours to standards, rules, rights, and arbitration procedures that are friendly to transborder investment, at the cost of peripheral-state autonomy. The governments of Canada and Mexico subsequently helped create a continental security arrangement through bilateral 'smart-border agreements', under which Washington is dependent on its neighbours for enforcement. As the United States shifted from hegemony to empire in the Middle East, resistance paradoxically increased in the periphery. From its new-won seat on the UN Security Council, Mexico refused to support

Washington's invasion of Iraq. Canada was more ambivalent, denying the war's legitimacy while participating in the command and control of US military operations through NORAD and supplying ships to buttress the US Navy in the Persian Gulf. In short, Uncle Sam's two peripheral states contribute substantially to US power, while trying to contain it when vital global issues are at stake.

Cédric Jourde analyzes the development of three pervasive American representations of Africa in the post–Cold War era, focusing particularly on the Bush administration and West Africa. Africa as a new battlefield in the 'global war on terror', Africa as a provider of strategic natural resources and Africa as a democratically weak region in need of external support are three dominant lenses through which the US administration now interprets African politics. These representations have made a set of US policies towards West Africa based on more robust military cooperation, narrow support for electoral processes, and financial and institutional support for US companies investing in oil-producing countries both thinkable and possible. At the same time, these representations exclude alternative policy paths.

André Laliberté looks into the security architecture that underpins American hegemonic stability in Asia, discusses the implications of the rise of China, the actor most likely to drive an eventual hegemonic transition, and surveys the strains on American security alliances in the region. Frictions within key bilateral agreements and poor prospects for further consolidation or expansion of the structure raise uncertainties about long-term sustainability, especially in view of the changing distribution of economic, political and military power. In particular, the rise of China is already undermining American hegemony and in the long term even Asian states traditionally close to the US, such as Japan and South Korea, may care more about the effects of China's economic prominence on their own prosperity than about American strategic interests. In other parts of Asia, American hegemony rests on the shaky foundation of states plagued by domestic unrest and problems of legitimacy.

Élisabeth Vallet and **Julien Tourreille** observe that in the aftermath of the US intervention in Iraq, surveys have found a sharp decline in the image of the US in Europe. However, while European perceptions of the US are predominantly negative, they are not uniform. Divergences and common points in European public opinion about the United States in general and US hegemony in particular, as well as tensions between Europe and the United States, have a long history and cool transatlantic relations are by no means a new phenomenon. Therefore, despite sharp and legitimate differences, Europe and the US must draw lessons from the Iraq crisis and create common structures and a shared agenda that reflect their community of values and interests. Complementary efforts, not balance of power, must be the guiding principle behind a renewed Atlantic alliance that remains central to international stability and prosperity.

Acknowledgments

A collection of this type requires both financial and human resources. We are grateful to all the individuals and organizations that gave us support.

First of all, we would like to acknowledge the assistance of the Social Sciences and Humanities Research Council of Canada (SSHRC), which provided primary funding and recognition of this research project on US hegemony and imperialism. We thank the Institut d'études internationales de Montréal (Institute of International Studies of Montreal) and the University of Québec at Montréal for their financial support. We are grateful to Katia Gagné, special projects coordinator, and Nicolas Riendeau, executive director of the Center for United States Studies for their devotion and hard work.

This book would not have been possible without the invaluable intellectual and research input provided by our contributors. We thank them for their genuine interest in this project and for their collective effort in this reflection on American power under the George W. Bush administration. We would like to express our indebtedness to the Ashgate reviewers for the painstaking task of copy-editing and indexing the work, and to our translator, the ever-efficient John Detre. We are most grateful to publishing editor Kirstin Howgate for her dedication. She showed a strong interest in this project throughout, gave us encouragement when we needed it, and demonstrated patience which, we hope, has been justified by the results of our efforts.

Charles-Philippe David
David Grondin

Introduction

Coming to Terms with America's Liberal Hegemony/Empire

David Grondin

[O]ur political imagination has been restricted by our uncritical acceptance of our own rhetorical construction of democracy, a construction that privileges free-enterprise capitalism and republicanism. Such a construction – limiting, as it does, our ability to understand both ourselves and others – needs to be rhetorically reconstructed to serve the needs of globalism as different nations struggle toward their own definitions, policies, and practices. The first step in such a rhetorical reconstruction is to become aware of our own language choices and the narratives and assumptions embedded in these choices.[1]

There is not a day that goes without American power being addressed or discussed in one way or another in the global media. Indeed, over the past five years, no subject has been more studied or discussed in world politics than the sheer extent of American power as imperialism, empire or hegemony, sometimes as praise but most frequently as resentment. A number of recent commentators and analysts have in fact noted the possibility of an imperialist turn in the conceptualization and prosecution of US foreign policy. Hence, several discussions of an 'American Empire' and a '*Pax Americana*' have garnished the political spectrum of many opinion-editorial pages of major papers across the globe, especially in the aftermath of the swift US military 'victory' in the 2003 Iraqi War. Sadly, in many cases, one can say that the emperor has been stripped of his clothes – and most of the time he was not even an emperor. The use of the term 'empire' has been a shortcut for any form of critique of US foreign policy at large since September 11, 2001, prior to the concept being discussed in a rigorous or serious way. In these instances, the galvanized epithet appears in itself as superfluous for the harsh criticism would have been levelled at the US no matter what.

One could put forth the idea that the US could be construed as an 'informal empire', a recurrent term in the literature on American imperialism. A fortiori, it sure possesses some analytical power, as it takes into account the importance of rules, norms and institutions. However, for many theorists, this dynamic would be better served by the term 'hegemony', which has the capacity to encompass both the

---

1 Martin J. Medhurst, 'Introduction: The Rhetorical Construction of History', in Martin J. Medhurst and H.W. Brands (eds), *Critical Reflections on the Cold War: Linking Rhetoric and History* (College Station, TX: Texas A&M University Press, 2000), pp. 3–19.

Gramscian concept of consensus and persuasion as well as the classical view that highlights the role of military power and coercion in the evolution of US foreign policy. This view is mostly associated with the work of John Ikenberry, Daniel Deudney, Andrew Hurrell and John Agnew. These scholars argue that 'it is analytically more useful to understand the United States as a hegemonic rather than an imperial power', especially since hegemony would be cast as being less an 'intrusive mode of control' than empire.[2] In fact, there is much leverage in this view that shall make it more compelling and attractive as a policy-oriented research agenda. All the more reason that most of the authors in this book implicitly or explicitly tackle the concept of US hegemony more than they take issue with empire. Perhaps it is John Agnew who put it best: 'Which word – empire or hegemony – best describes the role of the US in contemporary world politics? If it is an empire, it is a peculiarly incoherent and increasingly hollow one. It is better seen as increasingly subject to pressures from the very hegemony it has released on the world.'[3] That being said, if it makes more sense to use the concept of hegemony to understand how American power works in contemporary world politics, does it mean that if one considers American power in *longue durée*, by situating the rise of the US as a regional and then global power and by putting it in a broad historical context, empire and imperialism become more relevant concepts? Even so, there would still be nominal issues to consider.

The might of American power is so strong and extensive that it is impossible for any actor/agent of world politics not to feel threatened or beleaguered by the 'success story of the United States' as a nation-state. One cannot help but notice how sentiments of anti-Americanism have been expressed in several places where they could not have been thought possible or at an intensity never before reached. Some say that America's 'soft power' and its cultural appeal are decreasing and that the US is, 'again', on a declining curve. No matter what name American power has been given, whether it is empire, imperialism or hegemony, one must take a step back and reassess the exercise *and* representation of American power as well as its perception since George W. Bush took office.

Today's American hegemony/empire is more powerful than at any time in history. Yet it is under constant and even growing challenges in several spheres and ways. What has become of the US as the 'beacon on the hill'? According to the exceptionalist narrative, the United States has been anything but an empire. Therefore, it could, would and shall never be compared to other empires in history, present or past. This was and still is the essential leitmotiv behind an 'American exceptionalism'. Is it so far disconnected from its original 'covenant' as to bear no possible mention of its liberal and enlightened roots? Furthermore, has it come to a point that US nationalist expansion has become a sham (and shameful) quest for power? This book is most

---

2   Andrew Hurrell, '*Pax Americana* or the Empire of Insecurity?', *International Relations of the Asia-Pacific*, 5 (2005): 153.

3   John Agnew, *Hegemony: The New Shape of Global Power* (Philadelphia, PA: Temple University Press, 2005), p. 11.

certainly as much a study of American nationalism, hegemony and imperialism as it is of US sovereignty and state-building experiences.

America as a Place – and a Nation-State

The modern 'system of territorial division', of territorializations, made national states the primary locus of political, economic and cultural organization. This is the result of cartography, where territorial representation exists as a mental or illustrated map. With mapping, one proceeds to the reterritorialization of the world, as the state invests – reconstructs – 'its nation and people with new meaning'. Therefore, remapping participates in 'the fragmentation of the map of the contemporary world' through cartography.[4] Indeed, '[t]he undoubted success of the United States as a political-economic and cultural enterprise over the long term should not blind us to the limitations of the official story'.[5] When considering US global power, the resulting map is necessarily an approximation, an interpretation and a codification of reality. The globe in its entire cartographic representation is of interest to the US, because it has global power, responsibilities and interests. This is why, in the study of US power and of its redefinition, one needs to study both the US in its national context *and* abroad. But for that to happen, a dominant discourse writing the nation must be assessed for the United States of America. '[T]he national space of the United States is politically stabilized and homogenized through a dominant story, [...] [which] story is then widely accepted as a true account of the ways things operate, irrespective of empirical observations to the contrary.'[6] Maps shape a world that in turn shapes its maps: it is a recursive social process that renders modern cartographical practices epistemologically linked to the inscription of the nation/state in the spatial abstraction that embodied it and the territorial description that associated it with a national identity. The first part of this book is interested in one such particular 'state-space', that of the United States of America. We are thus interested in the narratives that construct the US as it exists as a political entity in its dominant story of a unified United States of America.

When we look at the space (space as controlled or commanded) of the United States in today's world order, it is as if we were looking down on the United States territory and people as outside 'observers'. This top-down approach construes space as an area where a collective entity is 'held together' in popular consciousness by a map-image and a narrative or story that represents it as a meaningful whole; it is as

---

4   Kennan Ferguson, 'Unmapping and Remapping the World: Foreign Policy as Aesthetic Practice', in Michael J. Shapiro and Hayward R. Alker (eds), *Challenging Boundaries: Global Flows, Territorial Identities* (Minneapolis, MN: University of Minnesota Press, 1996), p. 170.

5   John Agnew, 'Introduction', in John A. Agnew and Jonathan M. Smith (eds), *American Space / American Place: Geographies of the Contemporary United States* (New York: Routledge, 2002), p. 3.

6   *Ibid.*

if 'powerful actors [were] imposing their control and stories on others'.[7] However, when we look at its place, it is as if we were going from bottom-up, looking at the peoples. In considering global politics, because people matter, '[p]lace signifies their encounter with one another in the material reality (environment) that is construed as "space"'.[8] It refers to how everyday life is inscribed in space and takes on meaning for specified groups of people or organizations. Admittedly, '[t]he United States government can change entirely from decade to decade, but the need to make Americans, out of a land called America, continues in new and unexpected forms.'[9] American historian of the 'frontier experience' Richard Slotkin writes that 'so long as the nation-state remains the prevalent form of social organization, something like a national myth/ideology will be essential to its operation'.[10]

We are told that 'America was constituted in the space between law and outlawry, between legitimacy and rebellion, between the immediacy of the spoken word and the endurance of the written text. America is a nation where "law is king," yet the Americans are also "a people who think lightly of the laws".'[11] This constitutive contradiction marks the law as an axis in the structure of American identity. Contradictions are by all means at the core of American national identity as an 'empire of liberty'. One needs to assess the tensions of the actual United States with the ideal(ized) 'first new nation' that we find inscribed in the Declaration of Independence and the Constitution. It is this representational force of the Constitution over Americans, of the 'Homeland as a text', that allows Americans to compare their existence in the world as 'Americans' to their ideal existence written for eternity in the Constitution:

> Interpretation of the Constitution is thus an ambivalent communion, coupling the people and the text, the material and the ideal, aspiration and experience. In it the people recognize their ambivalent constitution between word and flesh. In it the people recall their authority. [...] Because it acknowledges the people as author of a text they know to have authored them, it invites them to recognize the dialectical nature of constitution. Because they are written into the text, as much in the name of the thing as in its content, it invites them to confirm that writing in the act and the acknowledgement of interpretation as a constitutional activity. It obliges them to be critical if they would be obedient, to comprehend the text if they are to be comprehended within it.[12]

Why is it so pregnant in American political culture to represent the US as the 'first new nation', as a 'revolutionary yet civilized' colonization as if it had had a

---

7   *Ibid.*, p. 4.

8   *Ibid.*, p. 5.

9   Kennan Ferguson, 'Unmapping and Remapping the World: Foreign Policy as Aesthetic Practice', p. 169.

10   Richard Slotkin, *Gunfighter Nation: The Myth of the Frontier in Twentieth-Century America* (New York: HarperPerennial, 1992), p. 654.

11   Anne Norton, *Republic of Signs: Liberal Theory and American Popular Culture* (Chicago and London: University of Chicago Press, 1993), p. 139.

12   *Ibid.*, pp. 136–38.

'clean break' from history?[13] Above all, in studying American expansionism in the post–World War II period, but especially since the end of the Cold War, one major concern of this book is that one does not need to adhere to or reassess American exceptionalism, which has been ruled out by numerous and rigorous historical studies of Early American history, of political theory, and of studies of American political development, even though it has never been able to reach a consensus in any of these aforementioned fields[14]. It does not mean however that one does not taken into account American exceptionalism.

Why Not Address American National Experience as an Empire?

As stated previously, this book does not share common views on the use of the terms 'empire' and 'hegemony' to refer to the United States' power, at least since WWII. However, what is more consensual is that there were US imperialist experiences at the turn of the 20th century in Cuba, Puerto Rico and the Philippines, among other places. Whether these experiences are limited in time and bear influences on actual US practices does not prevent us from addressing the empire as part of the American state experience. As will be seen in the individual chapters, where one starts and assesses American imperialism and hegemony is a matter of contention and debate.

---

13 John Agnew, 'Introduction', in John A. Agnew and Jonathan M. Smith (eds), p. 7.

14 As Early Americanist historian Joyce Chaplin explains:

> Above all, and as several non-Americanists have already pointed out, the *label* postcolonial makes little sense as a description of the United States, since the Revolution removed British *imperialism* only, not white *colonization* in America. The colonizing population left India by the midpoint of the twentieth century, but outside Nunavut (the semiautonomous First Nations' province recently created in arctic Canada), it still has not left North America. To apply the label postcolonial to the white settlers who made themselves independent of Britain is again to fetishize their experience as the center of North American history. (It may also demonstrate the paucity of Native American voices in the academy.) Independent Americans were postimperial, not postcolonial, and attention to the differing conditions in South Asia and North America would discourage the valorizing of accomplishments linked with one racial group that, if anything, continued the colonial legacy of the imperial era. Indeed, the United States probably never had a nonimperial moment, given that it made the Louisiana Purchase (and opened its 'empire of liberty') in 1803, even before the British finally relinquished aspirations to regain a foothold below Canada in 1815, with the Treaty of Ghent. In failing to take on the complex nature of postcolonial theory *or* by using the term postcolonial broadly, early Americanists will variously assert the myth of American exceptionalism: the triumphal view of American history and the focus on white settlers as heroes who overcame the British Empire.

Joyce E. Chaplin, 'Expansion and Exceptionalism in Early American History', *Journal of American History*, 89/ 4 (March 2003): <http://www.historycooperative.org/journals/jah/89.4/chaplin.html>.

But it is nevertheless a custodial concern of this book that all agree that the US was once an empire. For some, it may have been an empire in spirit or in the making, as it was foundationally presented as an 'empire of liberty' by Thomas Jefferson. However, the mere facts that there is so much talk of a (re)turn to imperialism serves as proof of contested views on experiences of American imperialism. For Stefan Heumann, when applied to the United States, 'The concept of empire transcends the disciplinary boundaries between foreign and domestic politics ... [because] domestic liberal institutions have to cope with imperial policies which originated from the encounter with the foreign.'[15] This imperial encounter in fact goes at the heart of a related and often belated theme, that of colonialism.[16]

In effect, the first concept one encounters when dealing with imperialism is that of colonialism (and now neo-colonialism). The problem most frequently encountered is taking colonialism for imperialism. In many instances imperialism is used as a synonym for colonialism, as if one were politically better than the other. If imperialism sure goes with colonialism, we should at least strive to nuance what colonialism was in conjunction with imperialism by refining the use of imperialism in such context. The generalization of imperialism over the theoretical span is unhelpful. For one thing, the US experience with imperialism was not the same everywhere. With most of Latin American countries, it tended to be more an informal imperialism, that is, the exercise of control by one sovereign state over another or others through various diplomatic, economic, political or military means and strategies. But in the Philippines, for instance, it did not materialize this way. Imperialism there turned into *colonialism*, for the Philippines became ruled by an apparatus constructed by the US and the US acted as an overseas colonial empire. Colonialism here is thus formal imperialism in contrast to the Latin American guise of American imperialism; it 'involves the explicit and often legally codified establishment of direct political domination over a foreign territory and peoples'.[17] The same went for Puerto Rico in 1898.[18]

As it is widely known there were debates, even fierce ones, over whether the US should follow the example of other European imperial powers by annexing the islands of the Philippines, Guam, Samoa, Puerto Rico, and on ascertaining

---

15 Stefan Heumann, 'Learning from the Past of the US Empire: Breaking Down the Boundaries between the Domestic and the Foreign', paper presented at the Graduate Seminar 'Strategies of Critique: Empire and its Discontents', Social and Political Thought, York University, Toronto, April 15, 2005. Paper made available by the author.

16 Roxanne Lynn Doty, *Imperial Encounters: The Politics of Representation in North-South Relations* (Minneapolis, MN: University of Minnesota Press, 1996).

17 Julian Go, 'Introduction: Global Perspectives on the US Colonial State in the Philippines', in Julian Go and Anne L. Foster (eds), *The American Colonial State in the Philippines* (Durham, NC and London: Duke University Press, 2003), p. 5.

18 Christiana Duffy Burnett and Burke Marshall (eds), *Foreign in a Domestic Sense: Puerto Rico, American Expansion, and the Constitution* (Durham, NC and London: Duke University Press, 2001).

formal colonial rule over overseas people.[19] What is certain, though, as historian Michael Adas relates, is that the first two governors of the Philippines that were sent by the US government in the newly created colonies of the Philippines of the American empire, William H. Taft and Luke Wright, viewed the British experience of colonization as 'the most obvious models for United States colonial policy'.[20] However, one must point out that in their minds a true sense of exceptionalism and manifest destiny was reactivated, as US colonial rule policy was seen as part of a civilizing process and missions that should aim at an 'an alternate regeneration' of the Philippines in America's image. There were frequent 'claims of exceptionalism grounded in misreadings of the colonial history of America's rivals, or in rather blinkered assessments of both the domestic situation in the US and the nature of colonial society in the Philippines'.[21] Most American stories were silent about the segregationist, paternalistic and racist influences in the US elite thinking. Indeed, American official discourse saw its colonial governing practices as distinctive and upscale when compared with European colonialisms. This exceptionalist thinking may owe a great deal to that teleological narrative 'that encompassed the history of the rise of the United States from an oppressed colony in its own right to its newly claimed positions as a global power'.[22] No matter how inaccurate it is in its representation of imperialist and neo-colonial practices of the US, this powerful narrative helps us understand how the whole civilizing mission in the Philippines took the form of an ideology of modernization and liberation of the rest of humanity in the height of the Cold War[23] and why it took a long time before being able to reinsert talks of American imperialism and empire in public discourse in the US.

The Study of American Imperialism/Empire

Any incursion in the study of imperialism comes with great pain for there are so many concepts to juggle with before even starting the analysis. This even gets harder when addressing US imperialism and its (un)likely empire. What are we dealing with when assessing the US as an empire? As historian Anders Stephanson stresses, the term has descriptive value:

---

19 See especially the thought-provoking and masterful study of historian Eric T. Love, *Race Over Empire: Racism & US Imperialism, 1865–1900* (Chapel Hill and London: University of North Carolina Press, 2004).

20 Michael Adas, 'Improving on the Civilizing Mission?: Assumptions of United States Exceptionalism in the Colonization of the Philippines', in Lloyd C. Gardner and Marilyn B. Young (eds), *The New American Empire: 21st Century Teach-In on US Foreign Policy* (New York and London: The New Press, 2005), p. 156.

21 *Ibid.*, p. 157.

22 *Ibid.*, p. 160.

23 Michael Adas, *Dominance by Design: Technological Imperatives and America's Civilizing Mission* (Cambridge, MA and London: The Belknap Press of Harvard University Press, 2006), p. 6.

That the United States does indeed possess a colonial empire overseas, whose aquatic area are equals that of the lower forty-eight lower states, may be a descriptive proposition; but it is also an interesting fact that demands exploration and explanation. Empire on that view signifies nothing but a legal and political form, and sometimes, with all the proper caveats, it is illuminating to describe a system as an empire. What is particularly interesting about the US variety is the obvious anomaly: *persisting, formal inferiority within a liberal framework, an official anti-colonialism that both recognizes and manages not to recognize the colonial fact.*[24]

How must we interpret the colonial appendages of the US? Do they fall within the parameters of imperialism? The denial – and absence – of an imperial structure does in fact render any question of an American empire somewhat problematic. Do we factor in the intent or the results? In this respect, what may qualify as an American empire? With the exception of Puerto Rico, Guam, the US Virgin Islands, the Northern Mariana Islands and American Samoa, now that (most) US colonies are independent, some make the compelling argument that to talk of American imperialism one must do it in a classical sense, that is, as European imperialism, and must limit its analysis to 1898 and its immediate aftermath, thus to what is constructed as 'America's imperialist moment' which is now said to '[have] come and gone'.[25]

To be sure, there may be some value to this line of argument. Imperialism is such an imbued concept that one always needs to know precisely how it is being used. One may even wonder whether the term has lost all relevant meaningful uses. For quite a long time, only the New Left historians of the 1960s, who argued along Marxist lines, and other Marxist theorists believed that the US had been an imperialist power since at least the 1870s (or even from its very birth). Yet this empire was not seen, with the exception of some specific cases (the Philippines, Puerto Rico, Cuba, among others), as a European-style colonialist empire, but rather as an informal economic empire – a capitalist power – interested in offshore markets, in Asia and China especially. Until recently, our understanding of the history and development of American power/hegemony was based on a conceptual definition that excluded empires because the US was constructed as being so exceptional that it was impossible to compare it with other empires.

Numerous Cold War historians, as well as International Relations (IR) scholars, that have now taken a more historical-materialist approach have suggested that considering the US as an empire through the use of the literature on globalization would provide some better historical and conceptual bases for both areas of thought, as well as providing some insight for the overall context of the present imperial discourse. Furthermore, combining an American empire with globalization could give us a more historicized version of globalization, and one that firmly brings power

---

24 Anders Stephanson, 'A Most Interesting Empire', Lloyd C. Gardner and Marilyn B. Young (eds), p. 255. Emphasis added.

25 Frank Ninkovich, *The United States and Imperialism* (Malden, MA: Blackwell, 2001), p. 247.

back into the equation, instead of taking globalization as a neutral and/or natural phenomenon.[26] It could also give a more adequate concept of the place of the US in the contemporary international system, and some basis for comparison with the past. This historical sociology argument thus makes bringing the US as an empire back into the IR discourse even more relevant, even if it may still be rejected afterwards. In truth, when comparing the United States with other empires one must not forget the context of global capitalism, and especially of globalization. Another thing to be aware of is that in so doing, in comparing US imperialism with other imperialisms from the 19th century onwards, the role of world order producer of the United States in the prevalent globalized neoliberal hegemony must be accounted for. In many respects, there seems to be intricate relations to be deciphered from the nexus of globalization, security and hegemony/empire that characterizes American power in our time. In effect, the identity politics of the US could diminish the added value of comparative historical analysis. As asserts Martin Coward, 'Often this has been in the unhelpful form of generalisations drawing upon models of imperialism that were designed to explain the colonialist expansion of capitalism in the eighteenth, nineteenth and twentieth centuries. And yet it is clear that such models are poorly suited to the analysis of American power in the early twenty-first century – *not least because America has always insisted, in its self identity, that it is an anti-imperial, anti-colonial power.*'[27] Drawing on the recent literature on a 'new American imperialism/empire', it would consequently become possible to undertake a critique of the new-found US imperial hegemony by way of taking cues from Hardt and Negri's *Empire* as a deterritorialized and borderless entity.[28] Entering the terrain of this Empire could indeed prove to be a good intellectual strategy if one wishes to understand the complexities of the networks of command and power relations at play in the reordering of global politics that has generally been subsumed under the title of 'globalization'.[29]

US Liberalism and Exceptionalism

Is US global dominance or its quest a call to empire? If not, why has the language of empire had such a 'new beginning' recently? As nicely put by the mainstream

---

26 Bryan Mabee, 'Discourses of Empire: The US "Empire", Globalisation and International Relations', *Third World Quarterly*, 25/8 (2005): 1363.

27 Martin Coward, 'The Empire Strikes Back: Permanent War and the Spatialities of Global Conflict after 9/11', Paper presented at the Global Justice/Political Violence Network, Sussex University, Brighton, UK, January 14, 2004, p. 2: <http://www.sussex.ac.uk/Users/mpc20/pubs/empire.doc>. Emphasis added.

28 Martin Coward, 'The Globalisation of Enclosure: Interrogating the Geopolitics of Empire', *Third World Quarterly*, 26/6, (September 2005): 855–71.

29 Amy Kaplan, 'The Tenacious Grasp of American Exceptionalism: A Response to Djelal Kadir, "Defending America Against its Devotees"', *Comparative American Studies*, 2/2 (2004): 162.

of American foreign policy ideologies, but especially by its arch-type, John Mearsheimer, the United States as hegemon may pursue a liberal world order, but must often do so through illiberal means. So this idea of a liberal empire brings back the issue of what liberalism is (American-style), and what recent US attempts are at reshaping the world order to its liking. And as Amy Kaplan puts it, 'In a dramatic turn away from the disavowal of its own imperial history, the embrace of empire across the political spectrum celebrates and normalizes US global dominance as an inevitable process. The notion of the homeland, with its nativist connotations, works to protect a sense of domestic insularity, always under attack yet cordoned off from the threatening outside world. While mainstream discourse places the homeland and the empire in separate spheres ... isolationism and internationalism in US policy today are two sides of the same imperial coin', as are American exceptionalism and universalism.[30]

American exceptionalism and the manifest destiny image are at the heart of any understanding of US imperialism/empire. The whole liberal imagination that so deeply characterizes the US – and that is mainly indebted to Louis Hartz's intellectual legacy in the American social sciences[31] – most assuredly accounts for the contradictions within the American republic, discarding the very idea of empire. The constant re-articulation of the ideal of the US as 'an empire of liberty' leaves no place for an American empire, even though it seems undisputable. If we understand US nationalist power and the project of an American liberal Republic as a different form of imperialism, it may become possible to address this issue of hegemony/empire without having to face the usual oppositions from Americans themselves and American academics especially. It may decidedly be one way to reappraise neoconservatism within the ideological web that renders it intelligible, that of American liberalism, for it helps us make sense of the discourse of a new American empire/imperialism.

As Anne Norton explains, 'Liberalism has become the common sense of the American people, a set of principles unconsciously adhered to, a set of conventions so deeply held that they appear (when they appear at all) to be no more than common sense. The capacity of liberalism to transform itself in America from ideology to common sense is the proof – as it is the means – of its constitutional power.'[32] American liberalism has evolved as the 'peculiar fusion of providential and republican ideology that took place after the Revolution' and stands as the civil and political religion that animates the powerful 'master narrative' of a manifest destiny, whereas liberalism becomes a 'manner of interpreting the space and time of "America"'.[33] Therein lays a unification of a sacred and secular conception of liberty,

---

30 *Ibid.*

31 Louis Hartz, *The Liberal Tradition in America: An Interpretation of American Political Thought Since the Revolution* (Orlando, FL: Harcourt, 1991 [1954]).

32 Anne Norton, *Republic of Signs*, p. 1.

33 Anders Stephanson, *Manifest Destiny: American Expansion and the Empire of Right* (New York: Hill and Wang, 1995), p. 5.

of a providential mission and sense of moral crusade that would identify 'America' and guide its action in the world.

America's peculiar situation had in many respects made it an object of universal interest.[34] In effect, the ideology of (American) liberalism goes even deeper:

> the presumption that liberal values are self-evidently true underscores the possibility that other societies could be more like America in practice given the proper incentives or tutelage. Hence the familiar spectacle of American presidents making appearances in foreign countries and pressing those countries to enact such liberal social institutions as a free market economy, the separation of church and state, and increased freedom of the press. While non-Americans resent such actions, in the United States, they are usually seen as the simple reaffirmation of things that Americans *know* to be true. America imagines the rest of the world as somehow, at base, just like America – if not for the distortion produced by ideology, corrupt regimes, and the historical effects of culture.[35]

It is in this American liberal ideological discourse that America acquires the status of a universal symbol for its values and its democratic system. The metaphorical global war on terror waged in the name of liberty and civilization delves into the same logic: 'To say that by attacking the United States the terrorists attacked the world is to suggest that America *is* the world – or, at least, is what the rest of the world aspires to become.'[36]

As stated by many scholars of American nationalism, the Bush administration's ambitious vision for America's role in the world is reminiscent of earlier moralistic statements of the antebellum period in US political history.[37] The post-9/11 era allowed it to reinvigorate the national security discourse with its manifest destiny and a sense of its exceptionalist mission of democratizing the world. Revealed most importantly by the neoconservative guise of US nationalism and liberal ideology, the Global War on Terror has been fuelled by an extremely vibrant and patriotic nationalist base that truly believes that America is invested with a providential mission and sense of moral crusade. This emanates from what Daniel Nexon and Patrick Thaddeus Jackson call the 'liberal imagination' in American political life, a powerful identity and ideological narrative in the American discourse on foreign policy which makes them overtly moralistic. It is often used to conflate the US and the world in the protection of liberal democracy and liberty.[38] It is however known

---

34 Anne Norton, *Alternative Americas: A Reading of Antebellum Political Culture* (Chicago: University of Chicago Press, 1986), p. 1.

35 Patrick Thaddeus Jackson and Daniel Nexon, 'Representation Is Futile? American Anti-Collectivism and the Borg', in Jutta Weldes (ed.), *To Seek Out New Worlds: Exploring Links Between Science Fiction and World Politics* (New York: Palgrave Macmillan, 2003), p. 146.

36 John Edwards, 'After the Fall', *Discourse & Society*, 15/2–3 (2004): 157.

37 Paul T. McCartney, 'American Nationalism and US Foreign Policy from September 11 to the Iraq War', *Political Science Quarterly*, 119/3 (2004): 400.

38 Patrick Thaddeus Jackson and Daniel Nexon, 'Representation Is Futile? American Anti-Collectivism and the Borg', p. 146.

that the suffusion of liberal values and ascription of a divine mission for the world bring about contradictions when confronted with some of the foreign policy actions of the United States. But this is of no concern for US nationalism; it is committed to an 'ideological construction of the nation that insists on the global relevance of the American project' and consequently claims 'its righteous entitlement to lead the world'.[39] This remapping of US nationalism is thus to be understood through a dialectical relationship of exceptionalism/universalism, and of a 'city upon a hill'/ crusader state. It is in this framing of US globalist nationalism that its neoliberal hegemonic global strategy tries to have it both ways, to remake the world in America's image, while assuming that its national interests are global interests, thereby conflating its national security with global security, as if the great aspirations of the US and of mankind were one and the same. In this light, the US–led Global War on Terror really becomes a nation-building project that has evolved into sort of a 'Global Leviathan', without its mandatory 'social contract' with the peoples of the world.[40]

Neoliberal Geopolitics as American Hegemony – and Informal Imperialism

All the fuss with empire/hegemony would not be as present and overwhelming if it were not for the neoconservative influence in the Bush administration. Does speaking of an American empire help us understand the reworking and transformations of American power that resulted from the Bush doctrine and the rising influence of neoconservatism in American politics? Maybe so, maybe not, but the imperial trope has been reactivated by self-declared neoconservatives and, on their own did they couch an argument for a better and stronger America in a 'New Rome' project, a *Pax Americana* for the 21st century.[41] Therefore, saying that things have changed since George W. Bush took office is a truism. We now need to consider the neoconservative fantasies of empire.[42] Moreover, it is happening in a country where the orthodox discourse has always maintained that there was no such thing as an American Empire. However, if some would like to make us believe that there is such a clash

---

39 Paul T. McCartney, 'American Nationalism and US Foreign Policy from September 11 to the Iraq War', p. 401.

40 Thomas P.M. Barnett, *The Pentagon's New Map: War and Peace in the Twenty-First Century* (New York: Putnam's, 2004), pp. 369–70.

41 For an in depth analysis of the neoconservative representations of American power through the discursive articulation of a new empire/'return to imperialism' thesis, see our article 'Une lecture critique du discours néoconservateur du nouvel impérialisme: La lutte globale contre le terrorisme comme *Pax Americana*' [A Critical Reading of the Neoconservative Discourse on the New Imperialism: The Global War on Terror(ism) as *Pax Americana*)], *Études internationales*, 36/4 (2005): 469–500.

42 Ellen Schrecker, 'Introduction: Cold War Triumphalism and the Real Cold War', in Ellen Schrecker (ed.), *Cold War Triumphalism: The Misuse of History After the Fall of Communism* (New York and London: The New Press, 2004), pp. 1–24.

in US foreign policy community that we might speak of a 'revolution in foreign policy',[43] in many ways it could rather be cast as an evolution, if not an extension of the long-standing neoliberal global strategy set forth for the 1945 post-war era and established within the Cold War's epithet, the 'national security state'.[44]

In highlighting a continuous trend, this does not mean that one believes that a rational project of a clear and well-designed foreign policy has been animating and driving US decision makers from 1945 onwards, but rather that there is some form of consensus on what US national interests and its national security objectives are (amongst decision makers and political and business elites). The conditions within which these objectives are put forth have changed, but the main principles of the strategy have not. Anyone interested in understanding the principles of neoliberal hegemony in US national security conduct since WWII cannot see the Bush foreign policy as a historical anomaly. In this very sense, one may say that the Bush doctrine represents an extreme version of the logic of US national security since WWII.[45] For neoconservatives, this military supremacy serves the interests of preserving the long-established hegemony. Even if the 2003 Iraqi War was not a public diplomatic success when we factor in the failure of the Bush administration to persuade a wide international audience of the legitimacy of its policies, there continues to be wide support for the promise of American values and ideals abroad.[46] At no point did neoconservatives reject the Cold War strategy, as their target was always the Clinton administration, which they usually criticize for having failed on capitalizing on the 'peace dividends' of the fall of communism at the end of the Cold War and for letting new challenges and threats emerge. Maybe it is differences that matter most, but it remains to be seen whether the neoconservatives were so revolutionary as to change US global strategy to bring its long-held hegemony to the ground. In contrast to what many observers and theoreticians assert, it still consists of a mix of a realism associated with fighting a 'foreign' threat (from Soviet communism to global terrorism), of a liberalism associated with financial international institutions and multilateral institutions such as the UN and NATO, and a commitment to free

---

43 Ivo H. Daalder and James M. Lindsay, *America Unbound: The Bush Revolution in Foreign Policy* (Washington, DC: Brookings Institution Press, 2003).

44 The term refers to the representation of the American state in the early years of the Cold War, with its very spirit and embodiment being enacted by the National Security Act of 1947, with the creation of the CIA, the Department of Defense, the Joint Chiefs of Staff, and the National Security Council. What appears vital to understand with the idea of the US 'national security state' (which is not to be conflated with garrison state) is that it designates both an institutionalization of a new governmental architecture designed to prepare the United States politically and militarily to face any foreign threat *and* the ideology – the discourse – that gave rise to as well as symbolized it. In other words, one needs to grasp the discursive power of national security in shaping the reality of the Cold War in both language and institutions.

45 Ellen Meiksins Wood, *The Empire of Capital* (London: Verso, 2003), pp. 157–63.

46 Rob Kroes, 'American Empire and Cultural Imperialism: A View from the Receiving End', in Thomas Bender (ed.), *Rethinking American History in a Global Age* (Berkeley and Los Angeles, CA and London: University of California Press, 2002), p. 299.

market ideology and the promotion of democracy. Today's American global strategy
still refers to the US neoliberal hegemony established after 1945. In that regard,
the discourse of a benign American hegemony and its associated neoliberal values
of free market, freedom and democracy remain powerful ideas outside the United
States. As political geographer Matthew Sparke argues, the differences in foreign
policy are not as far off as is alleged by both sides and should probably rather be
seen as two opposite sides of a coin: 'If we instead see the war planning and resulting
talk as a complicit mix of geopolitical affect and geoeconomic assumptions, such
contradictions becomes comprehensible as the contradictions of an informal
American imperialism being pushed in the direction of formality and force amid
globalized capitalist interdependency.'[47]

If one chooses to speak of American unipolarity and interprets American
military global power as 'one of the great realities of our age' and as a producer
of world order, indeed in going as far as to say that 'never before has one country
been so powerful or unrivaled',[48] what prevents a person from acknowledging an
American empire/imperialism? For such a person, John Ikenberry for instance, it is
the kind of world order *sought* in principle by the US that prevents any mention of
'imperialism'. The mere mention of empire as applied to what he sees as hegemonic
power from the US comes as a cursory and sketchy rendering. For them, it makes
no sense not to refer to our current era as unipolar and any talk that interprets it as
being imperial for one '[sees] the United States as an imperial power' is read as
unsound.[49] Since 9/11 and due to the rising influence of neoconservative ideologues
in the Bush cabinet, Ikenberry fears that the imperial logic threatens the post-war
American-led hegemonic order that has supposedly worked 'around open markets,
security alliances, multilateral cooperation, and democratic community'.[50] From
World War II onwards, Ikenberry depicts the Cold War US national security state as
having stopped short of any imperial endeavours. For him, talk of empire in the US
national experience goes back to the Philippines and the like, to 1898. Hegemony is
a better concept to account for 'the construction of a rule-based international order'.
In fact, neoliberal American hegemony was an open and democratic order premised
on rules, institutions and partnerships which have had 'an unprecedented array of
partnerships spread across global and regional security, economic, and political
realms.'[51] Matthew Sparke characterizes an informal American imperialism as the
geoeconomical and geopolitical logic of American hegemonic power in the global

---

47 Matthew Sparke, *In the Space of Theory: Postfoundational Geographies of the Nation-State* (Minneapolis, MN: University of Minnesota Press, 2005), p. 283.

48 G. John Ikenberry, 'Power and Liberal Order: America's Postwar World Order in Transition', *International Relations of the Asia Pacific*, 5/2 (2005): 133.

49 See especially Andrew Hurrell, 'Pax Americana or the Empire of Insecurity?'.

50 Takashi Inoguchi and Paul Bacon, 'Empire, Hierarchy, and Hegemony: American Grand Strategy and the Construction of Order in the Asia-Pacific', *International Relations of the Asia Pacific*, 5/2 (2005): 118.

51 G. John Ikenberry, 'Power and Liberal Order: America's Postwar World Order in Transition', p. 133.

capitalist system reaffirmed after 1945.[52] It is through these neoliberal geopolitics
– of American hegemony – that American *informal* imperialism could last, if not
be reinforced.[53] For Sparke, if this understanding of hegemony – which he does not
dispute but interprets as a form of informal imperialism – has been so powerful in
American political science as well as in policymaking circles over the past sixty
years, it is more a reflection of the pervasiveness of the 'liberal tradition in America'
that goes hand in hand with the exceptionalist narrative and with the Cold War
context of fighting Soviet communism and reading Marxist theorizing as product or
advocacy of the USSR. It is a sign of the exceptionalist roots of this rhetoric of denial
of imperialism that by choosing to focus on the depiction of the war in Iraq as an
aggressive attempt at American empire-building it is defused from recognizing that
this war '... has thematized and thereby also compromised the much more enduring
and informal form of market-mediated American hegemony'.[54] One could therefore
argue, as many (Walter Russell Mead for instance[55]) now do, that the US is a 'liberal
empire'; that in some encompassing ways American (neo)liberal hegemony *is* a
form of imperialism, albeit an informal one. The '(neo)liberal hegemony' thesis may
well be the best way to capture the US today, on the *longue durée* and in its present
conjuncture. Others will rather opt for the liberal empire idea, for it allows more the
exposition of the contradictions of the US state building and expansionist enterprise.
All of this is to say that it becomes crucial to see US nationalism through its many
different yet coexisting faces if one wishes to understand how US (neo)liberal
ideology permeates US state governmentality.[56]

The Global War on Terror as Fantasies of an Empire of Security

Following the collapse of communism, American strategists were at loose ends in
grappling with the development of a coherent security policy. While few, even in those
years of confusion, really doubted that America constituted the core of a global system
that was characterized by its hegemony, the shock of 11 September concentrated
minds. So something was added to the regnant assumption: neoconservative analysts
could now trumpet a new-found political will intended to translate the vision of
global dominance into reality. With the obvious evidence of American vulnerability,

---

52 Matthew Sparke, *In the Space of Theory*, p. 245.

53 *Ibid.*, p. 311.

54 *Ibid.*, p. 246.

55 Walter Russell Mead, *Special Providence: American Foreign Policy and How It
Changed the World* (New York: Alfred A. Knopf/A Century Foundation Book, 2002). In
1987 Mead was already depicting America's liberal hegemony as liberal imperialism. Walter
Russell Mead, *Mortal Splendor: The American Empire in Transition* (Boston: Houghton
Mifflin, 1987).

56 Matthew Sparke, *In the Space of Theory*, p. 281. See also Don H. Doyle, 'Manifest
Destiny, Race, and the Limits of American Empire', *Studies in Ethnicity and Nationalism*,
'Special Issue 2005: Nation and Empire' (2005): 39.

it became easy to legitimize a course of action that, absent the terrorist attacks on the country, would have smacked of old-fashioned imperialism. The clearest expression of this new will to power was found in the national strategy document unveiled in September 2002, and especially in the passages relating to preventive war.

According to the 2002 National Security Strategy (NSS) and the 2004 National Military Strategy (NMS), US military power must be ready to serve at any time if it is to have an impact. Both documents explicitly describe that the US will not only lead but dominate the strategically the world in trying to reach a *'full spectrum dominance across the range of military operations'*.[57] The US makes no attempt at dissimulating its global strategy in its self-declared Global War on Terror (GWOT). Its military might is there to maintain unilateral global dominance and hegemony by having the infinite possibility of waging war. Over what interests and values would this GWOT be fought? The answer to this question directly concerns the influence of neocons in US national security conduct.[58] At the turn of the millennium, influential neoconservative ideologues, figures like Paul Wolfowitz, Lewis Libby, Richard Perle, Stephen Hadley, Robert Kagan, and Irving and William Kristol, thought it was more than time for a more coherent, morally grounded, martial projection of US power falling under the auspices of a liberal benevolent empire using America's 'benign hegemony' to spread democracy rather than just extend the range of the free market.[59] In the first Bush administration, these neoconservative figures insisted that the US wanted to shape the world. They wanted 'an America that was genuinely imperial … not only because they believed it would make the world better, but because they wanted to see the United States *make* the world'.[60] It comes as no surprise then that one of the main organizations associated with neoconservatives is literally called the *Project for a New American Century*. If we are to believe US decision makers and neoconservative analysts, the US should be ready to deploy a 'democratic realism' in its national security conduct, a powerful rhetoric that reinstates the American commitment to an empire of liberty and of democracy. The axiom of democratic realism stipulates that the United States 'will support democracy everywhere, but we will commit blood and treasure only in places where there is a strategic necessity – meaning, places central to the larger war against the existential enemy, the enemy that poses a global mortal threat to freedom'.[61] How this would strategically translate

---

57 Richard B. Myers (Chairman of the Joint Chiefs of Staff), Department of Defense, US Government, George W. Bush Administration, *National Military Strategy of the United States of America*, Washington, DC, May 2004, p. 3.

58 See my article 'Mistaking Hegemony for Empire: Neoconservatives, the Bush Doctrine, and the Democratic Empire', published in *International Journal* in Spring 2006.

59 Corey Robin, 'Remembrance of Empires Past: 9/11 and the End of the Cold War', in Ellen Schrecker (ed.), *Cold War Triumphalism: The Misuse of History After the Fall of Communism* (New York and London: The New Press, 2004), p. 284.

60 *Ibid.*

61 This idea is from Charles Krauthammer, a political analyst close to neoconservative circles and associated with the think tank American Enterprise Institute, who many may know for his 1990 *Foreign Affairs* article 'The Unipolar Moment'. Krauthammer stresses that

is still fuzzy though. In so many ways this 'empire of liberty' evoked the idea of an 'empire of security'.[62] There is but a thin line separating hegemony from empire, and the former can easily become imperilled by the latter, with its stress upon militarism, arrogance, and above all, the growing threat to employ force. In effect, as Americanist Kousar Azam aptly puts it, 'The ethos of enlightenment that went into the foundational principles of the USA and promised mankind "an empire of liberty" is seldom reflected in US policies. The fractured discourses of American exceptionalism do not even promise that empire. On the contrary, the USA evokes the chimera of the return of empire that threatens to negate the notion of liberty and destroy in the process the very idea of sovereignty that makes liberty the basis of all civilized existence.'[63]

---

the US should apply a 'democratic realism' as its foreign policy in a 'unipolar era'. Charles Krauthammer, *Democratic Realism: An American Foreign Policy for a Unipolar World* (Washington, DC: AEI Press, 2004), p. 16. See also Charles Krauthammer, 'In Defense of Democratic Realism', *The National Interest*, 77 (Fall 2004): 15–25.

    62 Andrew Hurrell, '*Pax Americana* or the Empire of Insecurity?', p. 153.

    63 Kousar J. Azam, 'Resisting Terror, Resisting Empire: The Evolving Ethos of American Studies', *Comparative American Studies: An International Journal*, 2/2 (2004): 170.

PART 1
Representations of American Hegemony/Empire:
The Global and Domestic Implications of US Redefinition of Power

Chapter 1

Theory Wars of Choice:
Hidden Casualties in the 'Debate'
Between Hegemony and Empire

Robert Vitalis

For analyses of world politics since the George W. Bush administration's overthrow of the Taliban in Afghanistan and of Saddam Hussein in Iraq, the main hypothesis to be tested and if possible rejected is that the moment is one in which an old world order is dying and a new world order is being born. Thus it is easy to imagine a few of the key debates in advance. Some will argue for the signal importance of 9/11. Others will argue that the changes were obvious or nascent or incipient before the attacks on New York and Washington. Still others will argue that none of what we proclaim to be new is in fact new save at the margins, and certainly not in how power is being wielded and for what objectives. And though it won't be a main question among students of international relations, you can also imagine the argument turned on its head. We are witnessing a radical transformation in the American political economy, what Walter Dean Burnham calls with reference to earlier moments, the 1890s and 1930s, a 'critical realignment'.[1] Answering questions such as these correctly or even asking the right questions hinges on an adequate understanding of the institutions that make up the contemporary world system. The problem is that many journalists, scholars and activists have gotten it more wrong than right in lining

Author's Note: This article draws in part from the Foreword to a forthcoming book, *Kingdom: Race, State, and the Business of Mythmaking* (Palo Alto, 2007); a second, unpublished piece co-written with Ellis Goldberg, 'The Arabian Peninsula: Crucible of Globalization', European University Institute Working Papers, RSC No. 2002/9, Mediterranean Programme Series, 2002; a recently published book chapter, 'Birth of a Discipline', in Brian Schmidt and David Long (eds), *Imperialism and Internationalism in the Discipline of International Relations* (Albany, 2005); and from 'The Graceful and Liberal Gesture: Making Racism Invisible in American International Relations', *Millennium*, 29/2 (2000): 331–356. I'd like to thank the two editors, Charles-Phillipe David and David Grondin, and two of my colleagues, Ian Lustick and Brendan O'Leary, for sharp readings and commentaries on the draft.

1 See for example Thomas Ferguson, 'Holy Owned Subsidiary: Globalization, Religion and Politics in the 2004 Election', in William Crotty (ed.), *A Defining Election: The Presidential Race of 2004* (Armonk, 2005): 187–210.

up against the new, so-called American 'wars of choice'. Consider the confusion that emerges in discussions of something called empire and something else called hegemony. There are at least two kinds of analytical errors in current writings. One is the routine treatment of the two terms as synonyms, ignoring or ignorant of the work, starting with Immanuel Wallerstein, that shows how these two modes of international domination are different from one another.[2] Another, though, is a mistake that those who recognize the basic difference sometimes make. That mistake is to imagine that one mode of hierarchy is at work but not the other, although they are really co-existing, weaker and stronger tendencies in world politics.

Liberalism, Exceptionalism and Racism

At least two problems or blind spots affect the understanding of America's experience or practice of empire. One is the problem of exceptionalism – a standard way of viewing or narrating or thinking about the American experience.[3] American exceptionalism assumes the deep structural autonomy of that experience, that American history is unlike and unconnected with all others. Exceptionalism grounds, shapes and frames all the varieties of accounts purporting to prove American enterprise to be anything but agents of empire, of America being empire's antithesis, about the US acquiring an empire late or, as many political scientists are beginning to claim now, America is an empire but one that is unique in the annals of world politics.

The second blind spot is with respect to the power and robustness of beliefs about the naturalness of hierarchy to which Americans but not only Americans subscribe – more and less coherent ideologies that assign collective identities and places in an inegalitarian order on the basis of characteristics that people are purportedly 'born with' or 'inherit' or 'pass on' to their offspring.[4] Gender, ethnicity, nationality and even religion have served as grounds for exclusion in American political life, but no identity has mattered more than race in determining and justifying hierarchy. Thus, for the scholars who founded the discipline of international relations in the US at the turn of the twentieth century, the so-called races were fundamental or constitutive units of analysis. They treated the terms 'international relations' and 'interracial relations' as synonyms. Critics of the hierarchies built on the basis of skin color or facial features and the alleged inferior and superior abilities of such differently marked bodies coined a new term in the 1930s to characterize such practices. They called it 'racism', a variant on a term used first in the 1910s, 'racialism'.

---

2   Immanuel Wallerstein, *The Politics of the World Economy: The States, the Movements, and the Civilizations* (Cambridge, 1984).

3   You can do no better here than to turn to Daniel Rodgers, 'Exceptionalism', in Anthony Mohlo and Gordon Wood (eds), *Imagined Histories: American Historians Interpret the Past* (Princeton, 1998), pp. 21–40.

4   Rogers Smith, *Civic Ideals: Conflicting Visions of Citizenship in US History* (New Haven, 1997).

Racism is American exceptionalism's Achilles heel, the great contradiction at the heart of the 'storybook truth' about a country that Louis Hartz, the Harvard University political theorist and author of *The Liberal Tradition in America* (1955), imagined as 'eternally different from everyone else'.[5] A kindred contradiction runs through the work of those who today unselfconsciously reproduce Hartz's views in their accounts of a uniquely liberal and benign hegemonic order built by Americans after World War II – the one threatened by George W. Bush 'unbound'.[6]

Knowledge of the Ancestors

Empire and race (or what we might now say, a bit more critically, race formation or race-making) were widely understood as thoroughly intertwined problems by those scholars back at the turn of the twentieth century who began to call what they wrote and taught 'international relations'. They argued that the most pressing issues of the day demanded new interdisciplinary forms of knowledge. The men central to founding the field, raising funds for chairs and building departments and programs understood themselves as focused primarily on accounting for the dynamics of imperialism and nationalism. They sought practical strategies for better ways of administering territories and uplifting backward races, using what were seen as the progressive tools of racial science. The professors at the American Political Science Association and in their journals and book reviews depicted themselves as occupying a new intellectual space by right of the failure of the international legal scholars and antiquo-historians to deal adequately with the problems posed by empire. New race development and eugenics advocates vied and intersected with practitioners of *rassenpolitik* and with visionaries who predicted the inevitability of war between the Anglo-Saxons and one or more competing racial alignments.

The House That Exceptionalism Built

Exceptionalism is a narrative strategy that works to erase these realities of the centrality of empire and race formation to the so-called American experience. So, for instance, today white supremacy is not generally discussed either as a historical identity of the American state or an ideological commitment on which international relations is founded. Nor is empire understood as the context that gives rise to this specialized field of knowledge. To be a professional in international relations in the United States today means adopting a particular disciplinary identity constructed in the 1950s and 1960s that rests on a certain willful forgetting. By the 1980s, Michael Doyle, the Columbia University professor and advisor to United Nations Secretary General Kofi Annan, could claim that the discipline of political science in the United States had never shown much interest in empire and imperialism – even if its first

---

5   Hartz, as first quoted and then described by Rodgers, 'Exceptionalism', p. 29.

6   Ivo Daalder and James Lindsay, *America Unbound: The Bush Revolution in Foreign Policy* (Washington, DC, 2003).

organized subfield, also forgotten, was on comparative colonial administration. From the early 1990s critical margins of the field, Roxanne Doty insisted that it was less than thirty years earlier that a handful of other similarly positioned theorists first began to consider the role of race in world politics. She was their heir.[7] In truth, the lineage goes back a century or more.

The American intellectual historian, Thomas Bender, captures the irony in a moment when scholars like Hartz were constructing their exceptionalist accounts of America as a place apart while America's leaders oversaw the projection of power that is now talked about in terms of hegemony. Intellectuals after World War II, he says,

> were both explicitly aware of the new global position and responsibilities of the US, as they wrote. Yet so strong was the notion of American difference and autonomy that they looked inward, implying an American history unlike and unconnected with all others, even as they suggested the existence of a world economic system beyond the ken of the historical actors in their histories.[8]

Today, some younger, critical historians in foreign policy studies and diplomatic history recognize exceptionalism as one more intellectual construction of the Cold War. The rivalry with the Soviet Union goes far to explain the turn to imagining an America as 'different from other state actors and remain[ing] fundamentally apart from the historical relationships and processes that surround it and shape the nature of states and peoples with which it interacts'.[9] They might even concede that the long and unbroken history of American conquest and empire is denied or begins to be denied as part of the ideological struggle with communism. And they wouldn't be wrong.

Arguments about the Cold War origins of American exceptionalism give us only half the story, however. *Most* Cold War and post–Cold War historians of diplomacy and theorists of international relations continue to ignore racism when writing about transformations in the twentieth-century world order. The retreat or checkered course of white supremacy is not reducible to a story about America's containment of the Soviet Union, and it will not do to argue that the Cold War brought about white supremacy's end, as if it were the little extra push that liberalism needed for its redemption. The truth is, Cold War logics and imperatives often buttressed the forces of white supremacy globally.[10]

---

7   Michael Doyle, *Empires* (Ithaca, 1986), p. 11; Roxanne Lynn Doty, 'The Bounds of "Race" in International Relations', *Millennium* 22/3 (1993): 443–463.

8   From Thomas Bender's unpublished 'The Industrial World and the Transformation of Liberalism', ms, 2005.

9   From the introduction to Mark Bradley, *Imagining Vietnam and America: The Making of Postcolonial Vietnam, 1919–1950* (Chapel Hill, 2000), p. 7.

10   See Howard Winant, *The World is a Ghetto* (New York, 2002) and Thomas Borstelmann, *The Cold War and the Color Line* (Cambridge, MA, 2003).

Racism is a problem analytically separate from the problem of the Cold War, in the same way that the so-called end of empire or spread of the norms of decolonization and national self-determination are distinct from the Cold War. And both – decolonization and the partial defeat handed white supremacy – shaped the course of the twentieth century as much as the wars in Europe and the US–Soviet rivalry. This fact though goes unnoticed, especially in American IR theory, for reasons I have discussed.

From Empire to Hegemony to ... Empire?

Political science, historical sociology, international relations, and diplomatic history in the US have inherited and reproduced two analytical problems from the Cold War era, mistakes that have taken professors down a wrong path, although there are also some clues picked up along the way that promise a way out. One problem is the impoverished understanding of comparative empire building in place of some earlier, more sophisticated analyses of the interrelationships among late nineteenth-century processes of expansion, Jim Crow building and race development theory and practice. What was once known has been forgotten, and in its place is enshrined the relatively new, Cold War idea that America has never had an empire or else that America's version is 'empire lite'.

The second problem is the one identified by the writer Toni Morrison in her remarkable 'Black Matters', the first of her three 1990 Massey Lectures.[11] She analyzed the turn after World War II in the US to ignoring race. She calls it 'a graceful, even generous liberal gesture'. Postwar generations had been conditioned not to notice, she says. Morrison was writing about postwar literary critics and their silence about race and racism in the history of letters, the construction of literary canons and the criticisms worth making about the canonical texts. We can, however, easily extend the argument beyond the English and American Literature departments where, coincidentally, the study of empire has migrated. Theorizing in American departments of international relations after World War II involved a great deal of 'recoding'. Much of this work is itself a kind of escape from knowledge. The return in the 1960s of an old idea, hegemony, is something from the era that is worth holding on to, however.[12]

---

11 *Playing in the Dark: Whiteness and the Literary Imagination* (New York, 1993), pp. 9–10.

12 The concept did not appear in the *New York Times* or in other papers in the mid 1960s, whereas in a dozen or so academic journals it is found over 100 times. In 1969–1970, it is found 8 times in newspapers, but between 1971–1975, it appears in 89 stories. Use of the term exploded in the mid 1980s. Between 1986 and 1990 it appears 365 times; between 1991 and 1995, 730 times; and from 1996 until now, 983 times. The earliest references report Chinese foreign policy pronouncements denouncing Russian hegemony. As the Nixon administration pursued its *rapprochement* with the PRC the word entered the official vocabulary of American diplomacy, leading the Soviets to protest. Chinese premier Chou en-Lai was also first in the

Hegemony, Not Empire; Leadership, Not Domination

The first thing to note is that graduate students-turned professors in the US in the 1970s and 1980s who are teaching the canon in international relations now treat hegemony as a new theoretical concept. It is not, as the following editorial from the London *Times* in 1860 attests: 'No doubt it is a glorious ambition which drives Prussia to assert her claim to the leadership, or as that land of professors phrases it, the 'hegemony' of the Germanic Confederation'.[13] American scholars of foreign policy and inter-American relations in the 1920s conventionally described North America as exercising hegemony over the Caribbean. Great Britain exercised 'world hegemony' until around the time of World War I. And by 1937, according to the Austrian-Jewish émigré historian of City College, Hans Kohn, the growing power and industrial might of Japan, 'which seem to threaten the economic and political hegemony of the white races, have been discussed in many studies'.[14]

Among professors of international relations today the idea of hegemony most often refers to *the hierarchical order among rival great powers*.[15] To reproduce one frequently cited definition, hegemony is 'a situation in which one state is powerful enough to maintain the essential rules governing interstate relations, and willing to do so'.[16] This idea of an order among states represents a challenge to those who instead imagine international relations either as a kind of anarchy or else governed very loosely and fitfully via shifting alliances, referred to as the balance of power. An empire is another form of hierarchical international order, in which one state effectively seizes power and rules the subordinate societies. 'The domain of empire

---

New York Times to describe Nixon's August 1971 decision to suspend convertibility of the dollar as a sign that the US was 'losing its imperialist position of hegemony' (August 29, 1971, p. 19). Foreign affairs columnist C.L. Sulzberger agreed, analyzing the decline in hegemony of the dollar two months later (October 10, 1971, p. 4).

13 *Times*, May 5, 1860, p. 9.

14 Hans Kohn, 'The Europeanization of the Orient', *Political Science Quarterly* 52 (1937): 259–270.

15 The formalization of the professor's use of the concept and more accurately the 'theory of hegemonic stability' is usually credited to two eclectic scholars: Charles Kindleberger, an economist at MIT and Robert Gilpin, a political scientist at Princeton. To these twin canonical citations we should probably add a third by James Kurth, a political scientist at Swarthmore who presented a paper, 'Modernity and Hegemony: The American Way of Foreign Policy', at Harvard's Center for International Studies in 1971. See the discussion in Doyle, *Empires*, p.16, n. 16 and p. 40, n. 54. Kurth was the scholar most likely to be familiar with the late nineteenth-century references to Prussian hegemony. Note too that Robert Keohane was also teaching at Swarthmore with Kurth at this time, and he was the editor of the book in which Gilpin first began to lay out his account of the political economy of the post–World War II *Pax Americana*. See his 'The Politics of Transnational Economic Relations', in Robert O. Keohane and Joseph Nye, Jr. *Transnational Relations and World Politics* (Cambridge, MA, 1972). This collection first appeared in *International Organization* in 1971.

16 Robert Keohane and Joseph Nye, *Power and Interdependence* (Boston, 1977), p. 44.

is a people subject to unequal rule. One nation's government determines who rules another society's political life.'[17]

Hegemony is not so much a restrained and episodic form of interventionist politics by the US 'in' France or Britain or Japan as it is benevolent (or not) domination over the institutions that were established after World War II: the North Atlantic Treaty Organization, the General Agreement on Tariffs and Trade, the World Bank and the International Monetary Fund. The hegemon uses its power specifically in order to secure the cooperation of other states in building and maintaining the political architecture to support an open and integrated – 'liberal' – world economy.[18] Other states and classes consent because they gain more than token benefits. The hegemon pays a significant share of the costs of rule and acts with restraint rather than predatorily.[19]

Hegemony typically explains the two great periods of liberal market expansion in the mid nineteenth century – the *Pax Britannica* – and again in the mid twentieth century – the *Pax Americana*. In both periods, a single power builds and sustains a free trade regime that enmeshes its major rivals. The British case makes it easy to see the distinction between hegemony and empire, and why the distinction should continue to matter. First, virtually no one who writes on the nineteenth century treats any of the rival great powers – Russia, France, Austria, Prussia, the Ottoman state and more distantly the US and Japan – as part of Britain's 'informal empire' comprising various, protectorates, dependencies and clients. Second, there were multiple imperial complexes coexisting at the time of the *Pax Britannica*. And third, the decline of the first liberal order coincides with the 'imperial scramble' of the late

---

17 Doyle, *Empires*, p. 36.

18 There has always been some dissembling about the objectives of a project of this type, particularly when, as Gilpin notes, such arguments were hard to disentangle from the political challenge of new left social movements and, we would add, later, the force of opposition of declining northeast and rust belt regions. Still both those who defend postwar American hegemony as an example of 'enlightened self interest' together with those who began to condemn it as a costly campaign on behalf of a misguided 'ideological vision' point to important dimensions of a hegemonic order.

19 Today there is a small number of mostly European-trained scholars who bring Gramsci more centrally into theorizing about world order. The key works in this *fin de siecle* strand of Marxist IR theory include Robert Cox, *Production, Power and World Order: Social Forces in the Making of History* (New York, 1987); Enrico Augelli and Craig Murphy, *America's Quest for Supremacy and the Third World* (London, 1988); Stephen Gill (ed.), *Gramsci, Historical Materialism and International Relations* (Cambridge, 1993) and William Robinson, 'Gramsci and Globalization: From Nation State to Transnational Hegemony', *Critical Review of International Social and Political Philosophy* 8, 4 (December 2005): 1–16. The latter author is a sociologist. Needless to say, there is little prospect that these newest forms of structural Marxism will win many adherents inside the US, where Marxism is no longer taught and where the barely acceptable critical third position of 'constructivism' is sometimes offered up instead. What we can say is that as Gramsci's work has become better known in the Anglo-Saxon world, some IR theorists are more likely to reflect on the nonmaterial dimensions of hegemonic power.

nineteenth century, when these rival powers turned to increased exploitation and intensified – 'formal' – control over peripheral zones. 'Informal empires' quickly hardened into blocs.

Slippage

In the 1980s some scholars had returned to the earlier use of hegemony in analyzing various 'spheres of influence', for example, the US in Caribbean and Central America and the Soviet Union's domination of Eastern Europe.[20] Amid the clash of ideological anticommunists and the new left in the 1960s, empire and imperialism had been discredited and were not proper 'words for scholars' as Doyle put it. Extending the term hegemony made it somewhat more legitimate to compare modes of domination among the superpowers. And use of the recovered term works for some as a way, ironically, to distinguish our own era from a time when territorial conquest and the legal transfer of sovereignty were conventions of empire building – the problem being that many states practice non-territorial forms of domination presumably but only one state is ever described as a hegemon. For others the concept stands for a less extensive form of domination than found in empires of the nineteenth-century colonial-settler variety, although there are always (unconvincing) objections that domination is more insidious now in the guise of 'cultural hegemony' and the like. A plea for clarity and consistency may be futile at a time when public intellectuals and activists – let alone graduate students – dress up their opposition to US unilateralism using these very terms, but there may be some hidden value for those who might otherwise want to collapse the two ideas or modes of domination.

Neo-Colonial, Race-Blind, American Liberal Hegemony

Holding on to the distinction between empire and hegemony makes it easy to see how ascriptive hierarchy is reproduced over time. To put it in the simplest terms, a particular set of norms – call it hegemony – applies in relations among a superior caste of states and another set of norms – call it empire or dominion or dependency, terms used by North American scholars beginning in the 1920s – applies in dealings with a subordinate and inferior caste of states. Before World War II, policy makers, intellectuals and the white working class all defended the international caste system as a natural order among races. Now it is conventional to find international hierarchy defended as a natural order among states rather than races, with the same effect. 'The strong do what they will, the weak do what they must.' As Toni Morrison reminds us, it may be even more common to act as if hierarchy does not exist.

---

20 See Jan Triska (ed.), *Dominant Powers and Subordinate States: The United States in Latin America and the Soviet Union in Eastern Europe* (Durham, 1986).

A Norm against Noticing for the Twenty-First Century

Consider the exemplary explications of American liberal hegemony by John Ikenberry and his colleagues over the past dozen years. 'A remarkable aspect of world politics at century's end is the utter dominance of the United States.'[21] Ikenberry argues that it is the particular liberal characteristics of American hegemony that explains its durability. He describes the American century as a restrained and penetrated order, where other states possess an unusual degree of voice in American domestic politics, and where over time institutions came to lock in the partners. He contrasts this liberal settlement – that is, the creation of a new order after World War II – with the containment order or settlement with the Soviet Union.

What is thus truly remarkable in this account of world politics is the complete disappearance of what were once known as the inferior races. Thinkers like Mahan, Bryce and Adams, who Ikenberry describes as the original intellectual sources of American liberal hegemony, were among the country's great racial supremacists, and his account rehabilitates – doubtless unselfconsciously – an ex-*herrenvolk* (master race) democracy's ruling ideas. It is probably unselfconscious too about its embrace of international inequality, the missing third 'postcolonial' settlement. One has to read these works carefully to realize that rules of liberal hegemony apply to industrialized states only.

If Ikenberry would give some serious thought to America's dependencies and how they matter, he would have to acknowledge that different rules of world order apply across the entire twentieth century. After all, the varieties of embedded or structural liberalism theory, his included, that describe the postwar international order extend, again mostly unselfconsciously, Louis Hartz's influential beliefs about American culture to the western world as a whole, and Hartz himself accepted that illiberal institutions were a paradox that required explanation.[22] A standard explanation is that slavery or colonialism or racism is an atavism, a foreign import, a reflection of antiquated modes of production, and so on.

The present moment troubles many of the analysts and proponents of American liberal hegemony, obviously. They are troubled somewhat by the resurgent talk of assuming the burdens of empire. Much more troubling for most liberal internationalists, Brookings exiles and the like, however, are the implications of unilateralism for America's existing relationships with other advanced industrial nations. In *Foreign Affairs*, Ikenberry writes that

> If empire is defined loosely, as a hierarchical system of political relationships in which the most powerful state exercises decisive influence, then the United States today indeed qualifies.

21 G. John Ikenberry, 'Liberal Hegemony and the Future of American Postwar Order', in T.V. Paul and John Hall (eds), *International Order and the Future of World Politics* (Cambridge, 1999), pp. 123–144, 124.

22 Louis Hartz, *The Founding of New Societies: Studies in the History of the United States, Latin America, South Africa, Canada, and Australia* (San Diego, 1964), pp. 49–50.

If the United States is an empire, however, it is like no other before it. To be sure, it has a long tradition of pursuing crude imperial policies, *most notably in Latin America and the Middle East*. But for most countries, the US–led order is a negotiated system wherein the United States has sought participation by other states on terms that are mutually agreeable.[23]

Most countries – of the almost 200 today – included? With the Middle East and Latin America at some unspecified time the exceptions? Arguments such as this one depend, obviously, on not noticing a great deal, as is evident in his explication of what makes our world 'not empire … [but] a US–led democratic political order that has no name or historical antecedent'. For the analysis to work, it must exclude most of Africa, the Caribbean and Central Asia along with the Middle East and Latin America. Many if not most states in what we used to call the periphery have no 'voice opportunities' as he puts it, nor 'informal access to the policymaking processes of the United States and the intergovernmental institutions that make up the international system'. Saudi Arabia may be one of the few places in what we used to call the Third World where the model works, although voice in the case is not the result, as populists imagine it, of the Carlyle group or of Bush being an oilman or from Texas or having investments in common with the House of Sa'ud.[24]

Ikenberry himself is smart enough to recognize the anomalies in this Hartzian account of world order but apparently prefers to ignore the problems this recognition poses for the model. True, he says,

the United States has pursued imperial policies, especially toward weak countries in the periphery. *But US relations with Europe, Japan, China, and Russia cannot be described as imperial, even when 'neo' or 'liberal' modifies the term.* The advanced democracies operate within a 'security community' in which the use or threat of force is unthinkable. Their economies are deeply interwoven. Together, they form a political order built on bargains, diffuse reciprocity, and an array of intergovernmental institutions and ad hoc working relationships.

What is a paradox for Ikenberry is better understood as a constitutive feature of the contemporary – and constructed – world order. The fact doesn't trouble a generation that like the one before sees hierarchy as natural or else is unable or unwilling to see it at all. The more one emphasizes American hegemony's essentially consensual dimensions, the easier it is to see some of the basic and contrasting institutions and norms of empire – invasion, assassination, torture, bribery, segregation and the like.

---

23 G. John Ikenberry, 'Illusions of Empire', *Foreign Affairs*, March/April (2004): 144–156, emphasis mine.

24 See, from back in the days before Michael Moore's strange *Fahrenheit 9/11* my 'Closing of the Arabian Oil Frontier and the Future of Saudi-American Relations', *Middle East Report* No. 204 (1997): 15–21.

The Burdens of a New American Century

Consider the question one more time: What are most analysts most concerned with at the present juncture? For Ikenberry and many others in the universities and think tanks it is the infamous unilateralist turn, the trashing of the relationship among 'the advanced democracies' or what used to be called the Anglo-Saxon race and the possibly less than optimum strategy adopted by the US for 'preservation of power'. The land of the professors seems rather less troubled by the overturning of the weak norms against occupation of places that have resources that 'our' civilization requires. The best and the brightest are busy reinventing ideas about peoples that stand outside civilization, as was once asserted about states that through some artful nineteenth-century theorizing became 'tribes', and rushing to fine-tune those power point presentations that depict vast swaths of the world's 'failed states' in need of good governance, peoples in need of uplift and minorities in need of rescue.

Chapter 2

Geopolitics, Grand Strategy and the Bush Doctrine: The Strategic Dimensions of US Hegemony under George W. Bush

Simon Dalby

'The United States may be only the latest in a long line of countries that
is unable to place sensible limits on its fears and aspirations.'

Robert Jervis[1]

Geopolitics and Strategy

Geopolitics usually refers to the largest scale understanding of the arrangements
of world power. Invoking the term suggests both matters of importance and their
geographical arrangements, which in turn situate and constrain states in their
rivalries and struggles for power. Strategy is about the meshing of ends and means,
of attempting to attain ends with an economy of effort and the effective use of
the means available. Frequently the two meet in a discussion of 'grand strategy'
understood as the pursuit of the largest scale objectives by practitioners of statecraft.
In Colin Dueck's terms '"Grand strategy' involves a self-conscious identification
and prioritization of foreign policy goals; an identification of existing and potential
resources; and a selection of a plan which uses these resources to meet those goals.'[2]
Thinking about American hegemony in these terms is especially apt in an era that
has been termed by many as a 'war on terror', an era presided over by the self-
proclaimed 'war president' George W. Bush.

This chapter examines the geopolitical logic of the 'Bush doctrine' that drives
the *National Security Strategy of the United States* of 2002 and subsequent policy
statements. It is crucially important to take the doctrinal statements of George
W. Bush's administration seriously. If one reads them with assumptions that they
are naïve or some form of ideological smokescreen, then the possibility that the
speechwriters and intellectuals that form the core of George Bush's foreign and
defense policy team really aspire to what they claim gets occluded. Either invoking

---

1   Robert Jervis, 'Understanding the Bush Doctrine', *Political Science Quarterly*, 118/3
(2003): 365.

2   Colin Dueck, 'Ideas and Alternatives in American Grand Strategy, 2000–2004',
Review of International Studies, 30/4 (2004): 512.

conspiracy thinking or the intimation of ulterior motives may be very tempting for all sorts of reasons, but thinking in these modes about contemporary events is a mistake if it suggests that the public doctrine is a deliberate deception. There is a simple logic to the various articulations of 'the Bush doctrine' that is both obvious and important. It behooves scholars and analysts of geopolitics in particular to tackle this logic directly because strategic discourse is all about how global political space is domesticated and disciplined.[3]

The detailed history of the thinkers and policy makers that dominated American policy in the first Bush administration, and who have subsequently reemerged from the think tank and corporate boardrooms to take up the reins of power once again, the 'Vulcans' in their self preferred terminology, is beyond the scope of this chapter.[4] But an overview of their long-term thinking is essential as there are notable continuities in geopolitical thinking since the end of the cold war. It is also important to note that the Bush doctrine is not necessarily internally coherent, well meshed with other aspects of the Bush administration's policies, nor is it necessarily obvious from the doctrine how to conduct policy in any particular set of circumstances. But it does provide an overarching conceptualization of how the world is organized, of what is America's role in that world, and how American power is to be understood and used in that so specified context. The Bush doctrine was elaborated in the aftermath of September 11th in response to the events of that day drawing on existing geopolitical thinking and focused on 'war' as the primary response to what were understood as new 'global' dangers. Both the specifications of global and war are highly questionable, but they provided the key elements in American foreign and defense policy from late 2001 through the rest of George W. Bush's first administration.

Little of this geopolitical thinking is very new, although some innovations were obviously needed in a hurry in September 2001 given the novelty of Osama Bin Laden's tactics. The key themes of American supremacy, the willingness to maintain overwhelming military superiority over potential rivals and the proffered option of preventative war to stop potential threats from even emerging, were all sketched out in the first Bush presidency at the end of the cold war in the period following the war with Iraq in 1991 when Dick Cheney was Secretary of Defense, and Colin Powell and Paul Wolfowitz were at the heart of Washington's defense bureaucracy. The related key assumption that America has the right to assert its power to reshape the rest of the world to its liking also carries over from the early 1990s.

This chapter revisits the first Bush presidency to look at the debate then about what American strategy ought to be in the aftermath of the cold war. The point about

---

3   Bradley S. Klein, *Strategic Studies and World Order: The Global Politics of Deterrence* (Cambridge: Cambridge University Press, 1994).

4   See in detail James Mann, *Rise of the Vulcans: The History of Bush's War Cabinet* (New York: Viking, 2004); Stefan Halper and Jonathon Clarke, *America Alone: The Neo-Conservatives and the Global Order* (Cambridge: Cambridge University Press, 2004); Gary Dorrien, *Imperial Designs: Neoconservatism and the New Pax Americana* (New York: Routledge, 2004).

pre-eminence not being new is important; the logic of the Bush doctrine is obviously traceable to the end of the cold war and the triumphalism that pervaded the neo-conservative thinkers at the heart of the American foreign and defense establishment. As it turned out these people were once again in power on September 11th and the resulting 'Bush doctrine', clearly outlined in the 2002 *National Security Doctrine of the United States of America*, bears many of the hallmarks of the antecedent documents both in the first Bush administration and in the writings emanating from various lobby groups and think tanks during the Clinton presidency.[5]

After the Cold War

With the end of the cold war and the demise of the Soviet threat, planners in the American military establishment developed a series of ideas about the role for American forces in these new circumstances. In August 1990, just as the Iraqi invasion of Kuwait was occurring, George H.W. Bush announced a new strategy for American forces in a speech to the Aspen institute. Announcing that overall the US forces would be cut by 25% he argued that the new role involved preserving international stability and having the ability to intervene in regional threats to that stability. Variously known as the 'Aspen Strategy', the 'New National Security Strategy' or a 'Strategy for a New World Order' these statements outlined US military policy and priorities in the post–cold war world where a superpower conflict was seen as unlikely.[6]

The emphasis in this strategy was on military contingencies and the need to be prepared to fight a war with a well-armed Third World power. Obviously the war against Iraq in 1991 was a dress rehearsal for such a role for the US military in promoting 'the New World Order'. It was also, in retrospect, seen as the crucible for restructuring the US military organization. The mobilization and deployment provided the opportunity to cut across traditional bureaucratic 'turf' and promote the integration of the services in new ways.[7] It also allowed the extensive field trials of the new generation of high technology weapons including stealth fighters, 'smart' bombs and cruise missiles in non-nuclear roles.

These new strategic ideas were elaborated in official documents in the Defense Department then under Secretary Dick Cheney; the modified geopolitical priorities and force restructurings were fairly clear in outline.[8] First is the reduction in nuclear weapons, most obvious in the removal of tactical weapons from naval vessels, and

---

5   The White House, George W. Bush Administration, *The National Security Strategy of the United States of America* (Washington, DC, September 2002).

6   See in more detail Ola Tunander, 'Bush's Brave New World: A New World Order – A New Military Strategy', *Bulletin of Peace Proposals*, 22/4 (1991): 355–68.

7   H.G. Summers, *On Strategy II: A Critical Analysis of the Gulf War* (New York: Dell, 1992).

8   Dick Cheney, Department of Defense, George H.W. Bush Administration, *Report of the Secretary of Defense to the President and Congress* (Washington, DC, 1991); Joint

the consolidation of a smaller strategic arsenal combined with continued Strategic Defense Initiative (SDI) type developments in a new strategic configuration. Second was a continued presence of land forces in Europe and an Atlantic focus of both naval and heavy land based forces. The navy continued to dominate the Pacific region, albeit with a reduced number of carrier groups, while a flexible contingency force was planned along with the strategic transport capabilities to move it rapidly into any arena of conflict. Naval weapons such as the Seawolf class of submarines and the focus on anti-submarine warfare designed to defeat the Soviet navy were no longer deemed relevant; carrier task forces were elevated in importance to 'project power' anywhere around the globe.

The role of advanced technology in the success of the Gulf War also reinforced emphasis on maintaining a technological advantage over any likely adversary. Hence SDI and stealth programs were likely to be a keystone to any future armed force. So too was the continuation of reliance on reserves to flesh out the intervention forces. At least one prominent strategist at the time, Harry Summers, argued that restructuring forces to rely on reserves in time of war was important in garnering crucial political support for the military action in the Gulf in 1991. Further he argued that the Gulf War and the planning that led to it through the 1980s has marked a shift, in Clausewitzian terms, from the strategic defensive of the cold war to the strategic offensive in the post–cold war period. This marked, he suggested, a crucial reassertion of political will in the prosecution of foreign policy.[9]

Early in 1992 the scenarios that the force planning was based on became a series of *New York Times* headline news stories.[10] Among the crisis contingencies being considered were another Iraqi invasion of Kuwait and Saudi Arabia, a North Korean attack on South Korea, a coup in the Philippines, a Panamanian coup threatening the Canal Zone, and a war between Russia and Lithuania, Poland and Byelorussia with NATO intervention. Each of these would require flexible US contingency forces and the possibility, in at least the Lithuania scenario, of substantial heavy conventional forces. Critics argued that the Iraqi scenario was particularly far fetched given the recent destruction of the bulk of Iraq's military potential.

The clear emphasis in Pentagon planning, and in the 1994–1999 *Defense Planning Guidance* document in particular, on preventing the emergence of any other state as a rival to its global supremacy, generated considerable public debate.[11] While critics condemned the scenarios as unlikely and mere justifications for inflated military

---

Chiefs of Staff, Department of Defense, George H.W. Bush Administration, *Joint Military Net Assessment* (Washington, DC, 1991).

9   Summers, *On Strategy II.*

10   P.E. Tyler, 'As Fears of a Big War Fades, Military Plans for Little Ones', *New York Times* (3 January, 1992): 1; P.E. Tyler, 'Pentagon Imagines New Enemies To Fight in Post–Cold War Era', *New York Times* (17 February, 1992): 1; P.E. Tyler, 'War in 1990's: New Doubts', *New York Times* (18 February, 1992): 1.

11   P.E. Tyler, 'US Strategy Plan Calls for Insuring No Rivals Develop', *New York Times* (8 March, 1992): 1; P.E. Tyler, 'Senior US Officials Assail a "One Superpower Goal"', *New York Times* (11 March, 1992): 1.

budgets, the more interesting criticisms suggested that the more fundamental flaw in this kind of planning was the presumption that a US military force could or should unilaterally enforce a global order. Claiming victory in the cold war and in the Gulf War the *Defense Planning Guidance* suggested that the latter was a 'defining event in US global leadership'. While the Bush administration's opposition to a European security arrangement without US participation is not new, the Pentagon planning document suggested that any attempt by European powers, a rearmed Japan or a rebuilt Russian military to reassert regional leadership would be regarded suspiciously by the US military.

> Our first objective is to prevent the reemergence of a new rival, either on the territory of the former Soviet Union or elsewhere, that poses a threat on the order of that posed formerly by the Soviet Union. This is a dominant consideration underlying the new regional defense strategy and requires that we endeavor to prevent any hostile power from dominating a region whose resources would, under consolidated control, be sufficient to generate global power. These regions include Western Europe, East Asia, the territory of the former Soviet Union and South West Asia.[12]

Three additional objectives were enumerated to support this overall position. Firstly, the US should provide 'the leadership necessary to establish and protect a new order that holds the promise of convincing potential competitors that they need not aspire to a greater role or pursue a more aggressive posture to protect their legitimate interests'. Secondly, and beyond that, 'in non-defense areas, we must account sufficiently for the interests of the advanced industrial nations to discourage them from challenging our leadership or seeking to overturn the established political and economic order'. Thirdly, and in a most blunt assertion of global supremacy, the document argued that 'we must maintain the mechanisms for deterring potential competitors from even aspiring to a larger regional or global role'. Coupled to military advice that 'being as good as a potential adversary is not enough; winning means not only exceeding the strengths of the opponent, but dominating him so completely that the conflict is ended early with favourable results and minimal casualties', the claim to global supremacy could not be clearer.[13]

In its critics' eyes the argument for a new military 'Pax Americana' was more likely to raise fears of American hegemony in many places rather than reassure other states of the viability and desirability of the new world order, none of which augured well for a long-term political arrangement conducive to peace. There was no conception of the economic dimensions of either international economic issues or the long-term domestic budgetary constraints on military procurements in the world's largest

---

12 Department of Defense, *Defense Planning Guidance for the Fiscal Years 1994–1999* (Washington, DC, 1992); excerpts of the leaked 18 February draft as reprinted in *The New York Times* (8 March, 1992).

13 P.E. Tyler, 'Plans for Small Wars Replace Fear of Big One', *New York Times* (3 February, 1992): 6.

debtor nation.[14] In contrast the possibilities of multilateral alliance systems and an enhanced role for the United Nations and regional collective security arrangements were ignored. International security was understood as the unilateral imposition of US military force to maintain order in the international political system.

While the White House quickly distanced itself from the more controversial formulations in 1992, and some months later the Pentagon removed the offending 'one superpower' section from the 'guidance' document, the lack of a wider political vision in the US administration left room open for these scenarios and allowed strategic and geopolitical discourses to dominate political discussion. As one commentary at the time noted, in the absence of a clear political rationale for global politics after the cold war '… the defense debate has become a principal vehicle for discussing the much larger issue of the place of the United States in the post–cold war world'.[15] Indeed the rationale for global politics and what might be done now that superpower rivalry had faded away was little more than 'we won' and 'we intend to keep matters pretty much as they are for as long as we can'. With the arrival of the Clinton administrations these explicit formulations of geopolitical supremacy faded, but the use of military force abroad continued in Somalia, Bosnia and elsewhere.

The Project for a New American Century

The 'Vulcans' out of executive power in Washington after Bill Clinton's election, continued their advocacy of American primacy and formed a number of lobbying organizations the most high profile of which was 'The Project for a New American Century' (PNAC). This organization published a series of reports and open letters and was associated with a number of books produced by leading neo-conservative thinkers. Most notable was their 2000 report on *Rebuilding America's Defenses* which comes closest to a blueprint for the future.[16] The context of the late 1990s suggested to the PNAC authors that the 'happy situation' of American supremacy gained by what they considered America's victory in the cold war might not last:

> At present the United States faces no global rival. America's grand strategy should aim to preserve and extend this advantageous position as far into the future as possible. There are, however, potentially powerful states dissatisfied with the current situation and eager to change it, if they can, in directions that endanger the relatively peaceful, prosperous and free condition the world enjoys today. Up to now, they have been deterred from doing so by the capability and global presence of American military power. But, as that

14 J.Chance, 'The Pentagon's Superpower Fantasy', *New York Times* (14 March, 1992).

15 P.J. Garrity and S.K. Weiner, 'US Defense Strategy After the Cold War', *The Washington Quarterly*, 15/2 (1992): 57–76.

16 The Project for the New American Century, *Rebuilding America's Defenses: Strategy, Forces and Resources For a New Century. A Report of The Project for the New American Century* (Washington, DC, September 2000).

power declines, relatively and absolutely, the happy conditions that follow from it will be inevitably undermined.[17]

The PNAC report states that its approach explicitly builds on the documents from the latter part of the period when Dick Cheney was Secretary of Defense: 'The Defense Policy Guidance (DPG) drafted in the early months of 1992 provided a blueprint for maintaining US pre-eminence, precluding the rise of a great power rival, and shaping the international security order in line with American principles and interests.'[18] Looking ahead to the next presidency in a period of budget surpluses, which in PNAC's opinion obviated any financial reasons for constraining the defense budget, the authors offered their report as providing input into the next 'Quadrennial Defense Review' that the new administration would be expected to produce soon after the election. This PNAC blueprint was an explicit attempt to provide continuity with the earlier Cheney defense department planning in the first Bush administration. As such it provides a loosely consistent set of priorities and a geopolitical framework for a grand strategy based on military supremacy against any potential state rivals to American power.

The language suggests an imperial presence, and a world attuned to a Pax Americana:

> Today, the United States has an unprecedented strategic opportunity. It faces no immediate great-power challenge; it is blessed with wealthy, powerful and democratic allies in every part of the world; it is in the midst of the longest economic expansion in its history; and its political and economic principles are almost universally embraced. At no time in history has the international security order been as conducive to American interests and ideals. The challenge for the coming century is to preserve and enhance this 'American peace'.[19]

To counter potential challenges to this Pax Americana the PNAC authors suggested that American forces needed to be expanded. Four core themes were essential to the future defense policy, which they asserted needed to simultaneously:

- defend the American homeland;
- fight and decisively win multiple, simultaneous major theater wars;
- perform the 'constabulary' duties associated with shaping the security environment in critical regions;
- transform US forces to exploit the 'revolution in military affairs;'

This is an ambitions list for a military that PNAC argued needed to be expanded from 1.4m to 1.6m active service personnel. But by maintaining nuclear superiority and moving forces permanently to South East Europe and South East Asia the task could

---

17 *Rebuilding America's Defenses*, p. i.
18 *Ibid.*, p. ii.
19 *Ibid.*, p. iv.

supposedly be accomplished. Selective modernization of the forces could also be accomplished by canceling some expensive planned hardware innovations including the Crusader howitzer system and maximizing the use of new technologies to ensure the continued supremacy of American conventional forces. In addition cyberspace and outer space were arenas that needed American control. Missile defenses were also seen as essential to protect the American homeland and bases abroad. All of which required an increase of defense spending to between 3.5% and 3.8% of GNP. 'The true cost of not meeting our defense requirements will be a lessened capacity for American global leadership and, ultimately, the loss of a global security order that is uniquely friendly to American principles and prosperity.'[20]

Complaining that the Clinton administration had cut $426bn from defense equipment investments, and that none of the ten divisions were fully combat ready, the PNAC authors bemoaned the fact that military facilities are still in Germany when the security dangers are in South East Europe. The language of crises pervades the PNAC document, for which the opportunity to rebuild American power will be missed if the next president fails to adequately fund the defense forces and ensure the dominance of American arms into the future. The unipolar moment may pass and America face rivals for its hegemony if military readiness slips further and equipment and personnel are further neglected. The rhetoric is familiar from earlier days of cold war fears and from alarm at post-Vietnam force reductions; the late 1970s were replete with alarms about relative weaknesses and the need to rebuild the military; many of the neoconservatives who subsequently became influential were part of the Reagan presidencies where military spending was increased and weapons systems acquired.[21] The suggestion that American military supremacy won the cold war is a pervasive tendency in the rationalizations for new attempts to assert the supremacy. What is notably absent in all this discussion is any rival that might make American military dominance questionable. But, so the logic of the argument goes, ensuring that one is not even tempted to try is the only reliable way to assert Pax Americana – and yes, the PNAC report explicitly uses the phrase suggesting parallels with Rome and Britain in earlier periods.

Homeland defense takes priority in the PNAC document, especially the need for missile defense so that states which acquire ballistic missiles cannot deter American military action. This is the first priority. But the military must also preserve and expand the zone of democratic peace – according to much of the American liberal school of international relations thinking that ensues the democratic peace thesis – where democratic states apparently do not fight each other and are in one way or another aligned with the US, to ensure global prosperity. Where the forces in the cold war were primarily concerned with a conflict with the USSR in Europe, now in the post cold war they are concerned with fighting regional wars, but in a context where the potential strategic rivalries are focused in Asia. There is a very

---

20 *Ibid.*, p. v.

21 Simon Dalby, *Creating the Second Cold War: The Discourse of Politics* (London: Pinter; New York: Guilford, 1990).

different geography to American power now, and one that requires a refocused strategic posture. Constabulary duties, such as the deployment of American forces in the Balkans, are a clear part of the Pentagon's mandate too and require suitable force structures. Increasing the number of active forces and reducing reliance on reserve forces is seen as important, especially if constabulary duties are taken seriously. Nuclear weapons upgrades were apparently forgotten by the Clinton administration which was castigated for its negotiation of the supposedly ineffective comprehensive test ban treaty, which the Republican-controlled Senate defeated, leaving the treaty unratified.

There is a rich irony in the warning in *Rebuilding America's Defenses* where the authors wonder about the utility of aircraft carriers in the navy of the future. Will the navy carriers be rendered redundant by unmanned airplanes and guided missiles, in much the same way as carrier planes rendered battleships redundant at Pearl Harbor? Given that the PNAC document does not mention terrorism as a threat to American power, the adage about planning to fight the last war seems strangely apt. Alarm over the revolution in military affairs and the technological capabilities of potential future foes ignored the foes that actually did strike America on September 11th, 2001. The focus solely on rival states is noteworthy. It also structures a companion volume that Robert Kagan and William Kristol edited in 2000 that focused on potential threats to American power. Once again the rhetorical traditions of American thinking are reprised, this time in a volume entitled *Present Dangers*.[22] But states are the focus, and the rise of non-state threats are noticeably absent from the thinking.

A crucial dimension of this is how effectively this discussion of the future of American defense excludes from consideration global problems of economic and environmental matters and international humanitarian issues. The discursive structure on which all these play is the spatialized separation of cause and effect. Security problems are external to the fundamental operation of the essential elements of the 'Western system'. Military threats are not in any way related to matters of the economic injustices caused by the operation of the global economy. Existing boundaries are to a large extent considered legal and just even where they are not precisely demarcated (as in the case of the Iraq-Kuwait dispute). Responsibility for the difficulties to which military strategies are the answer is designated as originating in an external unrelated space. This radical separation, the spatialized 'Othering' of threats, acts to perpetuate geopolitical knowledge practices that emphasize conflict and militarized understandings of security.[23]

---

22 Robert Kagan and William Kristol (eds), *Present Dangers: Crisis and Opportunity in American Foreign and Defense Policy* (San Francisco: Encounter Books, 2000).

23 David Campbell, *Writing Security: United States Foreign Policy and the Politics of Identity*, rev. ed. (Minneapolis: University of Minnesota Press, 1998).

The Bush Doctrine

Subsequently the Bush doctrine formulated in response to the 9/11 attacks incorporated many of these themes. The most obvious and salient geopolitical points about the Bush doctrine are simple but very important, none more so than the immediate assumption that the struggle against terror was a matter best prosecuted as a matter of warfare rather than by diplomacy and police action. Once the events of September 11th were interpreted as a 'global' war on terror then the geopolitical categories from the first Bush administration and the PNAC documents shaped the subsequent prosecution of American policy. The specific geographies of Al Qaeda and struggles in the Gulf region were swept aside by the geographically inappropriate specifications of global struggle and the discursive repertoire of global security was awkwardly applied to the new circumstances in late 2001.

But as shown here these themes are not just an innovation of the second Bush presidency. Neither are they completely divorced from the prosecution of American power in the Clinton era. The shift in American thinking after the cold war from an overall policy of containment to one of enlargement in the Clinton years was a reversal of the spatial direction of policy. Instead of a negative formulation of holding the line against a supposedly expanding communist world, the democratic peace arguments supported a policy of democratization, of expanding the remit of liberal democracy in many places. Incorporating recalcitrant powers into the international trading and treaty organizations was part of the expansion of American influence in the 1990s and was in a most crucial way as if it meant following the 'lessons' of a liberal democratic peace which asserts that security is best arranged as incorporation within the international system rather than autarkic separation, a matter that has some substantial support in the pertinent scholarly literature.[24] This zone of democratic peace, to use the PNAC terminology, is seen as the core of America's power and its expansion becomes key to the logic of the Clinton administration, one usually more eager to use diplomatic than military power to effect its extension.

In the aftermath of the attack on September 11th the Bush administration issued a series of statements and speeches on what quickly became the 'global war on terror' (GWOT). The key elements in a new strategy were collected and issued as the 'National Security Strategy of the United States of America' in September 2002. Effectively this document acts as a codification of the 'Bush doctrine'. It is rich in American rhetoric, and in many ways can be read more as an assertion of American identity and aspiration, rather than as a strategic doctrine.[25] The restatement of Americanism, a virulent nationalism, is crucial to understanding the operation of the Bush administrations since September 11th. Although ironically in that second administration the Clinton themes of democratization abroad by political means

---

24 Etel Solingen, *Regional Orders at Century's Dawn: Global and Domestic Influences on Grand Strategy* (New Jersey: Princeton University Press, 1998).

25 Anatol Lieven, *America Right or Wrong: An Anatomy of American Nationalism* (New York: Oxford University Press, 2004).

are now once again being grafted onto the Bush doctrine by Condoleezza Rice as Secretary of State, suggesting another continuity in American thinking that is reasserting itself after the difficulties resulting from the military focus in the Bush doctrine.[26] It also, of course, reprises many earlier 'Wilsonian' idealist themes in American foreign policy.

Free trade, free markets, liberty and peace are the supposed universals in the National Security Strategy document and America is situated alongside all states seeking such goals. The obvious virtue of this is reprised in Fukuyama-style language of the demise of ideological competitors. But terrorism is worldwide too, and the homeland is vulnerable. Hence a new Department of Homeland Security that focuses on protecting America first and foremost. Regional partners in the hunt for terrorists and the spread of democracy are also a part of the strategy. The dangers posed by the proliferation of weapons of mass destruction are also a priority, and states that might supply them to terrorist organizations must be prevented from doing so. Africa's wars must be constrained, porous borders fixed to ensure that violence does not spread. Rogue states that hate America and everything it stands for have emerged and the danger of weapons of mass destruction is paramount. These are weapons of intimidation and threats to neighbours now, no longer the cold war weapons of last resort.

Crucially the NSS argues that in these cases deterrence no longer works: 'Traditional concepts of deterrence will not work against a terrorist enemy whose avowed tactics are wanton destruction and the targeting of innocents; whose so-called soldiers seek martyrdom in death and whose most potent protection is statelessness. The overlap between states that sponsor terror and those that pursue WMD compels us to action.'[27] This is of course half the logic for the invasion of Iraq in 2003. The NSS however is careful to suggest that ultimately such action is defensive. Invoking international law and the right of self-defense it argues that given the changed circumstances of these threats adaptation is necessary. 'We must adapt the concept of imminent threat to the capabilities and objectives of today's adversaries. Rogue states and terrorists do not seek to attack us using conventional means.'[28] Hence waiting for unambiguous evidence of imminent threat is no longer possible; preemption may have to come much earlier.

> The United States has long maintained the option of preemptive actions to counter a sufficient threat to our national security. The greater the threat, the greater is the risk of inaction – and the more compelling the case for taking anticipatory action to defend ourselves, even if uncertainty remains as to the time and place of the enemy's attack. To forestall or prevent such hostile acts by our adversaries, the United States will, if necessary, act preemptively.[29]

---

26 See 'A Conversation with Condoleezza Rice', *The American Interest*, 1/1 (2005): 47–57.

27 *National Security Strategy*, p. 15.

28 *Ibid.*

29 *Ibid.*

Keeping freedom of action open, the document further suggests that 'The United States will not use force in all cases to preempt emerging threats, nor should nations use preemption as a pretext for aggression. Yet in an age where the enemies of civilization openly and actively seek the world's most destructive technologies, the United States cannot remain idle while dangers gather.'[30] Hence the potential remains for the United States to act unilaterally in a preventive war mode, and without sanction from the United Nations or any other organization.

The enlargement of the global economy is also a key part of a national security strategy in this document, much more so than in previous security statements. While earlier documents in the Clinton years had added concerns with instabilities and environmental matters, the Bush doctrine is determined to reorganize the world with free markets and free trade. The acknowledgement that 'all states are responsible for creating their own economic policies' is nearly completely swamped in the effusive endorsement of 'economic freedom'.[31] This is the other half of the logic for invading Iraq. The assumption here is that removing dictators will immediately result in the emergence of an American style capitalist economy by people who have simply being waiting for the opportunity, which the marines have finally provided. In combination the assumption was apparently that invading Iraq would set off a demonstration effect in the region. That it has failed in this task in the region is one key argument against the Bush doctrine by its numerous critics.[32]

Interestingly too the NSS includes a claim that the United States seeks to reduce its greenhouse gas emissions and support environmental innovations broadly consistent with the Kyoto protocol even if the agreement itself is not specified. Likewise institutions of democracy are to be supported and built and economic growth supported by trade policy rather than aid. But China is chastised near the end for failing to follow its economic innovations by developing American style democracy. Its search for advanced weapons too is criticized as a threat to regional stability. International democracy does not however extend to the international criminal court which the NSS emphasizes does not have jurisdiction over Americans. Finally the strategy addresses the need for innovations in the military and the importance of institutional innovations to adapt to the new global security situation that the United States faces.

At the heart of such claims is a simple assumption that the United States is a different place, a unique state with its role in history as the overarching guarantor of the future. Although whether this is as the purveyor of globalization and interconnection in the form of a global economy that will end war by offering freedom to all, or the bringer of prophesied end times in some of the pre-millenarialist interpretations of American

---

30 *Ibid.*

31 *Ibid.*, p. 17.

32 Naomi Klein, 'Baghdad Year Zero: Pillaging Iraq in Pursuit of a Neocon Utopia', *Harpers* (September, 2004): 43–52. See also an especially trenchant critique of American imperial oil policy by Iraqi trade union leader Hassan Juma'a Awad in 'Leave Our Country Now', *The Guardian* (18 February, 2005); reprinted online by Commondreams.org.

fundamentalism, depends very much on specific interpretations of the overarching purpose of American power.[33] In these formations, contrary to assumptions in much American international relations scholarship, America is not a normal state, or a state like any other. It is not just a great power, or a temporary hegemon. Instead it has a unique and exceptional role to play in bending the world to its rule, for its own good supposedly. In short it is a formation with an explicit imperial mandate, however much such terminology may upset those who insist that they act on behalf of humanity as a whole. But of course this too is usually what empires claim to be doing as they bring violence to the 'dangerous' peripheries in their systems.[34]

Calling 911: The Bush Doctrine

It is important to read this sequence of documents, from the defense planning guidance documents through PNAC and on to the National Security Strategy of 2002, as having considerable continuity. Then it is easy to understand that 9/11 gave the neocons the pretext on which to make their strategy of military primacy the operational code for the American state.[35] The focus on Afghanistan and war as a response to 9/11 also follows because there was no conceptualization of terrorist organizations as separate from states. Neither was there any realization in the documents that the actions of America might cause intense opposition in many places, especially in the Middle East. The ethnocentrism and the focus on states perpetuates a much earlier understanding of international politics that, for all the talk of globalization in the 1990s, persisted in the halls of power, and was the discursive repertoire available on September 11th.

War provided a legitimacy to George W. Bush as president which his contested election in 2000 had not. The invocation of the term 'global' as the premise for the war on terror immediately confused matters in terms of the specific geographies of danger, but made sense in the terms of the PNAC formulation of America as the preeminent global power. The immediate emphasis on such things as National Missile Defense in the aftermath of 9/11, where had a system been operational it would have been quite as useless as any of the other weapons in the American military arsenal, makes sense once the overall view in the earlier documents is understood as the operational premise for decision making. The immediate hurry to invade Iraq, despite the absence of evidence of a connection with the 9/11 attacks, also suggests that this larger geopolitical framework was operational. But, that said, it is important to emphasize that while a general consensus on the geopolitics is

---

33 See Michael Northcott, *An Angel Directs the Storm: Apocalyptic Religion and American Empire* (London: I.B. Tauris, 2004).

34 See Derek Gregory, *The Colonial Present: Afghanistan, Iraq, Palestine* (Oxford: Blackwell, 2004).

35 Kenneth Waltz, 'The Continuity of International Politics', in Ken Booth and Tim Dunne (eds), *Worlds in Collision: Terror and the Future of Global Order* (New York: Palgrave Macmillan, 2002), pp. 348–53.

clear, the specifics are highly contested. Not least the difficulties that result over what to do with American policy with Saudi Arabia, where the House of Saud is seen by many neoconservatives as a dangerous and unstable regime that has funded all sorts of terrorist organizations indirectly for decades.[36]

All this is linked to the heart of the Bush doctrine specification of the world, the assumption that America was attacked on September 11th simply because terrorists hate freedom or the American people. If one understands that the actions on September 11th might have been a strategic action designed to have effect on American foreign policy, and that the attacks on the United States are related to American foreign policy in the Middle East, rather than an existential challenge to America, then matters take on a very different appearance.[37] Viewed in these terms Osama Bin Laden's formulations of the need for struggle against foreign troops and the comprador elites of the Arabian Peninsula follow a fairly simple logic of national liberation, a removal of the infidel troops from the land of the two Holy Places.[38] He uses numerous phrases to explain his antipathy to America, but it is all within a simple geography, a geography that is ignored in most of the discussions of the 'global war on terror'. Indeed it is ignored precisely because of the specification of that war as 'global'. It was assumed in the propaganda of the Bush administration in the aftermath of 9/11 that this was a global war, allowing for actions all over the globe. The Pentagon's cartographers have responded by redrawing the combatant commands to encompass the entire planet, including Antarctica.[39] The most obvious feature of the Bush doctrine is precisely the assumption implicit in its pages that America can and does operate on a global scale.

If indeed the enemy is specified as attacking America because of what it is, rather than what it does, then the logic of this makes some sense. However if Bin Laden's declaration of war text is taken seriously, and his strategic aims examined carefully, this makes much less sense. Bin Laden's aims are clearly the removal of the corrupt elite of the House of Saud and the infidels that support that regime and profit from its huge arms purchases, from the Arabian Peninsula. Read this way the attention is then directed at the regime in Riyadh, one that many of the neoconservatives also despise because of its appalling record on human rights abuses and its funding of fundamentalist organizations that have ironically been the breeding ground for recruits for Al Qaeda. How one specifies the geography of the contemporary strategic situation is crucial.

---

36 Victor Davis Hanson, 'Our Enemies: The Saudis', *Commentary* (July 2002).

37 See Simon Dalby, 'Calling 911: Geopolitics, Security and America's New War', *Geopolitics*, 8/3 (2003): 61–86.

38 Osama Bin Laden, 'Declaration of War against the Americans Occupying the Land of the Two Holy Places (Expel the Infidels from the Arab Peninsula)', (August 23, 1996): <www.terrorismfiles.org/individuals/declaration_of_juhad1.html>. This theme was repeated in his call to Westerners immediately prior to the November 2004 American election.

39 W.S. Johnson, 'New Challenges for the Unified Command Plan', *Joint Forces Quarterly* (Summer, 2002): 62–70.

There is more to Bin Laden's reasoning and his dislike for infidel civilization, but the theme of that dislike being explicitly linked to the actions of that civilization in the Middle East are key to Al Qaeda's struggle, and its appeal to Muslim youth. Getting this geography right suggests that the war on terror is one directly related to matters in the Middle East and the extraordinarily distorted societies based on huge oil wealth, a social order kept in place by American support, both directly in terms of security guarantees and a military presence, and indirectly in terms of business links, arms trading and training of security services of the elites in the Gulf and elsewhere.[40] But, and this is the key point, this is not the kind of analysis that is possible within the geopolitical categories used in the Bush doctrine with its focus on America and its specification of the world as in need of American leadership. Again the innovations in Condoleezza Rice's Middle East policy in 2005 and the explicit recognition that supporting authoritarian regimes at the expense of democracy there suggest that some of these issues are at least being finessed in the second Bush administration.

Imperial Geopolitics

What is especially clear in the discussion of GWOT is the refusal to accept that deterrence is any longer an appropriate logic for an American defense strategy. The reasoning is very simple: terrorists will not be deterred by American military force; they weren't on September 11th. Therefore taking the offensive and taking the war to them is the only possible strategy that makes sense; an argument repeated endlessly by George W. Bush in the presidential campaign in 2004. When linked to a doctrine of rogue states, and the supposition in strategic thinking that these states might supply weapons of mass destruction to terrorist networks, the notion of preemption then takes on a further important dimension. It implies the right of Americans to decide where and when to attack potentially dangerous powers. But whether a military response to terrorism is the most appropriate way to act is sidestepped in the doctrine with focuses on states and their leaderships rather than any other political entities.

The doctrine of preemption also runs into not inconsiderable obstacles given the difficulties of intelligence and prediction of what is deliberately concealed. In the period of the first George W. Bush presidency, American intelligence first failed to predict the attacks of September 11th and then incorrectly asserted that the Saddam Hussein regime in Iraq actually had weapons of mass destruction. Both times American intelligence was wrong; no wonder critics get so incensed when American politicians ignore international organizations and their attempts to find non-violent negotiated arrangements to security problems. The difficulty with preemption is made doubly awkward by the simple fact that the United Nations inspectors got it right with Iraq. American intelligence got it wrong. A policy based on such intelligence

---

40 See Michael Klare, *Blood and Oil: The Dangers and Consequences of America's Growing Dependence on Imported Petroleum* (New York: Metropolitan, 2004).

is obviously one that is likely to be suspect in the eyes of potential friends not to mention adversaries identified and targeted by such 'intelligence'.

But the strategy of preemption and the clear declaration that no other state will be allowed to emerge as a military rival suggests much more than ordinary international politics and the use of war as a strategy of statecraft. Such preeminence suggests to many people outside the United States, and many critics within, an imperial ambition. The arrogation of the right to decide on matters of international politics in the face of hostility from international organizations was roundly condemned in the lead up to the invasion of Iraq. The rhetoric in the 2005 State of the Union speech singling out Syria and Iran as potential targets, while notably ignoring North Korea, which really does have weapons of mass destruction and the ability to deliver them at least against Japanese targets, suggests a list of states that are to be brought into line with American policies in a way analogous with the Iraqi action.

While the temptation for further action in the Middle East may be considerable through the second Bush administration, there is a contradiction at the heart of the American efforts related to the innovations in the military capabilities trumpeted in the so called revolution in military affairs, the persistent argument in the American military that it is not in the nation building business, and George W. Bush's statement in the 2003 State of the Union address that America 'exercises power without conquest'. The rapid increase in high technology weaponry and its undoubted superiority on the battlefield is not however related to having a large number of soldiers available for garrison and pacification duties. America does not do nation building; it is not an empire after all, because it does not apparently conquer territory. What it can do and, as recently demonstrated in Yugoslavia, Afghanistan and Iraq, is willing to do, is to destroy regimes and the infrastructure that keep them in place. But the subsequent reconstruction and institutional rearrangements will be left to commercial enterprises and the troops of willing allies; it is not the task of the US military.

The relatively small size of the American forces, with less than two million, or one percent of the American population in uniform, has the advantage of reducing the casualty figures and keeps the professional salaries manageable in a budget that is still a relatively small percentage of GDP. But it does mean that troops in large numbers are not available to guard crucial facilities and do nation building after a war to accomplish regime change has finished its major combat phase. While the parallels with the British imperial hegemony of the nineteenth century are instructive, not least in how the British ran India with a relatively tiny bureaucracy, the small number of combat troops and limited availability of smart munitions do constrain what can be done using military means directly. In short the constabulary function in the wild zones of political crisis, which the PNAC suggested as one of the key functions of the American military, is one that the present military is not well equipped or adequately staffed to perform.

Hence the internal contradiction at the heart of the Bush doctrine: its ambitions to global security are limited by the 'constabulary' capabilities of its military and the inadequacies of its development and institution building capabilities.[41] Its global reach may destroy governments that it deems threatening, but it has great difficulty reconstructing the states after they are attacked. Preemption and the consequent denial of international law undermine support for American policies and hence exacerbate the difficulties of finding allied troops to do nation building. Thus instability requires continued military monitoring, an 'empire of disorder' in Alain Joxe's telling phrase.[42] The larger lesson of empire, that sound and competent administration of remote parts of the empire is the best assurance of stability, seems lost in a series of geopolitical and strategic formulations that cannot specify the world in a way that deals with the specific messy political realities of the Gulf and elsewhere. Above all else by using a geopolitical logic that simultaneously insists on American prerogatives to decide on acceptable and unacceptable political practices abroad, while simultaneously downplaying prior economic and political connections across those geopolitical boundaries in favour of short-term military considerations, long-term security for most of the planet's peoples is being compromised.

---

41 Many arguments on these lines have appeared in print but see in particular Wesley K. Clark, *Winning Modern Wars: Iraq, Terrorism, and the American Empire* (New York: Public Affairs, 2003) and Thomas P.M. Barnett, *The Pentagon's New Map: War and Peace in the Twenty-First Century* (New York: Putnam's, 2004).

42 Alain Joxe, *Empire of Disorder* (New York: Semiotexte, 2002).

Chapter 3

Representing Homeland Security

Aida A. Hozic

'I don't want our hands tied so we cannot do the number one
job you expect, which is to protect the homeland.'
From President G.W. Bush's remarks at Mt. Rushmore, August 15, 2002

On August 15, 2002, 11 months after the September 11 terrorist attacks on the United States and the establishment of the Office of Homeland Security, President George W. Bush chose Mt. Rushmore as a dramatic and profoundly symbolic setting to further his plan to construct a new Department of Homeland Security – the most significant reorganization of the US government since the 1947 National Security Act.[1] The new Department – a cabinet-level institution unlike its predecessor, the Office of Homeland Security – sought to centralize over a hundred previously dispersed government agencies into a single institution with 200,000 employees and at least five times as many civilian informers. According to the President's proposal, aside from coordination of homeland security efforts on federal, state and local level and with private and public agencies, the department was to have four primary tasks: information analysis and infrastructure protection; development of chemical, biological, radiological, nuclear and related countermeasures; provision of border and transportation security; and, finally, emergency preparedness and response. Consequently, folded under the wing of the new department would be the Immigration and Naturalization Service, Customs Service, Coast Guard, Animal and Plant Health Inspection Service, Federal Emergency Agency, Transportation Security Agency, Livermore National Laboratory, Plum Island Animal Disease Center, National Communications System of the Department of Defense, Computer Security Division of the National Institute of Standards and Technology and Critical Infrastructure Assurance Office of the Department of Commerce – to name but a few. Likening his efforts to those of President Harry Truman, who reorganized the previously fragmented US military services under the single Department of Defense in 1947 (a process completed with the 1949 Amendment to the 1947 National Security Act) to meet the 'visible enemy' of the Cold War, President Bush stated in his message to

---

1   The National Security Act of 1947 institutionally gave birth to the National Security State, although an idea of national defense apparatus was discussed already in 1938–1939. See Emily Rosenberg, 'Commentary: The Cold War and the Discourse of National Security', *Diplomatic History*, 17:2, 1993, pp. 277–84. Thanks to David Grondin for bringing the article to my attention.

the Congress that 'today our Nation must once again reorganize our Government to protect against an often-invisible enemy, an enemy that hides in the shadows and an enemy that can strike with many different types of weapons'.[2] And, speaking at Mt. Rushmore, flanked by the carved images of George Washington, Thomas Jefferson, Abraham Lincoln and Theodore Roosevelt, the President explained that 'the best way to protect the homeland, the best way to make sure our children can grow up free, is to hunt the killers down, one by one, and bring them to justice'.[3]

Sheltered by the magnificence of the monument, which had itself been identified as a prime terrorist target, the President reiterated the main tenets of his Administration's approach to security issues since September 11 – the novelty of war against terrorism as opposed to previous wars ('This isn't a war where these infantries go marching across the plains or hide in hedgerows, or formations of aircraft go streaming across our skies. This is a war where leaders hide in caves and send youngsters to their suicidal death.'); the indefinite (or infinite) time-frame of the war ('It doesn't matter how long it takes, as far as I'm concerned.'); the sense of historical mission and calling ('... history has called us. History has put the spotlight on America.'); the struggle of good versus evil and unquestionable superiority of American values ('out of the evil done to this great land is going to come incredible good, because we're the greatest nation on the face of the Earth, full of the most fine and compassioned and decent citizens'); the rationale for increased defense spending ('I want the message to be loud and clear to our friends and foe alike that we're not quitting, that the United States of America understands the challenge, that, no matter how long it takes, we're going to defend our freedoms.'); and, finally, the need for unrestrained government power in national security matters ('I don't want our hands tied so we cannot do the number one job you expect, which is to protect the homeland.').[4]

At the same time, the President introduced a new, culturally transformative vision of his government which suggested that individual identity and self-interest of American citizenry in this post–September 11 era should be made subservient to the interest of the state. ('More and more people understand that being a patriot is more than just putting your hand over your heart and saying the Pledge of Allegiance to a nation under God. ... more and more people understand that serving something greater than yourself in life is a part of being a complete American.'). Thus, much like the characters in one of the most celebrated Cold War films, Alfred Hitchcock's *North by Northwest*, whose grand finale also took place on Mt. Rushmore, Americans

---

2   Message to the Congress Transmitting Proposed Legislation to Create the Department of Homeland Security, June 18, 2002. Weekly Compilation of Presidential Documents. From the 2002 Presidential Documents Online via GPO Access [frwais.access.gpo.gov] [DOCID: pd24jn02_txt-12], pp. 1034–1038, Week Ending Friday, June 21, 2002.

3   Remarks at Mount Rushmore National Memorial in Keystone, South Dakota, August 15, 2002. Weekly Compilation of Presidential Documents. From the 2002 Presidential Documents Online via GPO Access [frwais.access.gpo.gov] [DOCID:pd19au02_txt-16], pp. 1376–1382, Week Ending Friday, August 16, 2002. Monday, August 19, 2002. Volume 38, Number 33, pp. 1335–1388.

4   *Ibid.*

were being urged to find their true and complete selves in places and institutions associated with their country's national interest. Perhaps unconsciously then (though nothing is unconscious in the world dreamed up by George Bush's key advisor, Karl Rove), the President's choice of Mt. Rushmore as the backdrop for the speech on homeland security was also a sign of his Administration's desire to turn the clock back and politically and symbolically re-create the 1950s, the time when American national security state first came into existence and when identities and individual aspirations of its citizens were deemed unstable or expendable unless subsumed under the cloak of patriotism and defense.

Just four years later, though, the carefully built edifice of George W. Bush's security apparatus seems to be crumbling. Delayed response to hurricane Katrina in New Orleans did not just expose the underbelly of American power – its impoverished African American citizenry – but also the institutional limitations of emergency management within the new Department of Homeland Security. The continued war in Iraq, on the one hand, and the troubled and overly dependent-on-gasoline economy, on the other, have brought President's approval ratings to unprecedented lows – just 2 per cent among African Americans and 35 per cent overall. Finally, the investigation of the 'CIA Leak' – the public outing of the CIA agent Valerie Plame as a retribution for her husband's criticism of the rationale for the war in Iraq – and the indictment of L. Scooter Libby, Vice President's Chief of Staff, revealed the degree to which the case for the replay of the Gulf War in 2003 depended on the cozy relationship between the Administration and the media, not just on the Machiavellianism of its creators.

Re-thinking American power under George W. Bush may, therefore, be less of an exercise in thinking about new political forms, most notably complex relations between sovereign and imperial powers, and more of an attempt to come to terms with a transparent and genuinely reactionary (and I do not mean this in normative terms) political project. The pre– and post–September 11 policies of the Bush Administration have aimed to re-inscribe the state into the international system, both in terms of centralization of domestic, political, economic and legal authority and in terms of its conduct of international affairs. As such they have revealed both the limits and potentialities of globalization, a phenomenon that was taken for granted throughout the 1990s. At the same time, Bush's policies have also consciously sought to erase the distinction between representation and reality, assuming that managing the former would be sufficient to control the latter. The making and unmaking of the White House authority – within and outside of the United States – force us, therefore, to think about categories of sovereignty, imperialism and hegemony not just as political, economic or military practices but also as representational ones – and, hence, about emperor's new clothes as much as about empires themselves. The Bush Administration, I will argue, has called itself into existence as an Empire, and attempted to affirm that Empire by simply calling itself one. The fact that its non-existent imperial cloak is so difficult to unveil brings up uncomfortable questions about the relationship between public complicity and propaganda, a slippery ground for both traditional and constructivist scholars of international relations.

North by Northwest: **From National Entertainment State to National Security State**

> I thought I would never be able to look at Mount Rushmore without Alfred Hitchcock sitting on my shoulder, reminding me of how Cary Grant and Eve Marie Saint dangle from the noses and cheeks of the presidents during the climax of the 1959 thriller *North by Northwest.*
>
> Susan Spano, 'Mount Rushmore', Los Angeles Times, August 8, 2002

Even if President Bush and his advisors chose Mount Rushmore because of the values that the monument is supposed to represent (the founding, growth and preservation of the United States), anyone who has ever seen Hitchcock's film *North by Northwest* will always think of Mount Rushmore as the place where Cary Grant and Eve Mary Saint discover their true selves in one of the most exciting chase scenes ever filmed.[5] But symbolic linkages between the film and President Bush's August 2002 address at Mount Rushmore run deeper than such free associations, reflecting a shift in both economic and cultural terms from what some observers have called 'national entertainment state' to a 'national security state'.[6]

North by Northwest is a film about Madison Avenue executive Roger Thornhill, played by Cary Grant, who is mistakenly taken for a government agent by a ring of (presumably pro-Soviet) spies, and who finally reclaims his own identity by acting as a government agent on Mount Rushmore. Along the way, Mr. Thornhill assumes the identity of George Kaplan, the non-existent CIA agent and a decoy for the spies, and, as he is – as Kaplan – chased across the country by both the spies and the government, he falls in love with a certain Eve Kendall (Eve Marie Saint), herself a double agent for the CIA. Together, and after a number of expected and unexpected turns, Thornhill and Kendall destroy the spy network and preempt an export of important government secrets to the Soviets. Needless to say, they also stay together happily ever after. Thus, as superficial and sexist as men come, twice divorced, and totally dependent on his mother – an empty Brooks Brothers suit with an Oedipal complex as J. Hoberman described him in the *Village Voice*[7] – Roger Thornhill transforms through the film into a principled and courageous man capable of love by becoming a CIA agent. Similarly, Eve Kendall, a blonde who's become

---

5   Recently, Michael Shapiro has written about Mount Rushmore as the contested site of Euro-American imperialism vis-à-vis Native Americans. See Michael J. Shapiro, 'The Demise of "International Relations": America's Western Palimpsest', *Geopolitics* 10, 2005, pp. 222–243.

6   The term 'national entertainment state' was first used by editors of *The Nation* as a title for the special issue on corporate publishing (March 17, 1997). On the re-emergence of the US national security state see David Grondin, '(Re)Writing the "National Security State": How Realists (Re)Built the(ir) Cold War', Occasional Paper 4, published by the Center for United States Studies of the Raoul Dandurand Chair of Strategic and Diplomatic Studies, University of Québec at Montréal, 2004.

7   J. Hoberman, 'City Limits', *The Village Voice*, October 20–26, 1999.

the spy master's mistress because 'she had nothing better to do that weekend', turns into a brainy woman worthy of being Thornhill's wife (*sic!*) by acting as a trump on government's behalf. Therefore, in the film in which not a single character has a stable identity, and shallowness appears to be the order of the day, the US government – or better the secret agencies of the US government – are the only institution capable of conferring a sense of self and purpose to these otherwise empty characters. To underscore this patriotic trail, Thornhill's and Kendall's search for identity takes place in a series of locations that are unmistakably 'American' – from the cityscapes of New York, the United Nations building and a modern railroad car ('a bedroom on the Twentieth Century') to the cornfields of Midwest and, ultimately, Mount Rushmore. Indeed, as Richard Millington has argued, 'the concept of an American "place" or "space" – America as a particular ideological location or configuration, and exercising a shaping power on what happens within it – drives the action and generates the meanings of the film'.[8]

The way in which this journey of self-discovery *qua* patriotic pilgrimage resonates with contemporary political discourses and policies is threefold. First, there is the already-mentioned emphasis on the need for cultural transformation in America. The President's insistence on assuming a purpose bigger than oneself – as a soldier, as a civilian informant or as an unquestioning citizen – in the speech delivered at Mt. Rushmore was a clear example of the neoconservative push for such a change. It also neatly dovetailed with the Right's traditional insistence on family values, duty, responsibility and, ultimately, Christianity. In the immediate post–September 11 period, there were also frequent media commentaries on the Clinton era – driven too by neoconservative assessments of the period of greatest economic prosperity in American history – as the time of shallowness, narcissism and consumerism. George Will called it America's 'decade long holiday from history'.[9] *New York Times* columnist Maureen Dowd famously lamented that September 11 showed us the limits of consumerism. The terrorists taught us, wrote Dowd, that 'we are more than the sum of our stuff' and embarrassed us in our search for material pleasures through Neimann Marcus catalogues.[10] In fact, one could easily imagine Roger Thornhill as the quintessential 'Friend of Bill' – a media executive, capable of selling anyone and anything with a witty spin, a cocktail party flirt, a Fifth Avenue shopper – who was forced to confront his own frivolity – and expandability – in the aftermath of September 11.

Centralization of state authority has also been made possible by the production of novel and different legal subjects. The quest for cultural transformation of citizens

---

8   Richard H. Millington, 'Hitchcock and American Character: The Comedy of Self Construction in *North by Northwest*', in Jonathan Freedman and Richard Millington (eds), *Hitchcock's America* (New York, Oxford: Oxford University Press, 1999), p.136.

9   George Will, 'US Faces New Reality', *Chicago Sun-Times*, September 12, 2001, Editorial, p. 79.

10   Maureen Dowd, 'Liberties: All That Glistens', *The New York Times*, October 3, 2001, Section A, Column 1, p. 23.

into patriots went hand in hand with the ironic erasure of citizens' rights through the appropriately named Patriot Act, whose lengthy title is – indeed – 'Uniting and Strengthening America by Providing Appropriate Tools Required to Intercept and Obstruct Terrorism (USA PATRIOT ACT) Act of 2001'.[11] The Act, and its subsequent update – Patriot Act II – increased authority of the government to conduct investigations and surveillance within the United States, access personal records of its citizens, detain those accused of terrorist conspiracy without notifying anyone,[12] deport lawful immigrants without proper hearings, expand the definition of terrorism to include acts of protest and civil disobedience. Similarly, the establishment of the legal category of 'enemy combatants,' which could also be applied to American citizens, and which allowed the state to detain them in military custody without any legal representation, turned all Americans into potential *homo sacri* – bare lives, people who could be killed without the killing being viewed as homicide. In Giorgio Agamben's terms, sovereign power produced its own subjects and its own infinite space of indistinction, where laws have been suspended and difference between legality and illegality erased.[13] Despite protests and legal objections, Guantanamo has become the frightening prospect of US citizens' relation to their state, not just an exception reserved for their enemies.[14]

Second, in this real-life parallel of Hitchcock's *North by Northwest*, the Bush Administration has also made a conscious effort to place entertainment (and infotainment) industries under the government control. While some scholars emphasize the continuities between the post–September 11 period and the period of close cooperation between Hollywood and Pentagon under Clinton, I would actually tend to stress the discontinuities.[15] Namely, the Clinton era represented a unique moment in the US domestic politics – but also in the projection of US hegemony abroad – when the entertainment industry all of a sudden took the lead in American economy, including development of information technologies affiliated

---

11 See the full text of the law at http://www.epic.org/privacy/terrorism/hr3162.html.

12 As *The New York Times* stated, 'An American citizen suspected of being part of a terrorist conspiracy could be held by investigators without anyone being notified. He could simply disappear.'

13 Giorgio Agamben, *Homo Sacer: Sovereign Power and Bare Life*, translated by Daniel Heller-Roazen (Stanford: Stanford University Press, 1998).

14 US Supreme Court, in Hamdi v. Rumsfeld (2004), decided that detention without counsel of US citizens is unconstitutional. However, the status of enemy combatants and treatment of prisoners is still the most contested issue of the Bush Administration, with important challenges to torture and disregard of the Geneva Convention now being raised by the Senate, thanks to the leadership of John McCain.

15 Some of the best writings about the post–September 11 were collected in a special issue of *Theory and Event* (Issue 5.4). On continuities of the Bush's foreign policies see in that issue contributions by James Der Derian, 'The War of Networks' and David Campbell, 'Time is Broken: The Return of the Past in the Response to September 11'. While my arguments in many ways follow in their footsteps, I place different emphasis on the role of the state in directing media activities under Bush as opposed to Clinton.

with defense. This is not to say that the US entertainment industry and Hollywood in particular have not historically played an important role in the production and reproduction of US hegemony. It is simply to underscore that entertainment and media industries have never before, and never to such a degree, been viewed as strategic sectors in the US economy.[16] Similarly, although Hollywood once again sheepishly cooperated with the Bush Administration, and although the traditional barter of relaxed ownership rules in exchange for self-censorship was even more emphatic now than in the past due to its links with other cable companies and broadcasters and, thus, more susceptible to FCC rulings, the relationship between Hollywood and the White House was very different than in the 1990s.[17] Its strategic importance to the Clinton Administration was well exemplified by its awarding the Pentagon's Medal for Distinguished Public Service to Steven Spielberg for his film about D-Day, *Saving Private Ryan*.[18] As I had previously argued, US hegemony during the Clinton years – just as hegemony in general – depended primarily on the obfuscation of major power lines, and the shift of political, public and even scholarly attention onto Hollywood at that time masked the continued militarization of the United States despite absence of any credible enemies.[19] The coverage of wars (Croatia, Bosnia, Rwanda, Kosovo) was viewed as a business both noble and profitable, and the un-masking of insidious links between representation and politics (including politics of violence), entertainment and warfare, could easily be seen as the key to understanding the way in which power operated both within and outside the US in the post–Cold War period.

In the world of George W. Bush, however, the roles of government and media, military and entertainment have once again been reversed. Not only have the media industries felt deprived of advertising revenue in the immediate post–September 11 period, they have also been put at a tremendous disadvantage by the Administration's insistence on 'invisible war' and 'invisible enemies'. In the war on terrorism, there was simply nothing to be seen. In addition, the strict control of access to the theaters of war and then embedding reporters (first in Afghanistan and then in Iraq)

---

16 See Aida A. Hozic, 'Uncle Sam Goes to Siliwood: Of Landscapes, Spielberg and Hegemony,' in *Review of International Political Economy*, Volume 6, Number 3, August 1999, pp. 289–312.

17 For a detailed analysis of the relationship between self-censorship and media ownership regulation see Aida A. Hozic, *Hollyworld: Space, Power and Fantasy in the American Economy* (Ithaca: Cornell University Press, 2003).

18 Some scholars have noted the symbolic and political importance of some films released in the aftermath of September 11, particularly of the war action movie *Behind Enemy Lines*. See Gearoid Ó. Tuathail, 'The Frustration of Geopolitics and the Pleasures of War: Behind Enemy Lines and American Geopolitical Culture', *Geopolitics*, 10, 2005, pp. 356–377 and Cynthia Weber, *Imagining America at War: Morality, Politics and Film* (London: Routledge, 2006). Once again, although the rushed release of the film is worth investigating, both the film and its author have hardly played the strategic role in American politics comparable to Spielberg's under Clinton.

19 See Hozic, *op. cit.*, 2003.

brought representation of warfare much closer to traditional propaganda than to the combination of virtual warfare and marketed violence of the past decade.[20] Under the guidance of Donald Rumsfeld, the notion of information warfare was expanded to include not just military communications systems or psychological warfare but also dissemination of (mis)information and propaganda. While the Pentagon's Office of Strategic Influence, formed to control such information flows, was eventually shut down, numerous other forms of state interventions into the media world have continued. Their list is too long for this paper but some examples include Condolezza Rice's stern instructions to broadcasters regarding Osama Bin Laden's tapes; restricting the publication of photographs of fallen soldiers' caskets and funerals; war on Al Jazeera; recalling Peter Arnette from Iraq because of his critical reporting of the first phase of the Iraq war; paying reporters to hail the Bush Administration's achievements in education and healthcare; placing decoy journalists into the White House Press Corps; restricting the broadcast of Steven Spielberg's film *Saving Private Ryan* on Veteran's Day ostensibly due to 'obscene language'; and hiring Charlotte Beers (former Madison Avenue executive and a self-proclaimed 'queen of branding') at the State Department to help sell the US image abroad. Ms Beers lasted 17 months, but the office has continued to exist and is currently occupied by Karen Hughes, a close associate of President Bush. Thus, while issues of 'events representation' are obviously of the utmost importance to the Bush Administration, their logic has been tremendously simplified over the past few years. Indeed, what we may be witnessing is the typical Žižekian paradox of fantasy – 'The Truth Is Out There' – the events (the political) representation and their relation to power have become so transparent that they elude us precisely because of their transparency, not because of their cover.[21]

Finally, under the Administration of George W. Bush, the structure of the US economy has been pushed back to its Cold War days, most evident in the resurgence of the military-industrial complex and oil industries and in the very material decline of all industries associated with the infotainment sector. The economic downturn of 2001–2002 was, to a great degree, a result of troubles in the new information economy. Many of the problems were associated with over-extension

---

20 On the use of propaganda in US war on terror and Iraq, see Sheldon Rampton and John Stauber, *Weapons of Mass Deception: The Uses of Propaganda in Bush's War on Iraq* (New York: Jeremy P. Tarcher/Penguin, 2003); Paul Rutherford, *Weapons of Mass Persuasion: Marketing the War Against Iraq* (Toronto, Buffalo, London: University of Toronto Press, 2004) and David Miller (ed.), *Tell Me Lies: Propaganda and Media Distortion in the Attack on Iraq* (London and Sterling, Virginia: Pluto Press, 2004).

21 Žižek's notion of fantasy is Lacanian, it is not a simple 'make-believe' but rather an organizing principle behind a fundamentally flawed, lacking reality. Hence, they are mutually constituting, and one cannot exist without the other. 'The Truth Is Out There,' borrowed from the *X-Files*, is a reminder that political falsification and ideology may not always be cloaked behind impenetrable veils – just like fantasy, they are the obvious, and precisely for that reason inaccessible, kernel of our everyday political life. See Slavoj Žižek, *The Plague of Fantasies* (London: Verso, 1997).

(telecommunications and entertainment industries in particular) but they were also a product of the shift in investment funds from infotainment sectors towards sectors traditionally affiliated with the Republican party (tobacco, energy and defense).[22] The initial protectionist measures of the Bush Administration (agricultural subsidies, steel tariffs) combined with the tightening of controls over science and technology R&D and their exports, as well as the focus on energy and oil – in other words, old economy – have effectively stopped the growth in all those sectors that were in one way or another regarded as the motors of globalization. With the notable exception of the Fox Corporation, whose profits have soared in conjunction with the fear factor and reliance on trivial (some would say obscene) entertainment, all other media companies have experienced serious losses and the downgrading of their shares since 2000.

The thread that links these three issues – the quest for cultural transformation, re-birth of propaganda and government control of media, and the decline of the new economy – is the attempt of the Bush Administration to place security issues back into the hands of the executive. While the defense budget was not nearly reduced as much as it could have or should have been in the Clinton era,[23] many traditional security analysts and cold warriors (many of them now in prominent positions in Bush Administration) perceived Clinton's security policy as a reckless commercialization of national security. Clinton's insistence on shifting the military-industrial complex into the market, de-regulation of science and technology policy, emphasis on development of dual technologies and links with entertainment industries disrupted many of the old patronage channels between government and industry and, at least according to some analysts, endangered the security of the United States.[24] It is indicative, for instance, that one of the first measures in the 'war on terrorism' was the withdrawal of Afghanistan's satellite pictures from the market, resulting in effect in the government's recapturing of a security industry that had commercially flourished in the Clinton era. The tightening of controls over dual-use technologies (DUTs) has become the centerpiece of the President's National Strategy to Combat Weapons of Mass Destruction (WMD), the so-called Proliferation Security Initiative (PSI). The PSI was hailed by no other than the controversial US Ambassador to UN, John Bolton, as 'one of the Bush Administration's most prominent innovations' and 'a muscular enhancement of our ability collectively to halt trafficking in WMD components'.[25] In the words of other analysts, however, thanks to PSI, 'it is no

---

22 Aida A. Hozic and Herman Schwartz, 'Who Needs the New Economy?' *Salon*, March 16, 2001.

23 See, for instance, Eugene Gholz and Harvey M. Sapolsky, 'Restructuring the US Defense Industry', *International Security*, 24:3, Winter 1999/2000.

24 On trade-off between dual technology and security see, for instance, Irving Lachov 'The GPS Dilemma: Balancing Military Risks and Economic Benefits', *International Security*, 20:1, 1995, pp. 126–148 and Vipin Gupta 'New Satellite Images for Sale' *International Security*, 20:1, 1995, pp. 94–95.

25 John R. Bolton, Under Secretary for Arms Control and International Security, 'The Bush Administration's Forward Strategy For Nonproliferation', Remarks to the Chicago

exaggeration to say that the war against Iraq was a war fought out of the fear of DUTs'.[26] Thus, to conclude, although 'national entertainment state' and 'national security state' have always been and continue to be mutually constitutive, the clear primacy of 'national security state' under the Bush Administration must be seen as a way of re-affirming the primacy of government, particularly of the executive and its centralized authority, in matters of state security.

We Are an Empire Now ...

So what is happening to America? Has it become an empire? Just several years ago, as the US and NATO were still recovering from the intervention in Kosovo, arguably the first violation of state sovereignty in defense of human rights, and as regrets over non-intervention in Rwanda and full-fledged intervention in Bosnia were still being heard, Antonio Negri and Michael Hardt's assessment of Empire seemed frighteningly accurate.[27] State sovereignty was vanishing or, better, it was being subsumed under the interests of the Empire; the US Empire – unlike the expansionist states under 18th and 19th century European imperialism – was not essentially territorial; the Empire embodied elements of the US constitutional order which made it both more complex and powerful and potentially vulnerable to upheavals and revolutions; the clearest manifestation of the Empire was the transformation of military into a police force, a pacifier of troubled zones and a border-control institution.

The domestic political landscape after September 11 and intervention in Afghanistan and Iraq means that the US no longer seems to resemble Hardt and Negri's Empire so closely. The transformation of the war against terrorism into the war against those who harbor the terrorists clearly brought states back into the picture where previously there might have been none. The wars in Afghanistan and Iraq, despite all the Bush Administration's claims to the contrary, have all the elements of state and nation-building. Indeed, it is widely accepted that the only way to stop terrorism from spreading is to re-establish state structures in those areas of the world where the state has failed – from Sudan and Somalia to Afghanistan, Indonesia, Philippines and, of course, Iraq. In addition, direct or indirect control of these areas by the United States is quite unapologetically territorial by nature, and focused on creation and affirmation of viable borders. The US constitutional order has not only been withdrawn into the boundaries of the US itself, but also increasingly restricted in its application even to US citizens. Finally, the military is once again a military, not a police, force, and now includes greater admissibility of the loss of lives in combat as the proof of manliness and noble heroism of American warriors.

Council on Foreign Relations, Chicago, IL, October 19, 2004 available at http://www.state.gov/t/us/rm/37251.htm.

26 Richard Re, 'Playstation2 Detonation: Controlling the Threat of Dual Use Technologies', *Harvard International Review*, Fall 2003, 25:3, pp. 46–50.

27 Michael Hardt and Antonio Negri, *Empire* (Cambridge: Harvard University Press, 2000).

The position of the current Administration towards the Hardt and Negri–style Empire can, therefore, be seen as reactionary. While elements of the US expansionist policies abound, and the US military has never been as over-stretched as it is now, imperialism *de jour* is far more state-centered in its nature than Negri and Hardt's Empire. Centralization of state authority at home has gone hand in hand with war making abroad, construction of homogeneity within has been premised upon the construction of the enemy without, and the markings of civilized and barbarian worlds are perpetually called upon to justify state violence and neglect of international norms. The power of choice is 'hard' not 'soft' – it is calculable in oil reserves, available missiles, number of reservists, defense budget, even the ability to prepare for hurricanes and avian flu. Its most transparent manifestation continues to be torture. The violence of September 11 has made possession of power and willingness to exercise it not only just but noble. In the US, sovereignty, too, once again appears unproblematic. Debates about Empire, empires and imperialism among policy makers and scholars may have brought our attention to a world much richer in forms of governance and political authority than the state-centered world of American realists,[28] but they are still, possibly, just a roundabout way of addressing tremendous power inequalities and unrepentant exercises of military force in the international system.

One notable exception, however, seems to rest in the self-understanding and self-representation of the Bush Administration. As Stefano Guzzini has recently written, American unilateralism is not necessarily a product of American supremacy, as most apologists of the Bush Administration would argue – rather, the unilateralism of the Bush Administration may be a way of producing and securing that supremacy in the world full of potential power competitors, once power and supremacy are understood as being far more complex than just military.[29] Similarly, in one of the most penetrating articles about the Bush White House, written just before the election of 2004, well-known journalist Ron Suskind cited a conversation with a senior advisor to the President, confirming the view that American Empire *de jour* has called itself into existence. The aide told Suskind that journalists like him lived

'in what we call the reality-based community,' which he defined as people who 'believe that solutions emerge from your judicious study of discernible reality.' I nodded and murmured something about enlightenment principles and empiricism. He cut me off. 'That's not the way the world really works anymore,' he continued. 'We're an empire now, and when we act, we create our own reality. And while you're studying that reality – judiciously, as you will – we'll act again, creating other new realities, which you can

28 See on this point Tarak Barkawi and Mark Laffey, 'Retrieving the Imperial: Empire and International Relations', *Millennium*, 2002, 31:1, pp.109–127 as well as responses to their article – Alex Callinicos, 'The Actuality of Imperialism', *Millennium*, 2002, 31:2, pp. 319–326; Martin Shaw, 'Post-Imperial and Quasi-Imperial: State and Empire in the Global Era', *Millennium*, 2002, 31:2, pp. 327–336; R.B.J. Walker, 'On the Immanence/Imminence of Empire', *Millennium*, 2002, 31:2, pp. 337–345.
29 Stefano Guzzini, 'Multilateralism and Power,' unpublished paper, 2005.

study too, and that's how things will sort out. We're history's actors ... and you, all of you, will be left to just study what we do.'[30]

Suskind's article caused a stir in the American media, but since it focused on the role of faith and religion in the White House, the above-mentioned quote was mostly interpreted as a sign of George W. Bush's blindness to the factual world due to his reliance on instinct, words from God or messianic beliefs. In other words, the statement of the President's aide was dismissed as yet another proof of the irrationality of the war-mongering Christian-based Presidency and, as such, entirely misunderstood. Bloggers critical of the President quickly started to identify themselves as being 'reality based' in cyber-space, implying, with their insistence on *reality*, a dedication to the forms of knowledge, and understandings of knowledge, that many postmodern scholars would find problematic. Their resistance to the Bush Administration – just like the resistance of the Democratic establishment and even of the Presidential candidate John Kerry –still relied on hope that the Truth and the Facts – about the Iraq war, about weapons of mass destruction, about the economy – would eventually catch up with the Administration, undermining the credibility of George W. Bush, and therefore his Presidency. Just one more declassified memo, just one more senate inquiry, just one more box of notes from the White House meetings – the anti-Bush bloggers seem to believe – and the Truth will be Out There. Thus, what has appeared most difficult to accept in the statement of President Bush's aide is the fact that the Truth is already Out There, for in political and media world there is none. The Administration has consciously applied Foucauldian power/knowledge nexus onto governance, fully aware of the constraints that it poses for any fact-based, reality-based, truth-based resistance. As Eric Alterman astutely noted several years ago

> objective and fair-minded reporting of the Bush Administration's policies requires pointing out repeatedly and without sentimentality that just about all the men and women responsible for the conduct of this nation's foreign (and many of its domestic) affairs are entirely without personal honor when it comes to the affairs of state. This simply isn't done in respectable journalism.[31]

Bush's Presidency, therefore, presents a much more fundamental challenge to our understanding of politics than the replacement of Empire with statehood or vice versa. It is not the form of political authority that is being re-defined in the Bush White House but the positivist logic of its interpretation, and with it our trust in autonomous power of empirically grounded arguments, in fact-checking standards of journalism, in 'objective and fair-minded' media, in democratic politics 'formatted through a dynamic of concealment and disclosure, through a primary

---

30 Ron Suskind, 'Without a Doubt,' *The New York Times Magazine*, October 17, 2004, p. 44.

31 Eric Alterman, 'Colin Powell and "The Power of Audacity"', *The Nation*, September 22, 2003.

opposition between what is hidden and what is revealed,'[32] in democracy 'imagined, practiced, and understood … as materialization of publicity'.[33] If the power of the Clinton Administration rested on granting strategic status to media industries and blurring the boundaries between entertainment and warfare, the power of the Bush Presidency rests on the intentional manufacture of secrets and just as intentional erasure of distinctions between representation and reality, imperial practices and imperial imaginary, reality-TV and reality-based communities on the Internet, Rush Limbaugh and *The New York Times*, *Faith in the White House* and *Fahrenheit 9/11*. Much more radically than any postmodern scholars could have done it, the Bush Administration has relativized the notion of The Truth, making it nearly impossible for its opponents to prove – despite their persistent attempts – that the Administration has ever engaged in production of lies.[34]

It is, perhaps, not surprising then that the greatest challenges posed to the Bush Administration have stemmed from the mismanagement of representations: leaking of obscene torture photographs from Abu Ghraib, images of African Americans at the Superdome in New Orleans, the cover up of the 'CIA leak'. It is as if the principal problem is always just a marketing campaign that has gone wrong, not the product that might have been faulty. Indeed, just in August of 2005, the President hired a famous marketing consultant to help him re-brand the war on terror itself. The story of the CIA leak – public outing of the covert CIA agent Valerie Plame as a retribution for her husband's, Ambassador Joe Wilson's, criticism of the rationale for the war in Iraq – may still prove to be the main stumbling block of Bush's Presidency. And yet that too is the story which restores the existing political order instead of problematizing it: an anti-Jacobin novel rather than an avant-garde statement. In a saga that has lasted nearly two years, involving senior White House Officials, CIA and the State Department, star journalists of major media outlets – *The New York Times*, CNN, *Time Magazine*, *Washington Post* – no one has come out looking particularly noble. The level of media complicity in the peddling of Administration's (mis)informations about Iraq is particularly troubling, even if one starts from a perspective critical of mainstream media and appreciative of the constraints under which they operate. And hence – at the end of the day – it is, at best, Valerie Plame and Joe Wilson – the Eve Kendall and Roger Thornhill of our Hitchcock movie – who will save the United States from further disgrace in Iraq. It is a strange day for American democracy and the critics of George W. Bush when the CIA reclaims the patriotic torch and folds us back under the wing of the same old National Security State.[35]

---

32 Jodi Dean, 'Publicity's Secret', *Political Theory*, 29:5, October 2001, pp. 624–650.

33 *Ibid.*, p. 626.

34 Not surprisingly, young Americans find Jon Stewart's 'fake news' on the Comedy Channel much more realistic than their serious and 'realistic' counterparts on major networks and cable channels.

35 David Grondin reminds me that 'the idea that scholarship on democracy and secrecy conveys is that history is always only "official history." It is why someone like Scott Armstrong, founder of National Security Archive in Washington, DC, would stress that 'the war over secrecy is democracy's most important low intensity conflict'. Indeed, he asserts

Conclusion: Limits to Representation and ... Interpretation

While traditional international relations scholars still firmly believe that 'threats' and 'security' are objective phenomena (and, therefore, can be assessed with reality-based empirical methods), constructivist international relations scholars see security as a 'speech act', an act of perpetual performance, produced and reproduced through language or visual imagery.[36] Security itself is difficult to represent – although idyllic visions of safe landscapes and homes exist in nearly every corner of the world – without representations of threat and danger. Thus production of security always depends on production and reproduction of insecurities – enemies, fears, known and unknown perils.[37]

It is the assumption of most constructivist approaches that such processes of securitization are not necessarily strategic or even intentional. Indeed, actors usually engage in the (re)production of threats and security options as a way of reproducing social order, their own power, sense of self or identity, boundaries of statehood, inside and outside of sovereignty. The threats that they speak about and the images or metaphors that they rely on come from available cultural and material repertoire; rarely are they completely invented. The discrepancies between representation and such cultural or material realities create possible openings for interpretative analyses of securitization – working backwards from representational frameworks we can learn about actors' identities, preferences, forms of authority and ways in which they tend to exercise their power, or referent objects of securitization. In short, representation of (in)security is a window into practices and subjectivities that would otherwise be difficult to grasp or destabilize.

American power under George W. Bush, and his Administration's security policies represent a puzzle for both traditional and constructivist scholars of international relations. In their own denial of reality as the basis for formulation of policies, the Bush Administration openly defies traditional security scholarship and its wisdom. At the same time, the Administration's conscious manipulation of images and symbols – not to mention perpetual play with color-coded threats – appears either too trivial or too conspiratorial to be worthy of any serious constructivist interpretation.

---

that 'Given the government's propensity to conquer, control and manipulate information, individual journalists, scholars and concerned citizens must fight an on-going low-intensity, guerilla war for government information.' See Scott Armstrong, 'The War Over Secrecy: Democracy's Most Important Low-Intensity Conflict', in Athan G. Theoharis (ed.), *Culture of Secrecy: The Government Versus the People's Right to Know* (Lawrence, Kansas: University Press of Kansas, 1998), pp. 141–142.

36 See Barry Buzan, Ole Waever, *et al.*, *Security: A New Framework for Analysis* (Boulder: Lynne Rienner, 1998); David Campbell, *Writing Security: United States Foreign Policy and the Politics of Identity* (Minneapolis: University of Minnesota Press, 1998); Ronnie D. Lipshutz (ed.), *On Security* (New York: Columbia University Press, 1995).

37 Jutta Weldes, Mark Laffey, Hugh Gusterson and Raymond Duvall, 'Introduction: Constructing Insecurity,' in Weldes *et al.*, (eds), *Cultures of Insecurity* (Minneapolis: University of Minnesota Press, 1999).

Yes, in many respects, we can think of the Bush Presidency as a series of staged events (from the famous announcement of 'Mission Accomplished' on the battleship to the address from the eerily empty square in New Orleans in the aftermath of the hurricane Katrina) and attempt to read its meaning thru politics of representation. How exactly did the Bush Administration make plausible its own version of the war on terror? How exactly did its officials sell the war on Iraq? Afghanistan? In the absence of real threats in Iraq, why did they engage in a war? How is the support for war perpetuated despite mounting number of deaths? But no matter how pressing, all such questions seem to presuppose a distinction between the 'public' and 'authority,' and provide us with hope that, following the trail of representation, the 'public' might be emancipated from the clutches of security games that have significantly restricted its democratic space.

But thinking about the Bush Administration as a series of staged events may also mean that the only way to address it is by assuming the politics of absolute transparency. There is really no need for a special prosecutor in order to establish that there were no links between Saddam Hussein and September 11. There is really no need for a senate inquiry to tell us that Halliburton received most of the noncompetitive contracts in every aspect of the war on terror. There is really no need for a congressional committee in order to see that most of the terrorists in September 11 attacks did not come from caves in Afghanistan. There is really no doubt that the Bush Administration officials produced realities that suited them, but isn't that the case with all power? The question, therefore, may not be – or at least not only – what did the Bush Administration do to make its security case(s), the question may also be why did so many Americans go along with it? And what – if anything – may lead Americans to acknowledge that the Emperor has no clothes and may have never had any?

Chapter 4

Revolution or 'Business as Usual'? International Law and the Foreign Policy of the Bush Administration

Shirley V. Scott

James Lindsay and Ivo Daalder have referred to a Bush 'revolution' in US foreign policy,[1] one aspect of which has been the US 'rejecting the traditional Wilsonian faith in international law and institutions' in favour of unilateral might. John Ikenberry has written of the Bush Administration's sweeping new ideas about US grand strategy by which the US is ultimately unconstrained by the rules and norms of the international community.[2] While it is certainly possible to find plenty of international law and institutional activity on which the US appears to have turned its back, there is also plenty that the US is right there in the midst of. Consider the growing number of bilateral free trade agreements, the US decision to rejoin UNESCO, or, for that matter, the enforcement of Security Council resolutions against Iraq. In seeking to ascertain whether the Bush administration may, indeed, have adopted an attitude towards international law fundamentally different to that of previous administrations, it is important to distinguish very clearly between criticism of the US engagement with international law and the scholarly analysis thereof. It is possible, for example, that some critics have condemned the overall approach of the Bush Administration towards international law as a way of critiquing specific policy choices. This chapter will suggest that the task of assessing the overall record of the Bush administration in relation to international law has been hampered by a theoretical abyss between conceptions of US power and international law. It will propose a means of overcoming this abyss before reaching its own conclusions as to whether there has been, and if so what the nature has been, of a Bush 'revolution' in the US relationship with international law.

---

1   James M. Lindsay and Ivo H. Daalder, *America Unbound: The Bush Revolution in Foreign Policy* (Washington, DC: Brookings Institution, 2003).

2   G. John Ikenberry, 'America's Imperial Ambition', *Foreign Affairs*, 81/5 (2002): 44.

The US and International Law

There is currently considerable disillusionment with the approach of the Bush administration to questions of international law. Much conventional wisdom has it that the US is two-faced in its attitude. On the one hand, the United States exalts the virtues of the rule of law and demands that other countries comply. But on the other, the United States does not seem to want to itself be bound by international law. Not only does the United States sometimes fail to comply with international law but it has not in recent years supported the growth and expansion of the system, as, for example, in the case of the Ottawa Landmines Convention or the International Criminal Court.

Dissatisfaction with the US attitude spans many branches of international law, including the environment, human rights, international humanitarian law, and arms control, although it is worth bearing in mind that in consideration of the political operation of international law use of force takes centre stage. The ultimate test of the 'real world' relevance of international law is generally assumed to be that as to whether international law has compliance pull over a powerful state deciding whether or not to use force. And hence, if there is one action or non-action of the US in relation to international law that encapsulates the apparent recent contempt of the US for international law and institutions it is the 2003 invasion of Iraq without explicit Security Council authorization, an action that some critics fear has dire consequences for international law as a whole.[3]

Criticism of the recent US attitude towards international law typically contrasts that attitude with US support for the expansion of the international legal order in the years post–World War II. Whereas the US was keen to establish the United Nations and the International Court of Justice in the 1940s, it has more recently acted in a way positively contrary to the establishment of the International Criminal Court. While the US was keen to use multilateral treaties to address arms control in the decades succeeding World War II, it now dismisses the very same regimes as inadequate to address the problems of today.

Elements of Consistency in the US Approach Towards International Law

It is in fact possible to discern a strong element of continuity in the post-1945 US attitude towards international law. This is perhaps most readily illuminated by removing the distinction commonly drawn between the pursuit of a liberal agenda focusing on international law and trade liberalisation on the one hand, and the realist preoccupation with the balance of power on the other. While it is generally assumed that the US has at certain times offered leadership in developing a liberal

---

3   'The immediate question ... [is not whether the 2003 invasion of Iraq is to be accepted as a valid legal precedent] but whether [international law] is to survive at all.' David Wedgwood Benn, 'Review Article. Neo-Conservatives and Their American Critics', *International Affairs*, 80/5 (2004): 969.

international order, the fact that the US has been so successful in the realist quest for increased relative power makes it reasonable to assume that the US has pursued what might broadly be termed a 'realist' foreign policy throughout the post–World War II years. Indeed, the US has used international law as a mechanism by which to increase its relative influence over the policies of others while seeking to minimize any external influences on its policies.

The lack of attention paid to international law in much realist theory does not necessarily mean that international law has not been in the picture.[4] It is possible to reconcile a realist understanding of foreign policy with international law. Rather than think of international law as something external to the United States, which the US at particular times may or may not have allowed to constrain its policy choices, we can view international law as integral to the pursuit of foreign policy objectives in the 'real world' of power politics.

If the United States had been seeking to maximize its relative power, understood in realist terms as the ability to influence the policies of other states more than they can influence those of the United States, it could be expected to have aimed to influence the substantive rules of international law as they evolved such that they serve to increase US relative power in a given issue area. Perhaps the most obvious example of this is the 1968 Treaty on the Non-Proliferation of Nuclear Weapons,[5] by which those states that had not already developed nuclear weapons pledged never to develop them, but those states that had already developed nuclear weapons did not have to renounce them. A state adopting a 'realist' approach to international law could also be expected to join a treaty regime only where it is positively in its interests to do so; if it proved more closely in the national interest to stay outside the regime or leave the regime, the state could be expected to do so. This would seem to be true of US behaviour in relation to the 1951 Refugee Convention,[6] or, to take more recent examples, of its failure to support the negotiation of the Ottawa Landmines Convention[7] and its 2001 notice of withdrawal from the Limitation of Anti-Ballistic Missile Systems (ABM) Treaty.[8]

A state adopting a realist attitude towards international law might also be expected to try to ensure that the rules regarding the functioning of the legal system are such as to permit it to change policy direction if it wishes to do so and to protect it from the policy advances of others. This would include aiming to be in a position to determine against whom, and when, rules of international law are enforced and to make sure that they are enforced against oneself as seldom as possible. Once again, it is not difficult to find examples of the US pursuing such a policy direction in relation to

---

4   Shirley V. Scott, 'Is There Room for International Law in *Realpolitik*? Accounting for the US "Attitude" Towards International Law', *Review of International Studies*, 30/1 (January 2004): 71–88.

5   729 UNTS 161.

6   189 UNTS 137.

7   26 ILM 1509 (1997).

8   944 UNTS 13.

international law which span the decades from the 1940s to the twenty-first century. Consider, for example, its safeguarding of the veto in the Security Council during the negotiation of the UN Charter, and its more recent desire to act via the Security Council – as, for example, in the case of UNSC 1540 on the non-proliferation of weapons of mass destruction and its preference for an explicit Security Council role in the verification of the Biological Weapons Convention.[9]

It might be expected that a state adopting a realist approach to international law would aim so far as possible not to give away the capacity to formulate and enforce the law applicable to US citizens in any particular issue area. The US tendency to not ratify optional protocols to human rights treaties could be considered an example here. And, if applied to a state's attitude towards international courts and tribunals, a state pursuing a realist approach to foreign policy might be expected to aim to be in a position to be able to have others answerable to judicial proceedings but to be much less accountable oneself. Here we can see examples in the US support for the ad hoc tribunals for the former Yugoslavia and for Rwanda versus its opposition to an ICC in which the US cannot determine which cases do or do not reach the Court.

This perspective on international law enables us to appreciate that it may be possible to reconcile power and international law in our understanding of the rise of the United States, something that the writers on liberal hegemony have advocated.[10] We can begin to appreciate just how administrations of both political persuasions have been able to harness international law and draw on it to facilitate its rise to sole superpower status. Not only has international law facilitated the US gaining a power lead over the rest of the world, international law has at the same time accorded US policies considerable political legitimacy. The US has, in turn, fostered that source of legitimacy by promoting the idea of the rule of law. By enhancing the idea of international law the US was ensuring a source of power that it could draw on to its own advantage.

Comparing the Administrations of Presidents Clinton and Bush

The previous section emphasized the element of continuity in the US approach towards international law since 1945 to demonstrate that international law and US power have not historically been separate and distinct. This is not to discard the possibility that since George W. Bush came to office the element of change has been greater than that of continuity. Let us now take up the challenge to see whether, if we look at specific aspects of foreign policy with an international legal dimension and which have spanned the administrations of Clinton and Bush, we can see a definable difference in their approach to international law. We will take several examples of actions for which the US under the Bush administration has met with

---

9   11 ILM 309 (1972).

10   See, *inter alia*, G. John Ikenberry, 'Power and Liberal Order: America's Postwar World Order in Transition', *International Relations of the Asia-Pacific*, 5 (2005): 133–152.

criticism, encompassing international environmental law, arms control, international humanitarian law, and the use of force.

The Kyoto Protocol

The problem of climate change was first addressed by international law in the United Nations Framework Convention on Climate Change,[11] which was opened for signature at the UN Conference on Environment and Development. The Third Conference of the Parties adopted the Kyoto Protocol to the United Nations Framework Convention on Climate Change on 11 December 1997.[12] This set individual emission targets for states in such a way as to meet a global outcome of a 5.2 percent reduction below 1990 levels of greenhouse gas emissions by 2008–2012. In the lead-up to Kyoto, the US had made it known that it expected the developing nations to contribute to the reduction. This was despite the fact that the Framework Convention had incorporated the principle of common but differentiated responsibility, which recognizes that, although all parties share certain common responsibilities in relation to the environment, developed countries have a particular onus to act. The Clinton Administration signed the Kyoto Protocol on 12 November 1998. Clinton announced, however, that he would not be seeking Senate support for ratification unless there were to be the meaningful participation of key developing countries.

The administration of George W. Bush reaffirmed US opposition to the Protocol, a position that, to critics, appeared to contradict the principle of common but differentiated responsibilities.[13] Environmental Protection Agency Administrator Christine Todd Whitman, Condoleeza Rice, and Bush himself all made comments to the effect that the Protocol was 'dead as far as the administration was concerned'.[14] Bush labelled it 'fatally flawed',[15] while proposing alternative initiatives. At an Association of South East Asian Nations (ASEAN) Regional Forum meeting in July 2005 the US, Australia, China, India, Japan, and the Republic of Korea presented a 'Vision Statement for an Asia-Pacific Partnership for Clean Development and Climate',[16] in accordance with which the partners may develop a non-binding compact designed to complement, but not replace, the Kyoto Protocol.

---

11 31 ILM 849 (1992).

12 37 ILM 22 (1998) (not yet in force).

13 Paul G. Harris, 'Common but Differentiated Responsibility: The Kyoto Protocol and United States Policy', *New York University Environmental Law Journal*, 7 (1999): 27–48.

14 Eric Pianin, 'US Aims to Pull Out of Warming Treaty' *Washington Post*, 28 March 2001, p. A1, cited in Murphy, p. 176 fn. 12 and Timothy Wirth, 'Hot Air Over Kyoto: The United States and the Politics of Global Warming', *Harvard International Review* (2002), <http://www.facstaff.bucknell.edu/pagana/mg312/kyoto.html>.

15 'President Bush Discusses Global Climate Change', press release of 11 June 2001, <http://www.whitehouse.gov/news/releases/2001/06/20010611-2.html>.

16 The vision statement is available at <http://www.dfat.gov.au/environment/climate/050728_final_vision_statement.html>. See also the Press Conference by Deputy

The Anti-Ballistic Missile Treaty

The 1972 US–Soviet Treaty on the Limitation of Anti-Ballistic Missile Systems (ABM) Treaty[17] was a cornerstone of bilateral efforts during the Cold War to prevent nuclear annihilation. Premised on the principle of mutually assured destruction, the treaty prohibited the development of an antiballistic missile system to protect the whole of either country or of an individual region, except where expressly permitted. Clinton believed that an emerging missile threat meant that there was an obligation to pursue a missile defense system that could enhance US security but advocated moving forward in the context of the ABM treaty. He unsuccessfully sought agreement from President Putin that the world had changed since the signing of the ABM treaty and that the proliferation of missile technology had resulted in new threats that might require amending that treaty.[18]

Although there was an attempt under the Bush administration to resurrect the idea of amending the treaty,[19] efforts to negotiate this with the Russians were unsuccessful. Publicly emphasizing the need to move beyond the constraints of the 30-year-old treaty, President Bush attempted to persuade Putin to jointly abrogate the treaty. When these efforts failed, the United States on 13 December 2001 submitted formal notification of its intention to withdraw from the treaty.

The International Criminal Court

The Clinton Administration had at first supported the establishment of the International Criminal Court but when it became clear during the diplomatic conference at which the text of the Rome Statute of the International Criminal Court was finalized that the US would not get the Court it wanted, the Clinton Administration became one of only seven states to vote against the Statute. Although Clinton later signed the Statute, he stated categorically that he would not, and would not recommend that his successor, submit the treaty to the Senate for advice and consent until fundamental concerns were satisfied.[20] When the US did sign, it was a strategic decision to do so, so as to enable the US to continue influencing the evolution of the Court.[21]

Secretary Robert Zoellick and others, 'Announcing the Asia-Pacific Partnership on Clean Development', 28 July 2005, <http://www.state.gov/s/d/rem/50326.htm>.

17 944 UNTS 13.

18 Remarks by the President on National Missile Defense, Gaston Hall, Georgetown University, Washington, DC, 1 September 2000, <http://www.clintonfoundation.org/index. htm.

19 Nikolai Sokov, 'US Withdrawal from the ABM Treaty: Post-Mortem and Possible Consequences', Monterey Institute of International Studies: CNS Reports, <http://cns.miis. edu/pubs/reports/2abm.htm>.

20 'Presidential Statement on Signature the ICC Treaty', 31 December 2000, <http:// www.clintonfoundation.org/index.htm.

21 *Ibid.*

On 6 May 2002 Bush 'withdrew' the US signature, and subsequently made it clear that 'one thing we're not going to do is sign on to the International Criminal Court'.[22] The Bush Administration went on to gain Security Council agreement to exempt US service personnel working on UN missions and to negotiate bilateral 'article 98' agreements exempting US nationals from ICC jurisdiction. Congress passed the American Service-members' Protection Act of 2002, which included a prohibition on US cooperation with the ICC.

Preemption

The 2002 National Security Strategy stated:

> The United States has long maintained the option of preemptive actions to counter a sufficient threat to our national security. The greater the threat, the greater is the risk of inaction – and the more compelling the case for taking anticipatory action to defend ourselves, even if uncertainty remains as to the time and place of the enemy's attack. To forestall or prevent such hostile acts by our adversaries, the United States will, if necessary, act preemptively.[23]

The international legal concept equivalent to that of preemption is anticipatory self-defense. While lawyers may differ over the details as to when anticipatory self-defense is legal few would accept that the threat Iraq posed to the US in 2003 was sufficient to justify its full-scale invasion and occupation by the US. In the event the US did not in any case justify the 2003 invasion in terms of anticipatory self-defense.

Preemption is generally characterized by its critics as a new strategy, but not all agree. John Lewis Gaddis has traced preemption to the earliest days of the republic,[24] while Max Boot cites as earlier instances of preemption, the 1965 invasion of the Dominican Republic to address the perceived threat from the rise of communism there and the 1983 invasion of Grenada to prevent its being cultivated as a Soviet and Cuban base.[25] According to Leffler, preemption is not new; it just has a special place in the thinking of Bush's defense advisers, who regard the post–September 11 game as one that cannot be won only with a strategy of defense.[26] According to this line of thought it is because the Administration does not want to be taken by surprise by a terrorist attack with WMD that there may be an increased willingness to act

---

22 'Remarks by the President to the Travel Pool During Tour', 2 July 2002, <http://www.whitehouse.gov/news/releases/2002/07/20020702-1.html>.

23 The White House, Washington, *National Security Strategy of the United States* (September 2002), p. 15.

24 John Lewis Gaddis, *Surprise, Security, and the American Experience* (Cambridge, MA: Harvard University Press, 2004).

25 Max Boot, 'Iraq Doesn't Discredit Wars of Preemption', *Weekly Standard*, 16 February 2004, <http://hnn.us/roundup/comments/3594.html>.

26 Melvyn P. Leffler, '9/11 and the Past and Future of American Foreign Policy', *International Affairs*, 79/5 (2003): 1053.

preemptively or even preventively rather than consider the use of force a last resort, but the difference is one of degree. With the assertion of the US right to preemption it became institutionalized policy under the Bush Administration.

The Use of Force Against Iraq

Following the expulsion of the Iraqi armed forces from Kuwait in 1991 by a coalition authorized to do so by Security Council Resolution 678, the Council passed Resolution 687 on 3 April 1991. This 'ceasefire resolution' required, amongst other things, that Iraq destroy or render harmless all chemical, biological, or nuclear weapons. A Special Commission was to be established for the purpose of carrying out on-site inspections in Iraq. As the 1990s wore on Iraq restricted cooperation with the Special Commission (UNSCOM) in protest at the sanctions to which it continued to be subjected.[27] Tensions increased, and, with UNSCOM unable to carry out its responsibilities effectively, the US and UK on 16 December 1998 commenced a 70-hour missile and aircraft bombing campaign against approximately a hundred sites in Iraq. The US continued to rely on Resolution 678 as legal justification for its actions; many international lawyers in the US and elsewhere questioned the validity of such 'ambiguous authorizations to use force'.[28] The actions were supported by a number of US allies but condemned by China, France, and Russia; Iraq charged that the bombing constituted aggression in flagrant violation of the UN Charter and principles of international law.[29] Between 1999 and 2001, United Kingdom and United States aircraft continued to attack Iraqi military sites approximately five to ten days every month.[30]

The US led a full-scale invasion of Iraq, commencing on 20 March 2003, for which there was once again no explicit authorization by the Security Council. The US has claimed the ongoing relevance of Resolutions 678 and 687 in combination with Resolution 1441 of November 2002. To legal critics 1441 did little to strengthen the claim to legality. The Resolution had concluded by stating that the Security Council would remain seized of the matter and the United States had made it clear at the time that it understood the Resolution to contain no 'automaticity' with respect to the use

---

27 Sean D. Murphy, *United States Practice in International Law*, Vol. 1: 1999–2001 (Cambridge: Cambridge University Press, 2002), pp. 409–410.

28 Jules Lobel and Michael Ratner, 'Bypassing the Security Council: Ambiguous Authorizations to Use Force, Cease-Fires and the Iraqi Inspection Regime', *American Journal of International Law*, 93/1 (1999): 124–54.

29 'Letter dated 2 August 1999 from the Permanent Representative of Iraq to the United Nations Addressed to the Security Council', UN Doc. S/1999/842 (quoted in Murphy in *The American Journal of International Law*, 1999, p. 102).

30 'Latest Bombings Are Part of a Long Campaign', *New York Times* (17 February 2001), p. A4, cited in Sean Murphy *United States Practice in International Law*, Vol. 1: 1999–2001 (Cambridge: Cambridge University Press, 2002), p. 416.

of force.'[31] President Saddam Hussein was captured and in 2005 was put on trial in Iraq, amidst ongoing violence which showed no sign of abatement.

Torture

The 1984 Convention Against Torture and Other Cruel, Inhuman or Degrading Treatment or Punishment (Torture Convention) requires a state 'to take effective legislative, administrative, judicial or other measures to prevent acts of torture in any territory under its jurisdiction'.[32] It expressly prohibits extraditing a person to another state where there are 'substantial grounds for believing that he would be in danger of being subjected to torture'.[33] The United States deposited its instrument of ratification with the UN Secretary-General on 21 October 1994 and the Convention entered into force for the United States on 20 November 1994. In its Initial Report to the Torture Committee, submitted on 15 October 1999, the US affirmed that it categorically denounced torture as a matter of policy and as a tool of state authority.[34]

It appears that, despite official US policy, the CIA had by then already initiated the practice of 'extraordinary rendition', by which it transferred prisoners to other countries, including Egypt, Morocco, or Syria, where they were then tortured. The practice was initiated with the approval of the Clinton Administration.[35] The practice of rendition has continued under the Bush Administration; in fact since President Bush announced the 'war on terror' there has apparently been a huge increase in its perpetration.[36] Official policy, as stated in the Second US Report to the Committee Against Torture, submitted on 6 May 2005, has continued to be that the US is unequivocally opposed to the use and practice of torture.[37] While the official policy as presented to the UN Committee has thus not changed from the Clinton to the Bush Administration, there has been evidence that during the 'war on terror' much

---

31 USUN Press Release #187 (02) (Revised). 'Explanation of Vote by Ambassador John D. Negroponte, United States Permanent Representative to the United Nations, following the vote on the Iraq Resolution, Security Council', November 8, 2002, web page of the United States Mission to the United Nations, <www.un.int/usa/02_187.htm>.

32 Convention Against Torture and Other Cruel, Inhuman or Degrading Treatment or Punishment, Dec. 10, 1984, art. 1(1) 23 ILM 1027.

33 Article 3(1).

34 *US Department of State Initial Report of the United States of America to the UN Committee Against Torture.* Submitted by the United States of America to the Committee Against Torture, October 15, 1999, <http://www.state.gov/www/global/human_rights/torture_intro.html>.

35 Jane Mayer, 'Outsourcing Torture: The Secret History of America's "extraordinary rendition" program', *The New Yorker* (14 February 2005), <www.newyorker.com/fact/content/?050214fa_fact6>.

36 *Ibid.*

37 *Second Periodic Report of the United States of America to the Committee Against Torture.* Submitted by the United States of America to the Committee Against Torture, May 6, 2005, <http://www.state.gov/g/drl/rls/45738.htm>.

ill-treatment and even torture has not only been 'outsourced' by US officials but
has been directly inflicted on detainees in Iraq, Afghanistan, and Guantanamo Bay.
Indeed, Government documents leaked during the course of 2004 suggested that
ill-treatment and torture had been envisaged in the early days of the 'war on terror'
and that Administration lawyers had laid the foundation for a shift in standards of
interrogation.[38] Memoranda gathered by Karen Greenberg and Joshua Dratel trace
the efforts of the Bush Administration to find a location secure from infiltration
and from intervention by the courts, to rescind the US's agreement to abide by the
proscriptions of the Geneva Convention with respect to the treatment of persons
captured during armed conflict and to provide an interpretation of the law which
would protect policy makers from potential war crimes prosecutions for the human
rights abuses and torture that followed.[39]

Findings

Daalder and Lindsay charged the Bush Administration with rejecting international
law and institutions in favour of unilateral might. 'Reject' is not a term of art in
international law. But if we interpret this phrase to mean 'being prepared to use US
military might even where it is illegal to do so and where a significant proportion
of the international community and/or the opinions of "mainstream" international
lawyers is that that use of force is illegal', then the levelling of the charge against the
Bush Administration has been appropriate. The mainstream view of the 2003 US–
led invasion of Iraq is undoubtedly that it was illegal; Kofi Annan himself declared it
such.[40] The catch is, that on this interpretation of Daalder and Lindsay's charge, the
Clinton Administration had also been guilty, so detracting from the sense in which
we could be said to be witnessing a 'revolution'. It is true that there was not the same
outcry from the scholarly community in the United States and US allies to the US
bombing of areas of Iraq between 1998 and 2001 as we have since 2003, but this
was likely due to several factors other than its legality: the bombing received much
less media coverage, it was overshadowed by other crises including Kosovo, and,
of course, it was not on the same scale as the 2003 invasion of Iraq. The scale of
the attacks is vastly different but the decision to use force without explicit Security
Council authorization or even the tacit approval of the other permanent members,
was no different. Nor does it seem that things would have been so very different in
relation to Iraq had Kerry become president. Kerry and his vice-presidential running

---

38 Amnesty International, *Report 2005*, <http://web.amnesty.org/report2005/usa-
summary-eng>.

39 Joshua L. Dratel, 'The Legal Narrative', in Karen J. Greenberg and Joshua L. Dratel
(eds), *The Torture Papers: The Road to Abu Ghraib* (Cambridge: Cambridge University Press,
2005), p. xxii.

40 UN News Centre, *Lessons of Iraq Underscore Importance of the UN Charter* (16
September 2004), <http://www.un.org>.

mate John Edwards had voted for the authorization of war and in his campaign Kerry vowed not to cut and run but to press on to 'victory'.[41]

Along similar lines, a policy decision to condone the torture of detainees had apparently been made under the Clinton Administration. Scheuer, a former CIA counter-terrorism expert who helped establish the practice, has claimed that, in the early days, the CIA's legal counsel signed off on each individual case; the system was designed to prevent innocent people being subjected to rendition.[42] But according to former FBI agent, Dan Coleman, the practice 'really went out of control' following September 11.[43] In legal terms, the legal-illegal line had already been crossed under Clinton; it is the difference in the scale on which the illegal behaviour has been conducted that presents such a stark contrast. As for the practice of 'stress and duress', by which captives are disoriented, humiliated, denied food and sleep and forced into agonizing positions for hours at a time in order to extract information and confessions; it is claimed that this was used – and taught to client armies around the world – under the Kennedy and Johnson Administrations.[44]

The other three examples considered above of the Bush Administration's practice in relation to international law did not relate to a legal-illegal division of behaviour. It is not illegal to decide against joining a treaty regime just as it is perfectly legal to withdraw from a treaty in accordance with the terms of the treaty. So it has not been the illegality of these actions that has caused such controversy. Nor could it really have been the substance of the policies in question. For it would seem that the substantive policies of the two administrations on the environment, arms control, and international justice and actions have not been dissimilar. Both administrations wanted to pursue missile defense, preferably with the acquiescence of Russia; neither wanted significant restrictions on US emission of greenhouse gases, especially without what it regarded as comparable requirements being imposed on the developing world; and neither was prepared to be a part of an international criminal court if the US were not going to be able to be the key influence over the operations of the Court.

The difference between the administrations, and the apparent source of the angst of so many commentators, lies in the way that the Bush Administration has gone about pursuing these substantive policy preferences. The Clinton Administration had already committed itself to developing a missile shield but was still talking in terms of amending the ABM treaty; under the Bush Administration, the US withdrew from the treaty. Although Clinton had said that the US would not ratify the Kyoto Protocol without necessary changes, Bush declared that the US would never ratify the Protocol. While Clinton left the way open for the United States to continue to try

---

41 Richard K. Betts, 'The Political Support System for American Primacy', *International Affairs*, 81/1 (2005), p. 10.

42 Jane Mayer, 'Outsourcing Torture: The Secret History of America's "Extraordinary Rendition"'.

43 *Ibid.*

44 Steve Weissman, 'Torture – From J.F.K. to Baby Bush' *Scoop Independent News*, <http://www.truthout.org/docs_04/123104A.shtml>, 18 April 2005.

to shape both the Kyoto Protocol and the International Criminal Court, Bush closed the door. Clinton seemed to want to minimize the appearance of conflict between US policies and existing or evolving international law while Bush has been prepared to clarify if not highlight the points of difference.

This observation accords with the views of a number of other writers on Bush foreign policy. Even Daalder and Lindsay, who have referred to a 'Bush revolution' in foreign policy, nevertheless emphasize that it is a revolution in methods, rather than goals.[45] Richard Betts has argued that the foreign policy of Bush is different in style – in how he goes about it, rather than in substance – from that of Clinton.

> Democrats push primacy with a human face, dressed up in the rhetoric of multilateralism, and they use military power with much hesitancy and hand-wringing. Republicans push primacy 'in your face', with unapologetic unilateralism, and they swagger brazenly. To a surprising degree, however, the two sides come out in the same place.[46]

The inclination to push primary 'in your face' has been evident in relation to, amongst other things, the attitude of the Administration to the issue of detainee abuse and torture. According to Steve Weissman, Bush, Rumsfeld, and Gonzales touted their rejection of the Geneva Conventions 'as a symbol of American resolve in fighting Islamic terrorists, [acting] as if they wanted the world to know. They wanted, it seems, to send "the ragheads" a message: "Don't Step on Superman's Cape"'.[47] The desire to 'swagger brazenly' has been seen in the reaction of the Administration to attempts by Republican Senators to prevent further torture. On 5 October 2005 the US Senate approved by 90 votes to nine the McCain-Graham-Durbin Amendment to the Defense Appropriations Bill, which established the Army Field Manual as the uniform standard for the interrogation of Department of Defense detainees and prohibited cruel, inhuman, and degrading treatment of persons in the detention of the US government.[48] A White House statement on the proposed amendment said that the President's advisers would recommend a veto if its language restricted the President's ability to effectively carry out the war on terrorism.[49]

What then of the other policy areas considered above in which illegality has not been at stake? What can be concluded here about the differences between the two administrations? If Clinton was still talking in terms of preserving but amending the ABM treaty, and Bush has withdrawn never to return, is this significant if the substance of each policy – developing a missile defense system – is the same? If only

---

45 Ivo H. Daalder and James M. Lindsay, *America Unbound: The Bush Revolution in Foreign Policy* (Washington, DC: Brookings Institution, 2003).

46 Richard K. Betts, 'The Political Support System for American Primacy', p. 2.

47 Steve Weissman, 'Torture – From J.F.K. to Baby Bush' *Scoop Independent News*, <http://www.truthout.org/docs_04/123104A.shtml>, 18 April 2005.

48 'McCain Statement on Detainee Amendments', 6 October 2005, <http://mccain. senate.gov/index.cfm?fuseaction=NewsCenter.ViewPressRelease&Content_id=1611>.

49 Press Briefing by Scott McClellan, 6 October 2005, <http://www.whitehouse.gov/ news/releases/2005/10/20051006-6.html#I>.

a 'thin red line' separated Clinton's rhetoric from a convincing legal justification for Kosovo[50] while the invasion of Iraq was unequivocally 'illegal', does this matter if the US intervention in both cases was strictly speaking not legal? If the Clinton and Bush administrations differ in their relationship with international law 'merely' in rhetoric or 'lip service', is that difference still a difference?

The Power of the Idea of International Law

Our answer to such questions will depend on 'what sort of a creature' we think international law is and where we think that creature resides in relation to the power of the United States. Discussions of US power usually have little to say about international law. Although some writers recognize that geographical factors including territory, natural resources, and population may contribute to US power,[51] focus is typically placed on the 'realist' military and economic dimensions, both supported by US technological superiority.

In an attempt to remind policy makers of the importance of less tangible forms of power, Joseph Nye has in recent years promoted the idea of soft power as a necessary accompaniment of the hard varieties.[52] Hard power is the ability to coerce but soft power lies in the ability to attract and persuade. It arises from the attractiveness of a country's culture, political ideals, and policies. While Nye makes mention of certain treaties and components of the international legal system, he does not systematically theorize the relationship of international law to US power. In his work on liberal hegemony, John Ikenberry similarly advances the view that contrasting power with institutions and ideas as sources of international order is a false dichotomy,[53] and yet Ikenberry's list of the dimensions of American global power makes no mention of international law.[54]

If international law is a system entirely external to international law lacking 'real teeth', something that can be the object of US disregard or on which the US can inflict actual damage but which is removed from the source of US pre-eminence,

---

50 Bruno Simma, 'NATO, the UN and the Use of Force: Legal Aspects', *European Journal of International Law*, 10 (1999): 1.

51 Bob Catley has defined the basis of US power as being a large, well-educated and fairly homogenous population, a substantial and well-located territory, the world's premier economy, and a state supported by its people and capable of mobilizing its resources for military conflict when the occasion has demanded. Bob Catley, 'Hegemonic America: The Arrogance of Power' *Contemporary Southeast Asia*, 21 (1999): 157.

52 Nye introduced the concept in *Bound to Lead: The Changing Nature of American Power* (New York: Basic, 1990), but has further developed and refined it in subsequent works, including *Soft Power: The Means to Success in World Politics* (New York: Public Affairs, 2004).

53 G.John Ikenberry *After Victory: Institutions, Strategic Restraint, and the Rebuilding of Order After Major Wars* (Princeton: Princeton University Press, 2000), p. 10.

54 G.John Ikenberry, 'Power and Liberal Order: America's Postwar World Order in Transition', *International Relations of the Asia-Pacific*, 5 (2005): 133.

then the differences in rhetoric and associated behaviour may not matter very much. But if we hold that international law, its inter-relationship with US policy and with other states, has been and may well still be, integral to US power, and if we believe that the source of the power of international law lies in the non-material world, then certainly it does.

International law has some material manifestations. There are buildings that house various international courts and tribunals, and there are many volumes of documents of international legal significance. But these things are not the essence of the system of international law. At the heart of international law is an idea, sometimes referred to as the rule of law. It is an idea about justice, about moderating the application of power. It is an idea about process, common expectations, and dignity. It is an idea that lends legitimacy to the exercise of power. That ideas, and their enunciation through language, matter, has been the most fundamental message of students of rhetoric, discourse analysts, Hegelian historians and philosophers, and ideology theorists.

If we accept that the essence of international law is an idea, or set of ideas, we have a basis on which to assess whether rhetoric and accompanying actions detract from the idea and power of international law. It has already been suggested that this idea is close to that of the rule of law and that it has been beneficial to the United States to associate its own policies with the idea of the rule of law. Let us now be more precise in specifying the constituent principle of the image of international law. They can be set out as follows:

- International law is ultimately distinguishable from, and superior to, mere politics.
- It is possible to distinguish objectively between legal and illegal action.
- The rules of international law are compulsory.
- International law is politically neutral or universal in the sense that it treats all states equally.
- International law is at this point of time (virtually) static.
- International law is (virtually) self-contained.
- It is possible to apply the rules of law objectively so as to settle a dispute between states.
- International law can deal with any issue that arises between states.[55]

According to a theorization of international law as ideology,[56] rhetoric that assumes these principles to be true reinforces this image of international law and hence its political power. During its rise to sole superpower status, the US has engaged in

---

55 Shirley Scott, 'Beyond Compliance: Reconceiving the International Law–Foreign Policy Dynamic', *The Australian Year Book of International Law* (1998): 44–45.

56 See S.V. Scott, 'International Law as Ideology: Theorising the Relationship Between International Law and International Politics', *European Journal of International Law*, 5 (1994): 313–25.

considerable rhetoric that upholds the idea of the rule of law which, in turn, has lent legitimacy to US policies and actions. On the other hand, rhetoric that undermines this image of international law thereby weakens the idea of international law. While these principles are not in a hierarchy per se, the most important is undoubtedly that of the distinction between law and politics. While it would be hard to deny that politics influences law, it is vital that there continues to be assumed the possibility of an ultimate distinction between them; otherwise law is no more than policy, which means that it can no longer serve as a referent point, a benchmark for the legitimate exercise of power. The basic point here is that rhetoric *does* matter; pursuing the same policy but justifying it in different terms *is* a difference.

The Rhetoric of George W. Bush Versus That of Ronald Reagan

It was earlier suggested that there has been considerable continuity in the US approach to international law since at least 1945. Many of the types of actions in relation to international law for which the Bush Administration has been criticized have precedents under previous administrations. Hence it does not seem possible to say that not ratifying treaties, or withdrawing from treaties, or not complying with certain treaties, or other specific types of action in relation to international law in themselves constitute a redefinition of US power. When some specific policies were compared against those of the previous Clinton administration it was further found that the examples could be divided into two groups. Those actions of the Bush administration that were 'illegal' had direct precedents under the Clinton administration but were being conducted on a much greater scale under Bush; those actions that were not illegal have shown continuity with Clinton policies but have been pursued with very different international law rhetoric under Bush. The chapter then went on to suggest a measure by which to gauge whether rhetoric and actions in relation to international law is damaging international law as a source of power in world politics. It was suggested that the source of the power of international law lies in a certain set of ideas about international law and that it is rhetoric and actions that point to these as not portraying reality that undermines the power of international law and that thereby tends to attract strong criticism. Rhetoric that does assume one or more of the principles to be true both strengthens the idea of international law and at the same time accords legitimacy to the policy in question. This gives us a more nuanced measure by which to compare the policies in relation to international law of different administrations.

My hypothesis is that the Bush Administration is much more willing to undermine that idea of international law than have been other administrations – certainly than was the Clinton Administration but possibly also previous republican administrations. Periodic reminders that the US is currently quite capable of doing what it likes, international organizations or law notwithstanding, such as Dick Cheney's comment that George W. Bush 'will never seek a permission slip to defend the American people',[57] detract from the image of international law as a standard apart from power politics.

The Clinton Administration, unable to provide a strong legal justification for its intervention during the Kosovo crisis, relied primarily on moral legitimacy to justify the campaign, whilst making passing reference to the United Nations and to international law. Five days after the bombing started, Clinton declared that if 'we and our allies do not have the will to act, there will be more massacres. In dealing with aggressors, ... hesitation is a license to kill. But action and resolve can stop armies and save lives'.[58] The Clinton Administration avoided giving a clear legal justification for a bombing campaign that did not fit readily within the parameters of the contemporary law on the use of force. Note here the distinction between compliance and upholding the idea that compliance is compulsory.

Even when the Reagan Administration needed to justify intervention in Grenada, the first announcement by Reagan in fact made no mention of a justification in international law but referred to the importance of protecting 'innocent lives, including up to 1,000 Americans whose personal safety is, of course, my paramount concern; second, to forestall further chaos; and third, to assist in the restoration of conditions of law and order and of governmental institutions to the island of Grenada'.[59] Such rhetoric stopped short of actually undermining the image of international law as a standard apart from politics with which a state must comply. In contrast, take these comments of Bush on the Kyoto Protocol:

> As you know, I oppose the Kyoto Protocol because it exempts 80 percent of the world, including major population centers such as China and India, from compliance, and would cause serious harm to the US economy. The Senate's vote, 95–0, shows that there is a clear consensus that the Kyoto Protocol is an unfair and ineffective means of addressing global climate change concerns.[60]

This statement undermines both the notion that all states must comply with international law obligations, and that international law treats all states equally. At the tenth session of the conference of parties, the chief American negotiator was scathing about the Kyoto Protocol which he claimed was based on bad science; he labelled it a political document;[61] the US has stressed that it is 'not sound policy'.[62]

57 Dick Cheney, '2004 Republican National Convention Address', 1 September 2004, <http://www.americanrhetoric.com/speeches/convention2004/dickcheney2004rnc.htm>.

58 The President's News Conference. 35 Wkly Comp. Pres. Doc. 471, pp. 25–26 (1999). The President later referred to Security Council Resolutions 1199 and 1203, although neither explicitly authorized the use of force.

59 Cited in Robert J. Beck, *The Grenada Invasion* (Westview Press, 1993), p. 55.

60 Text of a Letter from the President to Senators Hagel, Helms, Craig, and Roberts, 13 March 2001, <http://www.whitehouse.gov/news/releases/2001/03/20010314.html>.

61 'US Rules Out Joining Kyoto Treaty', BBC News, 7 December 2004, <http://news.bbc.co.uk/1/hi/sci/tech/4077073.stm>.

62 'Statement of the United States of America' by Paula Dobriansky, Under Secretary of State for Global Affairs at the resumed Sixth Conference of Parties to the UN Framework

Consider these comments on the draft verification protocol to the Biological Weapons Convention: 'we were forced to conclude that the mechanisms envisioned for the Protocol would not achieve their objectives, that no modification of them would allow them to achieve their objectives ...'.[63] By proposing that the long-running talks on a verification protocol be terminated because they were hopeless, the Bush Administration was undermining the idea that international law can address any issue that arises between states. Similar was the comment in relation to Kyoto, that the Protocol was 'fatally flawed', while comments regarding the ABM treaty having become out of date questioned the image of international law as virtually timeless.

This is not to suggest that rhetoric supportive of the idea of international law but divorced from reality will necessarily uphold the ideal strongly. Early US rhetoric regarding Iraq's lack of compliance with international law and Security Council resolutions functioned to uphold the image of a strict division between complying and not-complying and of the necessity of complying with international law; it was revelations of prisoner abuse that detracted from the notion that compliance is compulsory, and revelations that the US Administration had always wanted to 'get' Iraq, that not only pointed to but underlined in heavy ink the political nature of international law.[64]

Conclusions: Has There Been a Bush 'Revolution' in the US Attitude Towards International Law?

This chapter has sought to emphasize the need for some nuance in our analysis of what is new in the attitude of the current Bush Administration towards international law. It is too simplistic to make comments such as that the Bush Administration, unlike its predecessors, feels 'unconstrained by', or cares little about, international law. Many of the types of actions or inactions in relation to international law for which the Bush Administration has been criticized fall into a pattern that can be regarded as 'realist': that is, using international law as a mechanism by which to increase relative US influence over the policies of others while seeking to minimize any external influences on US policies. But to this extent the actions of the Bush Administration may be no different to those of most, if not all, US Governments since World War Two. And, while the Bush Administration has been prepared to

---

Convention on Climate Change, Bonn, Germany, 25 July 2001, <http://www.useu.be/ Categories/ClimateChange/ClimateChangeDobrianskyJuly25.html>.

63 Donald A. Mahley, Special Negotiator for Chemical and Biological Arms Control Issues, Statement to the Ad Hoc Group of Biological Weapons Convention States Parties (July 25, 2001), cited in Sean D. Murphy (ed.), 'Contemporary Practice of the United States Relating to International Law', *American Journal of International Law*, 95 (2001), p. 901.

64 See Shirley V. Scott and Olivia Ambler 'Does Legality *Really* matter? Accounting for the Decline in US Foreign Policy Legitimacy Following the 2003 Invasion of Iraq', *European Journal of International Relations*, forthcoming.

not comply with international law, even to the extent of engaging in the illegal use of force, this has also been a feature of previous Democratic as well as Republican Administrations.

In seeking to identify just what *is* new in the attitude of the Bush Administration to international law a comparison was made between the policies of the Bush and Clinton Administrations. The findings were analyzed using insights from a theorization of international law as ideology. From this it was hypothesized that the Bush Administration has been much more ready than the previous administration to undermine the 'idea' of international law via rhetoric and actions that fail to uphold the ideal of international law as a politically neutral set of standards and rules. It is not that no previous administration has ever undermined that ideal – when the ICJ found that it did have jurisdiction in the Nicaragua Case, the US agent said that the United States had been 'constrained to conclude that the judgment of the Court was clearly and manifestly erroneous as to both fact and law',[65] thereby undermining the notion that the rules of international law can be objectively applied so as to settle a dispute between states. But it is also true that, as the world is increasingly globalized and US power reaches around the globe, the scale of the US quest, and the reach of its influence, broadens.

It would not be wholly true to characterize the attitude of the Bush Administration towards international law as either a 'revolution' or as 'business as usual'. Rather, the US seems to have been on a slippery slide into an abyss from which it will be difficult for international law, and the US, to climb out. Rhetoric and action undermining the idea of international law has undoubtedly damaged the idea of the possibility of a world governed by international law.

Calls for the US to accord international law greater respect are not calls for altruism on the part of the United States. It was Weber who told us so clearly of the great advantage to the 'haves' of a sense of rule-based legitimacy: most basically, that if people believe in a particular set of 'rules of the game' they will comply with those rules even if to do so runs counter to their socio-economic, political, or legal interests. The bottom line of much of the criticism of US foreign policy under George W. Bush is that many of the dubious legal dimensions of the 'war on terrorism' are ultimately not in the best interests even of the United States. Removing terror suspects from the US legal system and treating them in ways forbidden by US and international law, for example, means that ultimately those individuals cannot readily be returned to be dealt with by that legal system.

Whether their focus has been on legitimacy and soft power – or, more provocatively, on unilateralism, domination and empire – commentators have been searching for ways to express what is in essence a very similar message: that the longer the task of repair is delayed and the more the damage is intensified, the more difficult will be the task of repair. What has not been so clear in much of the debate is

---

65 Letter from the United States agent to the Court of 18 January 1985: *Military and Paramilitary Activities in and Against Nicaragua (Nicaragua v US) (Merits)* [1986] ICJ Rep 17.

precisely how the US has damaged international law or precisely what the US needs to do differently in terms of international law in order to undertake that repair. It is to be hoped that this chapter has made a conceptual contribution to current debate on the exercise of US power by pinpointing the source of the power of international law and hence how US rhetoric and actions can weaken or strengthen that power and how the US can and does benefit from it. For, while specific actions or policies of the Administration as they relate to international law may have provided plenty of scope for criticism, it is in undermining the *idea* of international law that the Administration has been most reckless.

Chapter 5

Dealing with Hegemony at Home: From Congressional Compliance to Resistance to George W. Bush's National Security Policy

Frédérick Gagnon

In the United States, the US Congress plays a fundamental role in the foreign policy debate. Many US legislators, particularly the members of key congressional committees like the House and the Senate committees on Armed Services or the House Committee on International Relations and the Senate Committee on Foreign Relations, are prominent foreign policy experts. Just like the President of the United States or the members of the National Security Council, they discuss issues like the US policy in the Middle East, the solutions to protect the American people against terrorism or the best ways to diversify US sources of oil and natural gas. Members of Congress use many tools to influence US foreign policy: they appear in the media, write letters to the President and, most importantly, debate, make speeches and cast votes on Capitol Hill. To be sure, congressional influence on US international actions is much less important than the influence of the White House. However, Congress possesses many foreign policy powers, like the power to ratify treaties or the power to approve budgets. Therefore, scholars of US foreign policy should give attention to the impact of Congress on the elaboration of the war on terror, and on the way the United States deals with its hegemonic position in the world.

It is a widely held view that during George W. Bush's first term in office, the US Congress generally followed the White House's lead on foreign affairs issues.[1] It has been suggested that the President 'got exactly what he wanted' from the House and Senate,[2] and that Congress supported presidential proposals without substantially

---

1   See for instance James M. Lindsay, 'Deference and Defiance: The Shifting Rhythms of Executive-Legislative Relations in Foreign Policy', *Presidential Studies Quarterly*, 33/3 (September 2003): 530–46; Nancy Kassop, 'The War Power and Its Limits', *Presidential Studies Quarterly*, 33/3 (September 2003): 509–529 and Sabine Lavorel, *La politique de sécurité nationale des États-Unis sous George W. Bush* (Paris: L'Harmattan, 2003).

2   Ralph G. Carter's definition of 'congressional compliance' with the White House's proposals. See Ralph G. Carter, 'Congress and Post–Cold War U.S. Foreign Policy', in James

questioning, debating or modifying them.[3] We will argue that while it is true that the President was dominant and Congress largely compliant on the war in Afghanistan, increases in defence budgets, the passage of the USA Patriot Act, the National Security Strategy of the United States of America of September 2002, and the war in Iraq, negotiations between the White House and the Capitol became far tougher during and after the 2004 election on issues such as the reconstruction of Iraq, the confirmation of John Bolton as US Ambassador to the UN and the renewal of the Patriot Act. Thus far, the 109th Congress has been much less acquiescent than were the 107th and the 108th: the US legislators have stopped being accomplices of Bush's 'imperial temptation'.[4]

In this chapter, we will propose a theoretical explanation for Congress's stance on matters of national security during the Bush presidency and analyze why the congressional attitude towards Bush's policies has shifted from compliance to resistance. Our discussion is divided into three sections. First, we review the literature on congressional behaviour and the reasons behind it.[5] As shall be seen,

---

M. Scott (ed.), *After the End: Making U.S. Foreign Policy in the Post–Cold War World* (Durham, NC: Duke University Press, 1998), p. 110.

3   Frédérick Gagnon, 'En conformité avec la Maison-Blanche. Le Congrès et la politique de sécurité nationale des États-Unis durant le premier mandat de George W. Bush', *Études internationales*, 36/4 (December 2005): 501–25.

4   See Stanley Hoffman (with Frederic Bozo), *Gulliver Unbound: America's Imperial Temptation and the War in Iraq* (Lanham: Rowman & Littlefield, 2004).

5   Ralph G. Carter, 'Congressional Foreign Policy Behavior: Persistent Patterns of the Postwar Period', *Presidential Studies Quarterly*, 16 (1986): 329–59; *Idem*, 'Congress and Post–Cold War U.S. Foreign Policy'; Gerald F. Warburg, *Conflict and Consensus: The Struggle Between Congress and the President over Foreign Policymaking* (New York, Harper and Row, 1989); Thomas Mann (ed.), *A Question of Balance: The President, the Congress and Foreign Policy* (Washington DC, Brookings Institution, 1990); Eugene Wittkopf and James McCormick, 'When Congress Supports the President: A Multilevel Inquiry, 1948–1996', *Série Cahiers de l'Espace Europe*, 13 (May 1999): 15–40; Barry M. Blechman, *The Politics of National Security: Congress and U.S. Defense Policy* (New York, Oxford University Press, 1991); James M. Lindsay and Randall B. Ripley, 'Foreign and Defense Policy in Congress: A Research Agenda for the 1990s', *Legislative Studies Quarterly*, 17 (1992): 417–49; Donald R. Wolfensberger, 'Congress and Policymaking in an Age of Terrorism', in Lawrence Dodd and Bruce Oppenheimer (ed.), *Congress Reconsidered*, 8th edition, (Washington, DC: CQ Press, 2005), pp. 343–362; Barbara Hinckley, *Less Than Meets the Eye: Congress, the President, and Foreign Policy* (Chicago: University of Chicago Press, 1994); James M. Lindsay, *Congress and the Politics of U.S. Foreign Policy* (Baltimore and London: The Johns Hopkins University Press, 1994); *Idem*, 'Deference and Defiance'; Stephen Weissman, *A Culture of Deference: Congress's Failure of Leadership in Foreign Policy* (New York: Basic Books, 1995); Ryan C. Hendrickson, *The Clinton Wars: The Constitution, Congress, and War Powers* (Nashville: Vanderbilt University Press, 2002); James M. McCormick, Eugene R. Wittkopf and David M. Danna, 'Politics and Bipartisanship at the Water's Edge: A Note on Bush and Clinton', *Polity*, 30 (1997): 133–50; James M. Wittkopf and Eugene R. McCormick, 'Congress, the President, and the End of the Cold War', *Journal of Conflict Resolution*, 42 (1998): 440–67;

the analyses found in the literature can be divided into three broad categories: (a) domestic approaches that focus on internal factors; (b) systemic approaches that look at external factors and (c) multilevel approaches that ascribe equal importance to internal and external factors. Our conclusion is that multilevel approaches are more useful than domestic and systemic approaches for explaining congressional responses to the White House. Because they embrace both the external and internal environments, multilevel approaches enhance our understanding of how international events are perceived by members of Congress and how those perceptions are ultimately translated into congressional decisions.

In the second section, we apply a multilevel approach to analysis of congressional conduct on national security between 9/11 and the 2004 election. We will argue that congressional compliance with George W. Bush's national security policy is explained by the combination of three variables: international, domestic and individual. More specifically, it was due to the tendency of members of Congress to perceive US national security as being endangered by terrorism (the international factor), by Bush's high approval ratings in the United States (the domestic factor), and by the absence of powerful 'foreign policy entrepreneurs'[6] in Congress (the individual factor).

In the third section, we consider the resurgence of executive-legislative rivalry during and after the 2004 elections. Again, we use a multilevel approach to explain why the 109th Congress has not been as pliant as were the 107th and 108th. We will show that three factors have been decisive: the difficulties of Iraqi reconstruction (the international factor), George W. Bush's low approval ratings in the United States (the domestic factor), and congressional foreign policy entrepreneurs reasserting their power (the individual factor).

Three Approaches to Congressional National Security Behaviour

Three types of approaches are commonly used to explain Congress's behaviour on national security issues: (a) domestic; (b) systemic and (c) multilevel. All three attempt to identify the factors that account for congressional compliance with or resistance to the White House's national security agenda. We define congressional compliance as a situation in which the President 'gets exactly what he wants' from the House and Senate, and in which the legislators support presidential proposals without substantially questioning, debating or modifying them. We define congressional resistance as a situation in which Congress refuses to give the administration *exactly*

Marie Henehan, *Foreign Policy and Congress: An International Relations Perspective* (Ann Arbor: University of Michigan Press, 2000).

6   Ralph G. Carter, James M. Scott and Charles M. Rowling, 'Setting a Course: Congressional Foreign Policy Entrepreneurs in Post–World War II U.S. Foreign Policy', *International Studies Perspectives*, 5 (2004): 278–99.

what it wants, or even rejects the administration's proposals.[7] The main difference between the domestic, systemic and multilevel approaches is that they do not agree on the factors that account for congressional compliance or resistance.

Domestic Approaches

Domestic approaches focus exclusively or primarily on internal independent variables. On this view, the main reasons for congressional conduct are to be found within the American political and social environment. Ryan C. Hendrickson provides a good example of this approach: according to him, 'Congress's deference to the president ... is a pattern determined by political conditions at the time of the use of force, by the choices made by key individual members of Congress, and often by partisan considerations.'[8] Thus, to explain why President Clinton was able to use force in Somalia, Haiti, Bosnia and Kosovo, and against Osama Bin Laden and Saddam Hussein, all with only limited input from Congress, Hendrickson points to factors such as Clinton's leadership on foreign affairs, the readiness of Democrats in Congress to back a Democratic President and the absence of assertive individual leaders among Senators and Representatives.[9]

While Hendrickson focuses primarily on internal factors, he does not totally exclude external factors from his analysis. He admits that in the case of Iraq, members of Congress abdicated their war powers and deferred to Clinton because they widely agreed to define Saddam Hussein as 'the enemy'.[10] In other words, Hendrickson acknowledges that in some instances the way members of Congress interpret the international environment has an influence on the behaviour of Congress. But he does not consider external factors to be the most important determinants of congressional conduct: 'Prima facie', he argues, the end of the Cold War 'provided Congress the opportunity to serve as a stronger check on the commander in chief and break the pattern of deferential behaviour it had followed so frequently during the cold war'.[11] But Congress did not avail itself of this opportunity. This leads Hendrickson to the conclusion that we need to concentrate on domestic rather than international politics to understand why Congress has declined to assert its formal foreign policy powers.

While domestic approaches are useful for identifying some of the key determinants of congressional behaviour on national security issues (presidential leadership, absence of assertive foreign policy leaders in Congress, etc.), they

---

7   We base ourselves on Ralph G. Carter's definition of congressional 'resistance' or 'rejection' of administration policies. See Carter, 'Congress and Post–Cold War U.S. Foreign Policy', p. 110.

8   Hendrickson, *The Clinton Wars: The Constitution, Congress, and War Powers*, p. xiii.

9   For Hendrickson's application of these variables to explain why Congress chose to defer to the Executive in the case of Somalia, see *ibid.*, pp. 39–42.

10   *Ibid.*, p. 159.

11   *Ibid.*, p. xii.

have two important limitations when it comes to explaining why Congress initially supported Bush's policies and then became more resistant. First, they turn a blind eye to international factors. These cannot be neglected: it has become commonplace to argue that the 9/11 terrorist attacks have had a profound impact on US foreign policy.[12] Soon after 9/11, presidential historian Michael Beschloss commented: 'Now, George Bush is the center of the American solar system,' something that 'was not true ten days ago.'[13] Our analysis would therefore be incomplete if it were based on a domestic approach that failed to address the impact of the terrorist threat on congressional behaviour. Secondly, domestic approaches provide a relatively vague guide to identifying the different types of internal factors that influence congressional behaviour. To be sure, they point us towards domestic factors in general but they do not tell us exactly where to look. As shall be seen, a multilevel approach provides a more clear-cut framework and classifies domestic factors into categories (societal factors, institutional factors, individual factors, etc.).

Systemic Approaches

Systemic approaches turn the domestic approach on its head and concentrate exclusively or primarily on external variables to explain congressional security behaviour. On this view, 'the external source category, which refers to the attributes of the international system and to the behaviour of state and nonstate actors in that system',[14] contains the most important determinants of congressional support for or opposition to the foreign policies of the White House. James Lindsay provides an excellent example of the systemic approach.[15] He argues that the degree to which Congress aggressively exercises its national security policy powers 'turns foremost on whether the country sees itself as threatened or secure and to a lesser extent on how well the President handles foreign policy'.[16] According to Lindsay, when Americans and members of Congress believe they face few external threats, or when they think that international engagement could itself produce a threat, they see less merit in deferring to the White House on foreign policy and more merit in congressional activism. In this case, 'debate and disagreement are not likely to pose significant costs; after all, the country is secure'.[17] On the other hand, when Americans and Congress believe the United States faces an external threat, they quickly embrace the view that their country needs strong presidential leadership. 'Congressional dissent

12   For discussions of the impact, see James F. Hoge Jr. and Gideon Rose (ed.), *How Did This Happen? Terrorism and the New Year* (New York: Public Affairs, 2001); and Craig J. Calhoun, Paul Price and Ashley Timmer (eds), *Understanding September 11* (New York: New Press, 2002).
13   Quoted in Wolfensberger, 'Congress and Policymaking', p. 343.
14   Wittkopf and McCormick, 'When Congress Supports the President: A Multilevel Inquiry, 1948–1996', p. 18.
15   Lindsay, 'Deference and Defiance.'
16   *Ibid.*, p. 530.
17   *Ibid.*, p. 532.

that was previously acceptable suddenly looks to be unhelpful meddling at best and unpatriotic at worst',[18] writes Lindsay. Senators and Representatives do not want to be perceived as being on the wrong side, especially when they think it could hurt them in the next election.

In addition to these considerations, Lindsay argues, congressional behaviour also depends, to a lesser degree, on whether or not a President's foreign policy is successful. For instance, during the Cold War, Congress considered the gravity and urgency of the Soviet Communist threat to warrant a concentration of foreign policy powers in the hands of the President. However, Congress stopped deferring to the President coincident with the souring of public opinion on the Vietnam War. In short, Lindsay contends that the most important determinant of congressional assertiveness on foreign policy is the international environment (whether or not US national security is threatened). This factor is complemented by another external variable: the success or failure of US actions abroad.

While systemic approaches shed light on critical factors affecting congressional conduct in security matters (the existence of a global threat to US national security, the success of US actions abroad, etc.), they also suffer from two limitations. First, they overstate the influence of external events on decision-making in Congress. For instance, as shall be seen, it is true that the global threat of terrorism drove US legislators to accept Bush's policies on Afghanistan and Iraq, but since it is fair to argue that US Representatives and Senators continued to view terrorism as a significant threat after 2004, how then can we explain congressional opposition to Bush moves such as the nomination of John Bolton as US ambassador to the UN? Lindsay would probably argue that this is due to the problems in Iraq, another external variable. However, it is our contention that we also need to open up the United States' 'black box' and listen in on the conversations of the 'national security intellectuals'[19] in Congress to fully understand how external events translate into congressional decisions. For instance, to grasp the link between the difficulties in Iraq and congressional resistance to the national security policies of the White House, we need to consider the relationship between the situation in Iraq (an external factor) and internal factors such as Bush's low approval ratings and the 2006 mid-term elections.

The second limitation of systemic approaches is that they make little contribution to our understanding of the US Congress as an institution. In 1992, James Lindsay and Randall Ripley wrote an article in which they argued that research on the US Congress is underdeveloped: '[P]olitical scientists have paid surprisingly scant attention in recent years to congressional behavior on foreign and defense policy.'[20]

---

18   *Ibid.*

19   Amy Zegart defines 'national security intellectuals' in Congress as legislators who 'develop considerable expertise and devote serious attention to foreign policy issues and agencies'. Amy B. Zegart, *Flawed by Design: The Evolution of the CIA, JCS, and NSC* (Stanford: Stanford University Press, 1999), p. 32.

20   James M. Lindsay and Randall B. Ripley, 'Foreign and Defense Policy in Congress: A Research Agenda for the 1990s', *Legislative Studies Quarterly*, 17/3 (August 1992): 418.

We would suggest, however, that systemic approaches to congressional behaviour do little to fill the void: focusing on external variables to explain congressional decisions does not help students of the US Congress understand the actors, factors and mechanisms at work *within* Congress.

Multilevel Approaches

Multilevel approaches do two things that domestic and systemic approaches do not. First, they combine internal and external variables without ascribing greater importance to one than the other. For instance, Eugene R. Wittkopf and James M. McCormick aim to 'bridge the gap between the domestic and international arenas in explaining foreign policy processes – specifically congressional-executive interactions'.[21] Ralph G. Carter takes a similar approach: 'Like all foreign policy makers, members of Congress exist in a multifaceted setting and react to a wide variety of stimuli … international factors, societal factors, institutional factors, and individual factors.'[22] Secondly, advocates of multilevel approaches specify the types of internal factors that influence congressional decision-making. As we have seen, Carter identifies three categories of internal factors: societal, institutional and individual. Societal factors include the impact of public opinion, interest groups, ad hoc mass movements and the media on Congress's behaviour on foreign policy. Institutional factors refer to the impact of the President, bureaucracies, party leaders, congressional standing committees and caucuses. The crucial individual variables described by Carter are partisanship and the ideologies of members of Congress.[23] Similarly, Wittkopf and McCormick provide a clear breakdown of the internal factors that influence Congress's national security decisions, from 'societal variables', which they define as the 'various attributes of American society that affect the way the United States approaches the world'[24] (the President's popularity and the state of the economy fall into this category); to 'governmental' variables, defined as 'how the government is organized for the conduct of foreign policy, in particular the constitutional restraints on the various branches and the size and power of governmental institutions that deal with foreign policy'.[25]

Like the domestic and systemic approaches, multilevel approaches have shortcomings. For example, it could be argued that the categorizations proposed by Carter, Wittkopf and McCormick are not exhaustive, and that the authors neglect many important factors in congressional behaviour, such as strategic culture and the will of members of Congress to formulate sound policy. But as Steve Smith and John Baylis note, 'The basic problem facing anyone trying to understand … world politics is that there is so much material to look at that it is difficult to know

---

21 Wittkopf and McCormick, 'When Congress Supports the President', p. 18.
22 Carter, 'Congress and Post–Cold War U.S. Foreign Policy', p. 116.
23 *Ibid.*, pp. 117–129.
24 Wittkopf and McCormick, 'When Congress Supports the President', p. 20.
25 *Ibid.*, p. 22.

which things matter and which do not.'[26] And while they are not perfect, multilevel approaches provide a more comprehensive and precise understanding of the sources of congressional security behaviour than do domestic and systemic approaches. Consequently, multilevel approaches are more useful for explaining why Congress initially supported Bush's security policies and then began putting up resistance. On the one hand, unlike domestic approaches, multilevel approaches shed light on the link between external factors (threat of terrorism, difficulties in Iraq, etc.) and congressional conduct. On the other, unlike systemic approaches, multilevel approaches address, in addition to external factors such as the threat of terrorism and the difficulties in Iraq, the influence of political actors and mechanisms within the United States and Congress on congressional behaviour during the Bush presidency. As James M. Lindsay and Randall B. Ripley have argued, 'scholarship focused either on Congress as an institution or on the substance of foreign and defence policy has not prepared us to understand, let alone predict, what is likely to happen in Congress or as a result of congressional action'.[27] We believe we need to apply approaches that study congressional decision-making in greater depth than do systemic approaches.

The multilevel approach we will develop here considers three types of factors. First we look at international factors. While many commentators use the label 'external factors' to describe this type of variable, we prefer the term 'international factors' since 'external' suggests that there is a 'smoothly functioning mechanical transmission belt' between the international system and congressional decisions.[28] But US legislators are not rational actors who react to international crises, regional wars or the emergence of new national security threats in the same way. On the contrary, their responses to international events are influenced by character (their personal values, vision of the world, ideology, etc.). We therefore believe it is more useful to consider how members of Congress *perceive* international developments in order to explain congressional decision-making on security issues. It is not productive to study 'external events' in isolation from the way Representatives and Senators see, define and construct those events.

Secondly and thirdly, we study two sub-categories of 'internal factors': domestic factors, that is to say the impact of other American foreign policy actors (the President, public opinion, think tanks, etc.) on congressional decisions;

---

26   Steve Smith and John Baylis, 'Introduction', in *The Globalization of World Politics: An Introduction to International Relations*, 2nd edition (Oxford: Oxford University Press, 2001), p. 2.

27   James M. Lindsay and Randall B. Ripley, 'Foreign and Defense Policy in Congress', p. 436.

28   Gideon Rose develops the concept of a 'smoothly functioning mechanical transmission belt' in his 'neoclassical realist' theory of foreign policy. According to Rose, neoclassical realists reject the rationality assumption of systemic theories and 'argue that the notion of a smoothly functioning mechanical transmission belt is inaccurate and misleading. What this means in practice is that the translation of capabilities into behaviour is often rough and capricious over the short and medium term.' Gideon Rose, 'Neoclassical Realism and Theories of Foreign Policy', *World Politics*, 51/1 (October 1998): 158.

and individual factors, defined as the personal characteristics of US legislators (partisanship, ideology, assertiveness, etc.) and the impact of those characteristics on congressional behaviour.[29] Following Ralph G. Carter, Eugene R. Wittkopf and James McCormick, we argue that the 'internal factors category' encompasses a wide spectrum of diverse variables.[30] For instance, presidential approval ratings and the ideology of the Chairman of the Senate Foreign Relations Committee could both be labelled 'internal factors'. But interpreting the former as a feature of domestic politics (the impact of public opinion on congressional conduct) and the latter as an individual characteristic (the impact of legislators' ideologies on congressional conduct) provides a more precise picture of the operation of internal factors. We will now use this multilevel approach to analyze the issue at hand: why has Congress's attitude towards Bush's policies shifted from compliance to resistance? We will proceed in two steps. First, we will look at congressional-executive relations between 9/11 and the 2004 election. Second, we will consider Bush's second term.

Explaining Congressional Responses to the White House

Congressional Compliance with Bush's Security Policy

Between 9/11 and the 2004 election, Congress often accepted the administration's national security policies, beginning with Operation Enduring Freedom in Afghanistan, which Bush launched on October 7, 2001.[31] Just one day after 9/11, Vice President Cheney delivered to House Speaker Dennis Hastert a White House draft resolution authorizing the use of force against those responsible for the terrorist attacks.[32] The draft included these words:

> ... the president is authorized to use all necessary and appropriate force against those nations, organizations, or persons he determines planned, authorized, harbored, committed, or aided in the planning or commission of the attacks against the United States that occurred on September 11, 2001, and to deter and preempt any future acts of terrorism or aggression against the United States.[33]

In the face of some resistance from legislators such as Tom Daschle and Dick Gephardt, the Bush administration ultimately agreed to drop the last point ('and to deter and preempt ...') from the final resolution passed by Congress (S.J. Res.

---

29   Wittkopf and McCormick, 'When Congress Supports the President', p. 23.

30   Carter, 'Congress and Post–Cold War U.S. Foreign Policy'; Wittkopf and McCormick, 'When Congress Supports the President.'

31   We discuss this argument in more detail in Frédérick Gagnon, 'En conformité avec la Maison-Blanche. Le Congrès et la politique de sécurité nationale des États-Unis durant le premier mandat de George W. Bush'. Used with permission.

32   Wolfensberger, 'Congress and Policymaking', p. 346.

33   Quoted in *Ibid.*

23[34]). Despite such minor compromises, two points demonstrate the extent to which Congress was acquiescent in the case of Afghanistan: (1) it passed S.J. Res. 23 by overwhelming bipartisan votes (98–0 in the Senate[35] and 420–1 in the House[36]); and (2) it acted 'with uncharacteristic dispatch, bypassing its committee process and forgoing extended floor deliberations to complete action within three days of the attacks'.[37]

A second example of congressional compliance involves increases in military spending. As James M. Lindsay reports, when Bush asked for a $48 billion increase in the defence budget in February 2002, the request 'elicited few complaints from Congress, even though the bulk of the spending increase was targeted at funding defense programs that had been on the drawing boards for years rather than to meet new needs created by the war on terrorism'.[38] By contrast, during the presidencies of George H.W. Bush and Bill Clinton, there had been fierce debates between the White House and Congress regarding military spending. For instance, in 1992, US lawmakers used their power of the purse to cut Bush's requests for HARM missiles by 52%, high-speed cargo ships by 49%, and so forth. In 1993, Congress cut Clinton's requests for a 'National Launch System' for heavy payloads by 100%, F-16 fighters by 50%, etc.[39] But budget battles of this type were far less intense during George W. Bush's first term. When the White House proposed military budgets of $379 billion and $400 billion for FY 2004 and FY 2005 respectively, the House and the Senate made only 'modest changes in the Pentagon's plans to spend well over $1 trillion in the next decade on an arsenal of futuristic planes, ships and weapons with little direct connection to the Iraq war or the global war on terrorism'.[40]

In a third example of congressional compliance, on October 2, 2001, the Bush administration asked Congress to pass the USA Patriot Act. The 342-page act[41] was described by then-Attorney General John Aschroft as a 'package of tools urgently needed to combat terrorism', Jon B. Gould reported.[42] The primary objective of the law was to provide the government with effective tools to detect, deter and prevent

---

34   For the wording of S.J. Res. 23, see <http://www.law.cornell.edu/background/warpower/sj23.pdf>.

35   For complete results of the roll call vote, see the U.S. Senate website: <http://www.senate.gov/legislative/LIS/roll_call_lists/roll_call_vote_cfm.cfm?congress=107&session=1&vote=00281>.

36   For complete results of the roll call vote, see <http://clerk.house.gov/evs/2001/roll342.xml>.

37   Wolfensberger, 'Congress and Policymaking', p. 346.

38   Lindsay, 'Deference and Defiance', p. 540.

39   Carter, 'Congress and Post–Cold War U.S. Foreign Policy', p. 112.

40   Dan Morgan, 'Congress Backs Pentagon Budget Heavy on Future Weapons: Buildup Pricier than that in '80s', *Washington Post*, June 11, 2004, p. A23.

41   See H.R. 3162, 107th Congress, 1st Session, October 24, 2001: <http://frwebgate.access.gpo.gov/cgi-bin/getdoc.cgi?dbname=107_cong_bills&docid=f:h3162enr.txt.pdf>.

42   Jon B. Gould, 'Playing with Fire: The Civil Liberties Implications of September 11th', *Public Administration Review*, Vol. 62 (September 2002): 74.

terrorist attacks on American soil. For example, it loosened wiretap rules and let law enforcement agencies access an individual's Internet communications for the purpose of criminal investigations.[43] Though the USA Patriot Act was highly controversial, both the House and the Senate passed it with little debate. To be sure, Congress did amend the administration's proposal in some respects. One important change limited the Attorney General's proposed authority to hold immigrants suspected of terrorist activities.[44] However, as Nancy Kassop observes, Congress was particularly cooperative in passing the Patriot Act:

> The Patriot Act passed both houses of Congress with lightning speed … It bypassed most of the usual committee process in favour of high-level, closed-door, executive-legislative negotiations … It *did* receive some attention in the House Judiciary Committee, which marked it up on October 3, 2001, and passed a much-modified version, 36–0, but the bill on which the full House voted on October 12 contained a changed text (but same bill number) that had been secretly agreed to by Speaker Dennis Hastert (R-Illinois) and the White House, without any knowledge by the full committee. The Senate bill was negotiated by Judiciary Committee leaders with the administration, and never came before the full committee prior to the vote on the Senate floor … The final piece to this frenzy was the order by Senate Majority Leader Tom Daschle (D-South Dakota) to Russ Feingold (D-Wisconsin) to withdraw his amendments and fall in line behind the unanimous consent agreement, which permitted no amendments or debate.[45]

The act was passed by Congress on October 24, 2001 with only one Senator, Russ Feingold (D-Wisconsin), and 66 Representatives voting against it.[46]

A fourth example of congressional compliance was the response to the 'National Security Strategy of the United States' released by the White House in September 2002.[47] The document spelled out Bush's strategy of military preemption. Describing the urgency of the threat of international terrorism, the President stated:

> The greater the threat, the greater the risk of inaction – and more compelling the case for taking anticipatory action to defend ourselves, even if uncertainty remains as to the time and place of the enemy's attack. To forestall and prevent such hostile acts by our adversaries, the United States will, if necessary, act preemptively.[48]

43   *Ibid.*

44   Harry F. Tepker, 'The USA Patriot Act', *Extensions: Special Orders*: <http://www.ou.edu/special/albertctr/extensions/fall2002/Tepker.html>.

45   Kassop, 'The War Power and its Limits', p. 515.

46   In the House, 63 Democrats and 3 Republicans voted against the act. For complete results of the House roll call vote on the Patriot Act, see <http://clerk.house.gov/evs/2001/roll398.xml>. For the results of the Senate roll call vote on the same act, see <http://www.senate.gov/legislative/LIS/roll_call_lists/roll_call_vote_cfm.cfm?congress=107&session=1&vote=00302>.

47   See The White House, Administration of George W. Bush, *The National Security Strategy of the United States of America*, September 2001: <http://www.whitehouse.gov/nsc/nss.pdf>.

48   *Ibid.*, p. 15.

As scholars Michael E. O'Hanlon, Susan E. Rice and James B. Steinberg argue, while the doctrine of preemption can be useful in the fight against terrorism, it is a flawed foreign policy tool. For instance, it can send other countries, such as India and Russia, the signal that it is legitimate for them to use preemption to fight perceived threats to their own security.[49] Political scientist John Mearsheimer also criticizes the strategy of preemption: 'Such a policy alienates allies, tips off adversaries, promotes nuclear proliferation and generally makes states less willing to cooperate with the United States.'[50] Despite the debate within the Washington think tanks and academe, only a few members of Congress questioned Bush's philosophy of preemption. Probably the most prominent voices on this issue in the Senate were Robert C. Byrd (D-West Virginia) and Edward Kennedy (D-Massachusetts). Byrd noted that preemption 'appears to be in contravention of international law and the UN Charter'[51] and Kennedy termed it 'a call for 21st century American imperialism that no other nation can or should accept. It is the antithesis of all that America has worked so hard to achieve in international relations since the end of World War II'.[52] In the House, Barbara Lee (D-California) and 26 other Congressmen and women introduced a resolution 'disavowing the doctrine of preemption' on March 2003.[53] But the great majority of US legislators appeared to accept the principles and philosophy of preemption. For example, when Congressman John Larson (D-Connecticut) introduced a resolution calling for the establishment of a congressional commission to 'review the doctrine of preemption' and 'assess the consequences and implications of its adoption for foreign policy and military planning',[54] it gained no support in the House committees on International Relations and on Armed Services.

Bush's decision to overthrow Saddam Hussein provides a fifth example of congressional compliance. On October 16, 2002, Congress passed a resolution authorizing Bush 'to use the Armed Forces of the United States as he determines to be necessary and appropriate in order to – (1) defend the national security of the United States against the continuing threat posed by Iraq; and (2) enforce all relevant

---

49   Michael E. O'Hanlon, Susan E. Rice, James B. Steinberg, 'The New National Security Strategy and Preemption', *The Brookings Institution Policy Brief*, 113 (December 2002): 7.

50   John Mearsheimer, 'Hearts and Minds', *The National Interest*, 69 (Fall 2002): 16.

51   Robert C. Byrd, 'We Stand Passively Mute', Senate Floor Speech, Wednesday, February 12, 2003: <http://truthout.org/docs_02/021403A.htm>.

52   Edward Kennedy, 'The Bush Doctrine of Pre-Emption', *Truthout Issues*, October 7, 2002: <http://truthout.com/docs_02/10.09A.kennedy.htm>.

53   See H.Res. 141 'Disavowing the doctrine of preemption', 108th Congress, 1st Session, March 12, 2003: <http://thomas.loc.gov/cgi-bin/query>.

54   See H.R. 3616 'To Establish the Commission on Preemptive Foreign Policy and Military Planning', 108th Congress, 1st Session, November 21, 2003: <http://frwebgate.access. gpo.gov/cgi-bin/getdoc.cgi?dbname=108_cong_bills&docid=f:h3616ih.txt.pdf>.

United Nations Security Council resolutions regarding Iraq'.[55] US legislators began discussing a military intervention in Iraq after George W. Bush said in his 2002 West Point address that American security 'will require all Americans ... to be ready for preemptive action when necessary to defend our liberty and to defend our lives'.[56] But there were only a few days of debate on the Iraq Resolution (three in the House and five in the Senate) after the White House sent the first draft to Congress.[57] To be sure, a number of Congressmen and women spoke out against Bush's plans to overthrow Saddam Hussein. For instance, on October 8, 2002, Congresswoman Louise M. Slaughter (D-New York) said:

> I am deeply troubled by the administration's unwillingness to address the long-term strategy of Iraq. The President has failed to articulate any plan for dealing with the future of Iraq if and when Saddam Hussein is removed. Is Saddam's removal the final goal? Or will the United States be expected to engage in the reconstruction of Iraq?[58]

Robert C. Byrd (D-West Virginia), one of the most prominent critics of the war in Iraq, described the resolution as 'nothing more than a blank check given to the President of the United States'.[59] But although no satisfactory answers were ever provided to the questions 'Why Iraq?' 'Why now? and 'Where are the weapons of mass destruction?',[60] members of Congress acquiesced and voted in favour of the Iraq resolution by a wide margin (77–23 in the Senate[61] and 296–133 in the House[62]).

From the point of view of our multilevel approach, at least three factors were at play in this outcome. The first is an international factor: the tendency of members of Congress to believe that terrorism is a grave and urgent threat to US national security. Many experts on Congress have observed that the more threatening the international environment appears, the more US legislators tend to support the President's security policy.[63] For instance, during the first two decades of the Cold

---

55   See H.J. Res. 114 'To Authorize the Use of United States Armed Forces Against Iraq', 107th Congress, 2nd Session, October 16, 2002: <http://frwebgate.access.gpo.gov/cgi-bin/getdoc.cgi?dbname=107_cong_bills&docid=f:hj114enr.txt.pdf>.

56   George W. Bush, 'Remarks at 2002 Graduation Exercise of the United States Military Academy', West Point, New York, June 1, 2002: <http://www.whitehouse.gov/news/releases/2002/06/20020601-3.html>.

57   Kassop, 'The War Power and its Limits', p. 524.

58   *Congressional Record – House*, October 8, 2002, H7182: <http://frwebgate.access.gpo.gov/cgi-bin/getpage.cgi?dbname=2002_record&page=H7182&position=all>.

59   *Congressional Record – Senate*, October 4, 2002, S9959: <http://frwebgate.access.gpo.gov/cgi-bin/getpage.cgi?dbname=2002_record&page=S9959&position=all>.

60   Kassop, 'The War Power and its Limits', p. 524.

61   For complete results of the roll call vote, see <http://www.senate.gov/legislative/LIS/roll_call_lists/roll_call_vote_cfm.cfm?congress=107&session=2&vote=00237>.

62   See <http://clerk.house.gov/evs/2002/roll455.xml>.

63   See for example Lindsay, 'Deference and Defiance'; Jerel Rosati, 'Congress and Interbranch Politics', in *The Politics of United States Foreign Policy*, 3rd edition (Belmont:

War, fear of the USSR led members of Congress to accept that the White House was
the best institution to prevent 'communist contagion' around the world. According to
Michael Mastanduno, this had a clear impact on congressional-executive relations:

> Congress delegated authority and deferred politically to the Executive, on the grounds
> that only the presidency possessed the institutional resources, intelligence capability,
> and decision-making qualities – speed, steadiness, resolve, and flexibility – required to
> conduct the cold war effectively and lead a global coalition in the struggle against the
> Soviet Union and communism.[64]

In *The Powers That Be*, David Halberstam describes how the link between
communism and congressional compliance operated in the case of Sam Rayburn
(D-Texas), Speaker of the House from 1949 to 1953 and 1955 to 1961:

> [Rayburn] had, on most crucial issues, turned the House into an extension of the executive
> branch, making it an offering to the President. This was not a happenstance thing, it was
> very deliberative on his part. He talked often in great privacy about the limits of his
> knowledge, the limits of the knowledge – indeed, the ignorance – of his colleagues. Their
> backgrounds were terribly narrow and he was appalled by the idea of getting involved in
> areas of national security.[65]

It would appear that terrorism played a similar role in the minds of US legislators
after 9/11. In the words of Ivo H. Daalder and James M. Lindsay, 'In a replay of a
well-know phenomenon in American politics, the attacks shifted the pendulum of
power away from Capitol Hill and toward the White House.'[66] It was natural enough
for Republicans in Congress to give their fellow Republicans in the administration
all the leeway they wanted to fight terror. For example, Congressman Bill Young (R-
Florida) said that 'it is important that the Congress, the House, the Senate, [and] the
President … speak in one solid voice that we will not now nor ever tolerate the type
of terrorist activities that we saw brought upon our shores yesterday'.[67] But even
the Democrats were prepared to back Bush almost unconditionally. For instance,
ex-Senate Majority leader Tom Daschle (D-South Dakota) writes: 'I wanted to see
George W. Bush rise as well. Our differences, I can honestly say, were obliterated

---

Wadsworth, 2004), p. 331; and Steven W. Hook, 'Congress Beyond the "Water's Edge"', in
U.S. Foreign Policy: The Paradox of World Power (Washington: CQ Press, 2005), p. 128.

64   Michael Mastanduno, 'The United States Political System and International
Leadership: A "Decidedly Inferior" Form of Government?' in G. John Ikenberry (ed.),
American Foreign Policy: Theoretical Essays, 4th edition (New York: Longman, 2002), p.
238.

65   David Halberstam, *The Powers That Be* (New York: Knopf, 1979), p. 248. Quoted
in Rosati, 'Congress and Interbranch Politics', p. 300.

66   Ivo H. Daalder and James M. Lindsay, *America Unbound: The Bush Revolution in
Foreign Policy* (Washington, DC: Brookings Institution Press, 2003), p. 92.

67   See the U.S. House of Representatives website: <http://www.house.gov/young/
terrorism.htm>.

when that first airplane hit the first tower that morning ... I turned to our President just as every American did, to provide the leadership we all needed.'[68] Then-Majority Whip Harry Reid (D-Nevada) echoed that attitude on September 12, 2001, when he declared on the floor of the Senate: 'We in Congress stand united in our resolve to ensure that President Bush has every necessary resource as he leads our great Nation forward in the coming days and weeks and months.'[69] Even Robert C. Byrd, a strong critic of George W. Bush, admits that 9/11 made him feel 'empathy for this new young president, faced with such a calamity only eight months into his first term'.[70]

Thus, 9/11 created the conditions for a Cold War-like consensus in the United States, producing a general agreement among members of Congress that international terrorism is a global threat that the US government must confront.[71] This situation had at least two major consequences when it came to Congress's actions on security issues. First, it made legislators believe that the urgency of the danger warranted concentrating foreign policy powers in the hands of the White House. For instance, in the cases of the war in Afghanistan and the Patriot Act, members of the House and the Senate agreed to act quickly. They accepted an argument that was often made during the 1950s and 1960s to the effect that the legislative branch should not be overtly assertive in foreign affairs, for with 535 different personalities, egos and sets of interests, Congress is a body prone to gridlock and inaction, and this risks jeopardizing US national interests when quick response is needed against an external enemy.[72] Secondly, 9/11 eroded, for a time, the differences between the foreign policy visions of the Republicans and the Democrats. Interpreting terrorism as the new 'polar star' of American foreign policy, many Democrats stopped criticizing the White House and gave Bush the benefit of the doubt. For instance, Senators John Edwards (D-North Carolina) and John Kerry (D-Massachusetts) voted in favour of the resolution authorizing the administration to use force in Iraq.

The second determinant of congressional compliance in this instance was a domestic factor: Bush's popularity with the American people. As Figure 5.1 shows, Bush's approval ratings were only around 55% in August 2001. But 9/11 led Americans to rally around the flag and support the President.[73] When Bush launched

---

68   Tom Daschle (with Michael D'Orso), *Like No Other Time: The Two Years That Changed America* (New York: Three Rivers Press, 2003), p. 120.

69   *Congressional Record – Senate*, September 12, 2001, S9285: <http://frwebgate. access.gpo.gov/cgi-bin/getpage.cgi?position=all&page=S9285&dbname=2001_record>.

70   Robert C. Byrd, *Losing America: Confronting a Reckless and Arrogant Presidency* (New York: Norton, 2004), p. 83.

71   Frédérick Gagnon, 'A Cold War–like Consensus? Toward a Theoretical Explanation of US Congressional-Executive Relations Concerning National Security After 9/11', *Occasional paper 3 published by the Center for United States Studies of the Raoul Dandurand Chair of Strategic and Diplomatic Studies*, 2004, 33.

72   Ryan C. Hendrickson, *Clinton Wars*, p. 167.

73   For theoretical contributions to analysis of the 'rally around the flag effect', see Richard Stoll, 'The Guns of November: Presidential Reelections and the Use of Force, 1947– 1982', *Journal of Conflict Resolution*, 28/2 (1984): 231–46; and Barbara Hinckley, *Less Than*

Operation Enduring Freedom in Afghanistan and requested passage of the Patriot Act, his approval rating stood at 90%. When the White House released the doctrine of preemption and asked Congress to endorse the war in Iraq, nearly 70% approved of Bush's performance.

According to David Mayhem, 'All members of Congress have a primary interest in getting reelected. Some members have no other interest.'[74] It may reasonably be argued that offering resistance to the White House and criticizing its national security policies at a time when the President was riding high in the polls contradicted one of the primary goals of US legislators. Indeed, questioning the President's decisions could have been interpreted by the voters as opposing the public will. Since members of Congress must face the electorate regularly (every two years, the entire House and one-third of the Senate comes up for re-election), they want to avoid being labelled 'obstructionists' at any cost. Therefore, many Democrats who were against the war in Iraq followed public opinion and voted for the resolution authorizing Bush to overthrow Saddam Hussein. Similarly, Bush's popularity led to congressional compliance on the military budget. As Dan Morgan observed, 'The debate in Congress over the defense bill has largely skirted the budgetary or strategic implications of this buildup, largely because Republican and Democratic politicians are unwilling to appear weak on defense after the Sept. 11, 2001, terrorist attacks.'[75]

The third determinant of congressional compliance was an individual factor: the absence of any powerful 'foreign policy entrepreneurs' in Congress. Ralph G. Carter, James M. Scott and Charles M. Rowling define congressional foreign policy entrepreneurs as legislators 'who seek to enact their own foreign policy agendas'.[76] One type seeks to 'revise, refocus, or reformulate foreign policies' and 'generate alternative and replacement foreign policies'.[77] Between 9/11 and the 2004 election, however, these were relatively rare in Congress. As we have seen, the threat of terrorism and Bush's high popularity ratings gave US legislators little incentive to pursue this course. More importantly, those who did – like John Larson in the House or Robert C. Byrd in the Senate – had little clout. In the Republican-controlled House, Speaker Dennis Hastert (R-Illinois), majority leaders Dick Armey (R-Texas) and Tom Delay (R-Texas), Chairman of the House Committee on International Relations Henry Hyde (R-Illinois), Chairman of the House Committee on Armed Services Duncan Hunter (R-California) and other Republican leaders discouraged opposition by continually calling for unity between the House and the White House.

Meets the Eye: Foreign Policy Making and the Myth of the Assertive Congress (Chicago: University of Chicago Press, 1994).

74   David R. Mayhem, *Congress: The Electoral Connection* (New Haven: Yale University Press, 1974), p. 16.

75   Morgan, 'Congress Backs Pentagon Budget.'

76   Carter, Scott and Rowling, 'Setting a Course', p. 278.

77   *Ibid.*

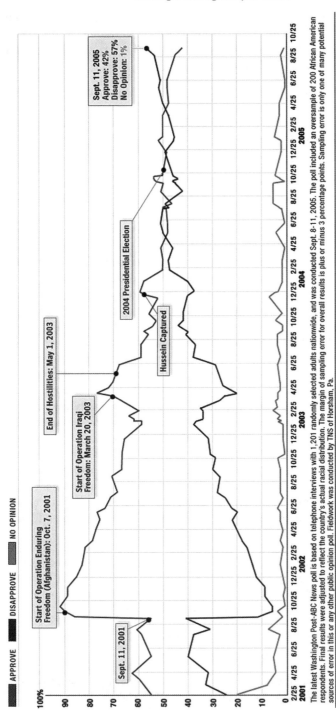

The latest Washington Post-ABC News poll is based on telephone interviews with 1,201 randomly selected adults nationwide, and was conducted Sept. 8-11, 2005. The poll included an oversample of 200 African American respondents. Final results were adjusted to reflect the country's actual racial distribution. The margin of sampling error for overall results is plus or minus 3 percentage points. Sampling error is only one of many potential sources of error in this or any other public opinion poll. Fieldwork was conducted by TNS of Horsham, Pa.

Figure 5.1 President Bush's Approval Ratings

As conservatives[78] who shared Bush's foreign policy vision, they often echoed the administration's attitudes. For instance, on September 25, 2003, in his opening statement at a hearing on US policy toward Iraq before the House Committee on International Relations, Henry Hyde declared:

> It is said by many that we had no option in Iraq, but that is untrue. For we always have options, both responsible and irresponsible. I, for one, am grateful that we have chosen the responsible one and hope that we have the endurance, despite all perils, to complete our task, even if we must do so alone.[79]

The Republicans in the House also used their institutional powers (more floor time, more power to set the agenda of the House, to manage committee budgets and agendas, etc.) to prevent radical revisions or reformulations of Bush's national security policies. According to Lawrence C. Dodd and Bruce I. Oppenheimer, 'Republican leaders [used] the Rules Committee to limit the time available for debate and voting on amendments, as well as limiting the amendments that may be offered.'[80] They also perfected a strategy of 'limiting Democratic participation until their party members are fairly united'. Indeed, 'Committee markup sessions at times have taken on a pro forma appearance, as differences among Republicans have already been resolved in committee caucus sessions or in informal negotiations with the leadership.'[81]

Thus, it was difficult for the Democrats to modify bills at the committee level because little debate occurred and party line votes were the norm. The Democrats also lacked power and could hardly act as 'congressional foreign policy entrepreneurs' in the Senate. They did control the chamber between May 2001 and January 2003, but Senate Majority Leader Tom Daschle (D-South Dakota) and his party enjoyed only a thin majority of 51 Democrats versus 49 Republicans. And at a time when the public, the Republican-controlled House and most Republican Senators backed Bush's foreign policies, Democratic leaders had little choice but to fall in line. Furthermore, the institutional powers of the Senate Majority leader are limited in comparison with those of the Speaker of the House. As C. Lawrence Evans and Daniel Lipinski observe, 'By chamber precedent, the majority leader receives priority recognition on the floor. But unless there are sixty votes to invoke cloture, the right to filibuster

---

78   Between 2001 and the 2004 election, their individual liberal voting records (according to Americans for Democratic Action) never exceeded 15%, whereas their individual 'conservative lifetime scores', according to the American Conservative Union, were Delay 96%, Hastert 93%, Hyde 84% and Hunter 93%. See <http://www.adaction.org/votingrecords.htm>. and <http://www.acuratings.org/default.asp?ratingsyear=2001>.

79   See Committee on International Relations, House of Representatives, 108th Congress, 1st Session, Hearing on the *US Policy Toward Iraq*, September 25, 2003: <http://commdocs.house.gov/committees/intlrel/hfa89534.000/hfa89534_0f.htm>.

80   Lawrence C. Dodd and Bruce I. Oppenheimer, in Lawrence Dodd and Bruce Oppenheimer (eds), 'A Decade of Republican Control: The House of Representatives, 1995–2005', *Congress Reconsidered*, 8th edition (Washington, DC: CQ Press, 2005), p. 49.

81   *Ibid.*

a bill or nomination into oblivion gives rank-and-file senators (especially members of the minority party) enormous leverage.'[82] Therefore, Democratic Senators were hesitant to propose drastic alternatives to Bush's foreign policies, since they knew the Republican minority could block such efforts by using delaying tactics such as filibusters. It became even more difficult for the Democrats to attempt to revise, refocus or reformulate Bush's security policies after they lost control of the Senate in the 2002 mid-term elections. Strong allies of the White House then secured the key national security positions in the Senate and sought to turn the chamber into an extension of the executive branch. For instance, the Chairman of the Senate Armed Forces Committee, John Warner (R-Virginia), unequivocally supported Bush's request for an increase in the military budget:

> At this critical time in the war against terror, when we are asking so much of our uniformed personnel and their families, and when we are seeking the continued cooperation of our allies, what message do we want to send? We must send a message of continued commitment and resolve by supporting the level of funding for defense requested by the President. Our military deserves no less.[83]

Congressional Resistance to Bush's Security Policies

Though Congress generally accepted Bush's security policies between 9/11 and the 2004 election, there is extensive evidence that its attitude has changed since 2004. In the interim, Congress has resisted the White House in at least three cases.

First, legislators from both parties have questioned, debated and criticized Bush's handling of the reconstruction of Iraq. In May 2004, for instance, Jane Harman (D-California), the top Democrat on the House Intelligence Committee, declared that 'the one thing that's clear is that our oversight needs to be strongly improved – it's inadequate'.[84] At a Senate Armed Services Committee hearing, John McCain (R-Arizona), said: 'I'll give $50 billion, I'll give $100 billion. But it seems to me that we do have an oversight responsibility as to where this money is spent. I don't think that all of that money has been well spent in the past.'[85] House Minority Leader Nancy Pelosi (D-California) expressed similar misgivings in stronger language: 'I believe that the president's leadership in the actions taken in Iraq demonstrate an incompetence in terms of knowledge, judgment and experience.'[86]

---

82   C. Lawrence Evans and Daniel Lipinski, 'Obstruction and Leadership in the US Senate', in Dodd and Oppenheimer (eds), *Congress Reconsidered*, p. 229.

83   See Senator John Warner, 'Chairman Warner Leads Successful Fight to Restore Defense Funds in Senate Budget Bill', March 10, 2004: <http://www.senate.gov/~warner/pressoffice/pressreleases/20040310c.htm>.

84   Quoted in Chuck McCutcheon, 'Congress Vows to Improve Its Oversight on Iraq', *Newhouse News Service*, May 15, 2004: <http://www.newhouse.com/archive/mccutcheon051704.html>.

85   *Idem.*

86   Dana Milbank and Charles Babington, 'Bush Visits Hill to Reassure Republicans', *Washington Post*, May 21, 2004, p. A04.

Those criticisms continued and intensified after the 2004 election. For instance, verbal fireworks attended Secretary of Defense Donald Rumsfeld's appearance before the Senate Armed Services Committee in June 2005.[87] While its Chairman, John Warner (R-Virginia), continued defending Bush's policies, other committee members, such as Edward Kennedy (D-Massachusetts), argued that the White House had made 'gross errors and mistakes' in Iraq.

Also, many members of Congress have sought to offer alternatives to Bush's policies. Joe Biden (D-Delaware) called on the Bush administration to set goals in a number of areas, including security, reconstruction and governance, and report to Congress monthly on whether the benchmarks had been met. Congressman Walter Jones (R-North Carolina) called for the withdrawal of US troops to begin by October 2006.[88] Senator Russ Feingold (D-Wisconsin) introduced a resolution 'expressing the sense of the Senate that the President should submit to Congress a report on the time frame for the withdrawal of United States troops from Iraq'.[89] These attitudes contrast sharply with congressional reactions to Bush's earlier decisions concerning Iraq.

A second example of congressional resistance was the response to Bush's request for Senate confirmation of John Bolton as US ambassador to the UN in March 2005. In May 2005, after heated debate in the Senate Foreign Relations Committee, its Chairman, Richard Lugar (R-Indiana), sent the nomination to the full Senate without a recommendation. Lugar was forced to make the rare move when one of the Republican members of the committee, George Voinovich (R-Ohio), joined with the Democrats and refused to endorse the choice, stating, 'It is my opinion that John Bolton is the poster child of what someone in the diplomatic corps should not be.'[90] When Bolton's nomination was sent to the full Senate for an up or down vote, the Republicans fell short of the 60 vote supermajority needed to cut off debate, because the Democrats refused to support Bush's choice.[91] Faced with the stalemate, Bush was forced to side-step the Senate and use his recess appointment power to name John Bolton United Nations ambassador.[92]

The renewal of the USA Patriot Act is a third example of congressional resistance. In June 2005, Bush called on Congress to reauthorize the sixteen provisions of the act that were slated to expire at the end of the year. While the House complied on July 22, 2005 by a 257–171 vote, many Congressmen and women, mostly

---

87   Bennett Roth, 'Battle on the Hill Is Raised Over Iraq', *Houston Chronicle*, June 24, 2005: <http://www.chron.com/cs/CDA/ssistory.mpl/politics/3238990>.

88   *Ibid.*

89   See S. Res. 171, 109th Congress, 1st Session, June 14, 2005: <http://frwebgate.access. gpo.gov/cgi-bin/getdoc.cgi?dbname=109_cong_bills&docid=f:sr171is.txt.pdf>.

90   BBC News, 'Bush Suffers Blow on UN Choice', May 12, 2005: <http://news.bbc. co.uk/2/hi/americas/4539623.stm>.

91   Yochi J. Dreazen, 'Senate Democrats Engineer a Delay of Vote on Bolton', *The Wall Street Journal*, May 27, 2005, p. A3.

92   Christopher Cooper, 'Bush Appoints Bolton to UN Post, Bypassing Senate', *The Wall Street Journal*, August 2, 2005, p. A3.

Democrats, criticized the application of the Patriot Act and expressed concerns about infringements of civil liberties. For instance, on June 10, 2005, during an oversight hearing in the House Judiciary Committee, John Conyers (D-Michigan), the ranking Democratic member, complained that the government's legal authorities to prosecute the war against terror 'have been abused'.[93] After repeated criticism of the White House, Committee Chairman Jim Sensenbrenner (R-Wisconsin) gavelled the hearing to a close and walked out while Democrats continued to testify, with their microphones turned off.[94] Five days later, the House decided to limit the scope of the Patriot Act, passing an amendment introduced by Congressman Bernard Sanders (I-Vermont) to prevent the Justice Department from using the Patriot Act to search library records, by a vote of 238–187.[95] There was also considerable opposition to the Patriot Act in the Senate, most notably the introduction by Senators Larry Craig (R-Idaho) and Dick Durbin (D-Illinois) of the Safety and Freedom Enhancement Act of 2005 (SAFE),[96] which sought to amend the Patriot Act to limit the use of roving wiretaps, modify traditional authority to delay notification of a search, and limit the ability of law enforcement and intelligence officials to secure business records relating to terrorist activity.[97] There was no consensus in favour of the proposals in the Senate. However, it is clear that the Senate's behaviour with respect to the Patriot Act has changed since the law was passed in October 2001. Many Senators have joined Russ Feingold (D-Wisconsin), the only Senator to vote against the Patriot Act in 2001, and are now questioning, criticizing or trying to revise Bush's homeland anti-terrorism program. For instance, in April 2004, Senator John Sununu (R-New Hampshire) declared:

> I think we need to take a step back, look at the Patriot Act in its totality and try to make it work better and try to strike a better balance between the protection of the civil liberties we all cherish as Americans and the tools we do believe are necessary for law enforcement and intelligence agencies to conduct the war against terror.[98]

---

93   See John Conyers, Jr., 'Statement at a Democratic Hearing on "Reauthorization of the Patriot Act"', June 10, 2005: <http://www.house.gov/judiciary_democrats/patriotdemhrgstmt61005.pdf>.

94   Mike Allen, 'House Chairman Shuts Down Patriot Act Hearing after Democrats, Witnesses Criticize Administration', June 11, 2005: <http://www.detnews.com/2005/politics/0506/17/polit-212115.htm>.

95   See *The Hill*, 'Vote of the Week', June 16, 2005: <http://www.hillnews.com/thehill/export/TheHill/News/Frontpage/061605/patriot.html>.

96   See S. 737, 109th Congress, 1st Session, April 6, 2005: <http://frwebgate.access.gpo.gov/cgi-bin/getdoc.cgi?dbname=109_cong_bills&docid=f:s737is.txt.pdf>.

97   See Edwin Meese III and Paul Rosenzweig, 'The SAFE Act Will Not Make Us Safer', *The Heritage Foundation*, Legal Memorandum #10, April 30, 2004: <http://www.heritage.org/Research/HomelandDefense/lm10.cfm>.

98   John Sununu, 'Remarks about SAFE Act on Senate Floor', April 7, 2004: <http://www.sununu.senate.gov/floor_statements04-07-04.htm>.

According to our multilevel approach, at least three factors explain the congressional resistance we have described. The first is an international factor: the difficulties of Iraqi reconstruction. According to James M. Lindsay, 'how aggressively [the legislative branch] exercises its formal foreign policy turns foremost on ... how well the president handles foreign policy'.[99] For instance, in the wake of the US failure in Vietnam War, lawmakers were much more prepared to challenge the White House than they had been during the 1950s and 1960s. In 1973, Congress overrode President Richard Nixon's veto to pass the War Powers Act, which 'sought to restrict the president's power to engage in prolonged military excursions'.[100] Since Bush declared the 'end of major combats' in Iraq on May 1, 2003, a number of developments have led members of Congress to question US national security policy. First, the White House has been unable to prove its two main arguments for going to war. No weapons of mass destruction have been found and no clear link has been established between Saddam Hussein and Al-Qaeda. Second, the costly occupation of Iraq helped push the federal budget deficit to a record of $413 billion in 2004.[101] Thirdly and most importantly, by July 2006 more than 2,500 American soldiers had died in Iraq.[102] Thus, while 9/11 continues to generate support among members of Congress for the view that measures such as increased military spending and the Patriot Act are necessary to protect Americans against terrorism, the problems in Iraq have led many to doubt whether Bush made the best possible response to 9/11. And if it is true that the US legislators 'make an honest effort to achieve good public policy',[103] then it is not surprising that the difficulties in Iraq have led members of Congress to question, criticize or revise Bush's national security program. For instance, much of the opposition for John Bolton's confirmation as Ambassador to the UN stemmed from the fact that Senators associated him with the neoconservative movement that convinced Bush to overthrow Saddam Hussein.

The second factor in congressional resistance is a domestic factor: Bush's low approval ratings in the United States. As Figure 5.1 shows, Bush's popularity dropped from 90% to around 40% between 9/11 and the end of 2005. It oscillated around 50% during the 2004 election year and sank below 50% after the re-election of the President, due to the ethics controversy involving House Majority Leader Tom Delay (R-Texas), the CIA leak scandal surrounding Dick Cheney, Karl Rove and Lewis 'Scooter' Libby, the slow federal response to Hurricane Katrina, high gasoline prices, and the handling of the Iraq war. Moreover, influential lobbies have begun criticizing Bush's security policies. For instance, the American Civil

---

99   Lindsay, 'Deference and Defiance', p. 530.

100   Hendrickson, *The Clinton Wars*, p. ix.

101   See *USA Today*, 'Government Says 2004 Deficit Was Record $413 Billion', October 14, 2004: <http://www.usatoday.com/news/washington/2004-10-14-deficit_x.htm>.

102   See CNN, 'Forces: US & Coalition Casualties': <http://www.cnn.com/SPECIALS/2003/iraq/forces/casualties/>.

103   Mark Carl Rom, 'Why Not Assume That Public Officials Seek to Promote the Public Interest?', *Public Affairs Report*, 37 (July 1996): 12. Quoted in Roger H. Davidson and Walter J. Oleszek, *Congress & Its Members*, 10th edition (Washington, CQ Press, 2005), p. 8.

Liberties Union (ACLU), Patriots to Restore Checks and Balances, Americans for Tax Reform, the American Conservative Union and the Eagle Forum have formed a liberal/conservative coalition to fight the renewal of the Patriot Act.[104]

According to Eugene Wittkopf and James M. McCormick, these developments have played a critical role in the mounting congressional resistance to the White House, for 'the more popular a president is with the American people, the more likely [it is that] members of Congress will support his foreign policy bids'.[105] The connection between Bush's low approval ratings and the newfound willingness of many US legislators to challenge the President's security policies is of an electoral nature.

On the one hand, Republicans knew it was difficult for them to win re-election on Bush's coattails in the 2006 mid-term elections, as many did in 2002 when Bush's popularity was still above 65%. Now, with many Americans questioning, criticizing or calling for changes to Bush's policies, GOP legislators sometimes have little choice but to part company with the White House if they want to keep the support of voters. For instance, Congressmen Roscoe Bartlett (R-Maryland), Timothy V. Johnson (R-Illinois) and Ray Lahood (R-Illinois) all represent dovish districts in their states and all voted against the renewal of the Patriot Act in July 2005. While their seats were not competitive in 2004, it appears that one of the reasons for their votes was concern about their re-election chances in 2006. Similarly, Senator Lindsey O. Graham (R-South Carolina) has expressed concerns about the GOP's prospects of retaining control of the Senate in 2006. He told Donald Rumsfeld that 'in the most patriotic state that I can imagine, people are beginning to question. And I don't think it's a blip on the radar screen. I think we have a chronic problem on our hands'.[106]

On the other hand, the Democrats also had reason to think that 'challenging the president's foreign policies could actually help them at the ballot box by enabling them to stake out positions that their constituents favour'.[107] In September 2005, for instance, 62% of Americans disapproved of the way Bush was handling the situation in Iraq.[108] It has therefore become easier for the Democrats to spin arguments such as 'Bush made a mistake', 'Iraq is an intractable quagmire' or 'we have to rethink our presence there'.

A third cause of congressional resistance to Bush is an individual factor: the growing impact of foreign policy entrepreneurship in Congress. To be sure, the GOP held control of the House and Senate in 2004 and has continued to use its institutional powers to limit expression of criticism and prevent changes to Bush's

---

104 James G. Lakely, 'Conservatives, Liberals Align Against Patriot Act', *The Washington Times*, June 14, 2005: <http://www.washtimes.com/national/20050614-121304-2787r.htm>.

105 Wittkopf and McCormick, 'When Congress Supports the President', p. 20.

106 Quoted in Bradley Graham, 'Rumsfeld Under Fire on the Hill', *Washington Post*, June 24, 2005, p. A1.

107 Lindsay, 'Deference and Defiance', p. 534.

108 Michael A. Fletcher and Richard Morin, 'Bush's Approval Rating Drops to New Low in Wake of Storm', *Washington Post*, September 13, 2005, p. A8.

proposals. For example, in October 2005, Jay Rockefeller (D-West Virginia), Vice Chairman of the Senate Committee on Intelligence, expressed outrage after Majority Leader Bill Frist (R-Tennessee) 'unilaterally cancelled' a briefing that was to have provided all Senators with detailed classified information on Iraq from the National Intelligence Council.[109] But at the same time, the difficulties in Iraq and Bush's low approval ratings have eroded the legitimacy of Republican leaders and their ability to marginalize or silence foreign policy entrepreneurs in Congress. For example, on June 10, 2005, James Sensenbrenner, Chairman of the House Judiciary Committee, agreed to let the ranking Democratic member, John Conyers (D-Michigan), choose the witnesses and the topic for a hearing, which ended up examining the executive branch's abuse of legal authorities to prosecute the war on terrorism.[110] A week later, the House Republican leadership could not prevent Conyers from organizing a small conference in the Capitol basement about the 'Downing Street Memo', a British memo that some believe proves that the Bush administration 'fixed' the intelligence and 'distorted' the facts to promote its bid to dislodge Saddam Hussein, and therefore supports the argument that US intelligence on Iraq prior to the intervention was trumped up rather than simply mistaken.[111]

Foreign policy entrepreneurs have also raised their voices in the Senate and forced the GOP leadership to address points that challenge Bush's policies. For example, while the Senate voted 85–13 to confirm Condoleezza Rice as Secretary of State, many Democrats used the debate on her nomination to draw attention to the difficulties in Iraq. At the Senate Committee on Foreign Relations hearings on the nomination, Barbara Boxer (D-California) said Rice had 'not acknowledged the deaths' in Iraq or 'laid out an exit strategy for Iraq', and was not 'willing to admit mistakes', including 'going to war over weapons of mass destruction found later not to exist'.[112] It can be expected that in the presidential election of 2008, Senators such as Russ Feingold (D-Wisconsin), Hilary Clinton (D-New York) and Joe Biden (D-Delaware) will be tempted to criticize Bush's policies and propose alternatives. As James M. Lindsay notes, 'Senators with an eye on the White House seem particularly eager to establish their credentials on foreign policy.'[113] It is therefore likely that the difficulties encountered by US national security policy, combined with Feingold's, Clinton's and Biden's ambitions, will prompt them to become congressional foreign policy entrepreneurs in the near future. Russ Feingold has already taken a firm stand

---

109   Jay Rockefeller, 'Rockefeller Expresses Outrage that Majority Leader Frist Cancels Intelligence Briefing on Iraq', October 5, 2005: <http://rockefeller.senate.gov/news/2005/pr100505a.html>.

110   Committee on the Judiciary, House of Representatives, 109th Congress, 1st Session, 'Hearing on the Reauthorization of the USA Patriot Act (Continued)', June 10, 2005: <http://judiciary.house.gov/media/pdfs/printers/109th/21913.pdf>.

111   Dana Milbank, 'Democrats Play House to Rally Against the War', *Washington Post*, June 17, 2005, p. A06.

112   CNN, 'Rice Spars With Democrats in Hearing', January 19, 2005: <http://www.cnn.com/2005/ALLPOLITICS/01/18/rice.confirmation/index.html>.

113   Lindsay, *Congress and the Politics of U.S. Foreign Policy*, p. 42.

against the Patriot Act and the Iraq War. In a statement prepared for delivery from the floor of the Senate in September 2005, he declared:

> Too often, too many of my colleagues are reluctant to challenge the Administration's policies in Iraq for fear that anything other than staying the course set by the President will somehow appear weak. But the President's course is misguided, and it is doing grave damage to our extraordinarily professional and globally admired all-volunteer United States Army.[114]

Understanding the Domestic Politics of US Hegemony: Directions for Future Research on the Impact of Congress on US National Security Policy

We have explored the factors involved in congressional compliance with Bush's national security policy between 9/11 and 2004, and growing congressional resistance to the White House since 2004. To this end, we have compared three types of analyses of congressional national security behaviour: domestic approaches, systemic approaches and multilevel approaches. We have concluded that multilevel approaches, though not exhaustive, enjoy many advantages over domestic and systemic approaches. They bridge the gap between internal and external factors and offer a clear overview of the types of internal factors that contribute to congressional compliance with or resistance to the White House. Applied to the war in Afghanistan, the increase in the defence budget, the passage of the USA Patriot Act, the release of the National Security Strategy of the United States of America of September 2002 and the war in Iraq, our multilevel approach leads to the conclusion that between 9/11 and 2004, Congress followed Bush's line on national security policy for three main reasons: (a) US legislators tended to perceive terrorism as a serious global threat to US national security; (b) Bush was highly popular with the American people and c) there were no powerful foreign policy entrepreneurs in the House and Senate. The multilevel approach has also shown that the difficulties of Iraqi reconstruction (an international factor), Bush's low approval ratings in the United States (a domestic factor) and the new assertiveness of congressional foreign policy entrepreneurs (an individual factor) account for the increasing executive-legislative rivalry since 2004. This rivalry is illustrated by congressional opposition to the White House on policy towards Iraq, the nomination of John Bolton as US ambassador to the UN, and the renewal of the Patriot Act.

While the theoretical explanation developed in this chapter adds to our understanding of congressional behaviour, it also has limitations. First, it could be argued that it focuses on Bush's popularity and congressional foreign policy entrepreneurship to the neglect of other domestic factors, such as the fact that one party controls both the White House and Congress, and the ideology of members of

---

114 Russ Feingold, 'The President's Policies in Iraq Are Breaking the United States Army', Statement as Prepared to Be Delivered from the Floor of the United States Senate, September 28, 2005: <http://www.truthout.org/docs_2005/092805R.shtml>.

Congress. We would agree that such factors could also be useful for explaining the behaviour of Congress. For example, as we have noted, one reason why congressional foreign policy entrepreneurs had little influence between 9/11 and 2004 is that the House was controlled by GOP leaders who shared Bush's foreign policy vision and core beliefs. Therefore, the 'one-party government' factor (a GOP-controlled House) and the 'ideological factor' (GOP leaders who share Bush's vision and core beliefs) were in play.

A second caveat that must be raised is that we have no evidence as to which of the factors posited by the multilevel approach has the greatest weight in this case.[115] One way to address this point would be to attempt to construct a general theory of congressional security behaviour. Using the scientific deductive method, we could test the hypotheses we have developed here over a longer period in the history of congressional-executive relations and attempt to determine the effectiveness of each of the independent variables we have identified (congressional perceptions of threat, congressional perceptions of foreign policy failure, the President's popularity, the presence or absence of powerful foreign policy entrepreneurs in Congress) in explaining Congress's conduct with respect to security issues since the birth of the American Republic. Hypotheses such as 'the greater the perceived threat to US national security, the more likely Congress is to accept presidential security policies' and 'the lower the President's approval ratings, the more likely Congress is to challenge presidential security policies' would have to be tested over the history of congressional-executive relations since 1776. We would no doubt find some hypotheses to be more consistent with the empirical evidence than others. Eugene Wittkopf and James McCormick have performed just such an analysis for the 1948–1996 period.[116] Their conclusion is that 'congressional support for the president on foreign policy cannot be understood solely by focusing on any one domestic or international source category'.[117] The existing literature indicates that it would be difficult to abandon either of those sources in our analysis since both have been important in driving Congress's behaviour on national security since the end of World War II.

We believe that future multilevel accounts of national security behaviour could make contributions to our understanding of Congress and foreign policy in at least two areas:

1. They could help reconcile the systemic and domestic approaches to analysis of congressional security behaviour. As we have seen, the former holds that it is not necessary to open the United States' 'black box' in order to understand Congress's conduct while the latter argues that the international environment has only a marginal impact on congressional decisions. However, our analysis

---

115 I would like to thank Professor Joseph M. Grieco for drawing this problem to my attention.

116 Wittkopf and McCormick, 'When Congress Supports the President.'

117 *Ibid.*, p. 30.

shows that investigating internal factors and interpreting the impact of international events on US legislators are both essential. Therefore, multilevel approaches will clear away unnecessary barriers to the development of our knowledge of Congress and foreign policy.

2. Multilevel approaches can help congressional scholars develop analyses that emphasize factors in congressional decision-making other than the 'classic' electoral factor. Since the publication of David Mayhem's *Congress: The Electoral Connection* in 1974, it has become commonplace to argue that 'members of Congress are single-minded seekers of reelection' and that 'the electoral assumption alone is sufficient to explain the great bulk of congressional behavior'.[118] But Mayhem himself recognized that US legislators have goals aside from re-election. It is reasonable to argue that students of Congress need to develop analytical tools that shed light on what has been left unsaid by Mayhem's theory. The relationship between voters and members of Congress is not the only factor that explains congressional behaviour and multilevel approaches can help fill the gap left by Mayhem.

Also, future political events will produce new dynamics for congressional scholars to investigate. For instance, should Americans elect a Congress and a White House controlled by different parties in the near future, we will have to study how the President deals with partisan opposition in the Senate and the House. New terrorist attacks against the United States could also drive changes in congressional behaviour on security matters. Despite their dissatisfaction with the situation in Iraq, members of Congress would likely react to another 9/11 just as they did after the attacks against the World Trade Center and the Pentagon; many would follow the lead of the White House and argue that 'politics stops at the water's edge'.

Conclusion

In sum, any discussion of US national security policy should integrate considerations about Congress and the US legislators. As we saw in this chapter, US Senators and representatives adopted Bush's foreign policy vision after 9/11. In the case of Iraq, they became accomplices of Bush's imperial temptation when they decided not to question or criticize the White House. It is reasonable to argue that these developments temporary jeopardized the checks and balances system the Americans regularly praise as part of their democracy. Indeed, the Founding Fathers' ideal of balance of powers was profoundly shaken: Bush and his cabinet became almost entirely free to conduct US foreign policy the way they pleased; congressional requirements for executive accountability became almost inexistent. But there are good reasons to think that Bush will never enjoy such a freedom of action again. Many members of Congress now share Robert C. Byrd's view that 'no president

---

118 On this issue, see Lindsay, *Congress and the Politics of U.S. Foreign Policy*, pp. 33–52.

must ever again be granted such license with our troops or our treasure'.[119] Thus, even if US hegemony gives the White House an incomparable freedom of action in the international system, and even if the Bush administration is prone to develop ambitious national security goals because it wants to protect the American homeland against terrorism, the power arrangements between the Congress and the president ensures a certain degree of restraint. At least when (and as long as) the checks and balances work properly in Washington, America's imperial ambition will be reduced or slowed down in the global arena.

---

119   Robert C. Byrd, *Losing America*, p. 214.

PART 2
Perceptions of American Hegemony: The US Redeployment of Power and its Regional Implications

Chapter 6

In Search of a Policy Towards Islamism: The United States at War Against Global Terror

Onnig Beylerian

Despite the apparent militancy of the Bush Administration and President Bush himself, the United States remains ambivalent towards the war against global terror it declared in the aftermath of the destruction of the twin towers and the attack on the Pentagon. It is now generally understood that this war is waged against the Jihadi faction of the Islamist international movement. The choice of the term 'war' by the Bush Administration[1] is not fortuitous: it represents a comprehensive effort to mobilize American national power in order to achieve major strategic goals.

America under George W. Bush is waging a war against an adversary whose sources of power have not been adequately identified. The failure to fully understand the bases of power can be seen in the articulation of American strategic goals. In spite of the loss of human lives and capital that have been spent to prosecute this war, the principal Jihadi network, Al-Qa'eda, still remains elusive and deadly, as the recent London suicide bombings have shown.

In this chapter we show that the Administration's ambivalence in waging war against global terror resides in (1) the difficulty in identifying and articulating the nature of the threat, (2) the highly uncertain outcome of Iraq's rehabilitation and (3) the tentative and yet highly ambitious nature to reform political institutions and processes in the Arab-Islamic world.

The Nature of the Adversary

The United States could have chosen not to react with a declaration of war against global terrorism. Similar European countries which experienced terrorist acts (but at a considerably lesser scale), the Bush Administration could have responded through

---

1   'The deliberate and deadly attacks which were carried out yesterday against our country were more than acts of terror. They were acts of war.' George W. Bush, 'Remarks by the President in Photo Opportunity with the National Security Team', September 12, 2001, <http://www.whitehouse.gov/news/releases/2001/09/20010912-4.html>.

a joint police and military operation around the globe without resorting to such a comprehensive response.

But the horror and surprise of 9/11 was reminiscent of Pearl Harbor.[2] This time it was not an attack against US forces deployed at the periphery of continental United States, but against significant symbols of US power. Clearly, Bush felt he could not afford to respond through law enforcements agencies only. War appeared a more appropriate response. But war against whom? This was not the case of a maritime power seeking to knock out its competitor, but a terrorist organization with bases in Afghanistan. Al-Qa'eda was not unknown to US intelligence agencies. In fact Al-Qa'eda confederates had previously tried to destroy the twin towers in the first months of the Clinton Administration. They would apply the same approach with the new Bush Administration, also was caught off guard at a time when it was putting together key elements of its administration.[3] The sheer destructive magnitude of 9/11 along with previous well-planned terrorist bombings and attacks led Bush to perceive an adversary so powerful and pervasive as to declare war against it.

To begin combating Al-Qa'eda, an immediate target was found in the elimination of the Taliban regime and Al-Qa'eda's operational bases in Afghanistan.[4] During subsequent months and years, Bush continued to speak about global terror, which had now become a keyword for identifying a phenomenon with imprecise features, one difficult to explain to an American public who remained traumatized by 9/11 and alarmed by the constant expansion of this war.

Complexity of the Adversary

In its quest to explain the complexity of the threat to the public, Bush confronted several problems. First, Bush depicted this war as a combat against a phenomenon, a scourge that befell humankind or a war against a group of sophisticated global killers.[5] During his first term, Bush failed to explain how Americans could continue to support a prolonged struggle against a phenomenon and not against a clearly identifiable enemy. Terrorism is not impersonal: it represents a method that an

---

2   George W. Bush, 'The Budget Message of the President', 4 February 2002, <http://www.whitehouse.gov/news/releases/2002/02/20020204.html>; for a discussion comparing Pearl Harbor and 9/11 and the similar historical position shared by Franklin Roosevelt and George Bush, see John L. Gaddis, 'Grand Strategy in the Second Term', *Foreign Affairs*, 84/1 (2005): 2–15.

3   See the stunning narrative regarding the Administration's lack of concern in deciphering the intentions of the Jihadists on the eve of 9/11: Condoleezza Rice before the 9/11 Commission on the Memorandum of August 6, 2001, <http://www.9-11commission.gov/archive/hearing9/9-11Commission_Hearing_2004-04-08.pdf>, 13.

4   George W. Bush, 'Address to a Joint Session of Congress and the American People', 20 September 2001, <http://www.whitehouse.gov/news/releases/2001/09/20010920-8.html>.

5   See Commission 9/11, 'National Commission on Terrorist Attacks Upon the United States', *The 9/11 Commission Report*, August 2004, <http://www.9-11commission.gov/report/911Report_Ch12.pdf>, 362.

antagonist uses to reach an end. In the case at hand, terrorism is used by a set of radical Islamist movements, or more exactly Jihadists, who espouse the most extreme form of Islamism. The strategic objective of Jihadists is to overthrow through violence existing regimes in all Arab and Islamic countries and replace them with Taliban-like or theocratic regimes. The ultimate goal is to restore the Caliphate and convert all states into Islam.[6]

Yet right after September 11, Bush did not abstain from referring to bin Laden and his networks as the main enemy. He also did not hesitate to identify him as well as other Islamist armed organizations as inheritors of totalitarian ideologies.[7] But he represented bin Laden and Al-Qa'eda as a phenomenon detached from its geopolitical and historical context. Bin Laden is far from being a common terrorist or the chief of a Baader-Meinhof gang. He was a useful and occasionally indispensable ally of the United States in its covert war against Soviet occupation of Afghanistan.[8] Thanks to his years of close collaboration with the United States, bin Laden was able to observe and learn from his US mentors covert methods of war. Nor has bin Laden worked in an unknown terrain: the Islamist radicalization of Muslim populations dates back to the 1970s when nationalist Arab regimes[9] began to co-opt Islamists as a means to bolster their diminishing legitimacy. Bin Laden also maintains close contacts with members of ruling elites of several Arab and Islamic countries, mainly through financial and banking ties.[10] If in the 1980s he assumed simple tasks such as recruiting Islamist volunteers for Afghanistan, today he figures in Arab opinion as a major political personality and inescapable factor in inter-Arab and Islamic politics.

A second problem for the Bush Administration was that it abstained from carefully analyzing Al-Qa'eda's sources of power situated in the Arab-Islamic

---

6   Henry Kissinger, 'America's Assignment: What Will We Face in the Next Four Years?', *Newsweek*, November 8, 2004, 144/19: 32–38. See also Letter from al-Zawahiri to al-Zarqawi, July 9, 2005, from the Office of the Director of National Intelligence, <http://www.dni.gov/letter_in_english.pdf>.

7   Reiterated recently by his national and homeland security advisers, Stephen Hadley and Frances Fragos Townsend, 'What We Saw in London', *The New York Times*, July 23, 2005: A2/13.

8   Steve Coll, *Ghost Wars: The Secret History of the CIA, Afghanistan, and Bin Laden, from the Soviet Invasion to September 10, 2001*, New York, 2004.

9   See for example the case of Syria, Scott Wilson, 'Religious Surge Alarms Secular Syrians: Islam's Clout Among Frustrated Youth Challenging Governments Across Mideast', *Washington Post*, January 23, 2005: A21; Nicholas Blanford, 'Syrian Islamic scholar preaches moderation', *Daily Star*, January 18, 2005, <http://dailystar.com.lb/article.asp?edition_id=10&categ_id=2&article_id=11901#>; Ibrahim Hamidi, 'Can Syria keep its Islamist genie in the bottle?' *Daily Star*, January 12, 2005, <http://dailystar.com.lb/article.asp?edition_ID=10&article_ID=11740&categ_id=5#>.

10   See for instance *Update on the Global Campaign Against Terrorist Financing, Second Report of an Independent Task Force on Terrorist Financing Sponsored by the Council on Foreign Relations*, 2004. See also John R. Bradley, 'Al Qaeda and the House of Saud: Eternal Enemies or Secret Bedfellows?' *Washington Quarterly*, 28/4: 139–152.

public space largely dominated by Islamists. The range of Islamist influence in Arab civil societies is now considerable.[11] If the majority of Islamist parties and movements began their political careers by providing social assistance and Quranic primary education to local communities, their actual zeal is entirely devoted to an ideology which includes social renewal requiring the demise of autocratic regimes supported by the United States and its Western allies. In this perspective, Israel is seen as a main obstacle that has imposed itself on the Arab and Islamic world by disfranchising Palestinians from their lands and advocating an ideology buttressed by a formidable military power.

Islamism as ideology and political movement is not new. Without getting into a long description of the evolution of this ideology,[12] the international Islamist movement is now based on an elaborate system of social, economic, cultural and political ideas, which vies to build a society substantially different than that advocated by Western Liberalism.[13] It therefore competes with Liberalism since it offers an alternative to Western social and political doctrines.[14] If the United States and Europe failed to pay due attention to the scope and breadth of Islamism it is because none of the Islamist movements challenged the West through force. Indeed, the majority of Islamist groups directed their political activities inwards, to their respective states. These groups were not interested in leading their activities outside Arab and Islamic countries, in contrast to Jihadists who began to stage terrorist attacks

---

11   A broad definition adopted by the majority of observers could be found in Graham Fuller, 'Islamists in the Arab World: The Dance around Democracy', Carnegie Papers No. 49, Carnegie Endowment for Peace, September 2004, <http://www.ceip.org/files/pdf/cp49. fuller.final.PDF>. According to this definition, Islamism holds that the Koran and the Hadith, and the traditions set by the life of the Prophet, his actions as well as his words, contain important principles that must govern the *Umma*. There cannot be a separation between Islam and politics. This definition of Islamism includes a large group of individuals and groups that self-identify according to the degree to which politics can be separated from Islam. This can range from moderate Islamist parties with a secular face, such the Development and Justice Party in Turkey now in power, to armed Islamist groups such as the Palestinian Hamas and the Lebanese Hezbollah. For a general description of relations between Islam and Islamism see Vartan Gregorian, *Islam: A Mosaic, Not A Monolith*, Washington, DC, 2003, 74–89.

12   Gilles Kepel, *Jihad : Expansion et déclin de l'islamisme*, Paris, 2003; Olivier Roy, *L'Islam mondialisé*, Paris, 2003; and Olivier Carré, *Mystique et politique : le Coran des islamistes : commentaire coranique de Sayyid Qutb (1906–1966)*, Paris, 2004.

13   See for instance Timur Kuran on Islamist economic thought which he finds wanting, 'Islamism and Economics: Policy Implications for a Free Society' in Sohrab Behdad and Farhad Nomani (eds), *Islam and Public Policy* [International Review of Comparative Public Policy, vol. 9], Greenwich, 1997: 72–102; 'The Genesis of Islamic Economics: A Chapter in the Politics of Muslim Identity', *Social Research*, 64 (Summer 1997): 301–338; 'The Economic Impact of Islamic Fundamentalism', in M. Marty and S. Appleby (eds), *Fundamentalisms and the State: Remaking Polities, Economies, and Militance*, Chicago, 1993: 302–341.

14   Thomas Butko, 'Unity Through Opposition: Islam as an Instrument of Radical Political Change,' *Middle East Review of International Affairs*, 8/3 (December 2004): 33–48.

both in Arab and Western countries a few years after the end of the Soviet occupation of Afghanistan. Lastly, Western countries were largely indifferent to Arab social and political development but interested in securing the supply of cheap energy.

It is important not to confuse Jihadists with Islamist political formations. Bin Laden and his associate al-Zawahiri present themselves as the vanguard and power builders of Islamism. Their goal is to lead the international Islamist movement, populated by a constellation of groups and individuals claiming one form or another of Islamism. If mainstream Islamists have serious reservations with respect to Jihadist methods and strategy, their goals nevertheless converge in many ways since both oppose US policies. It is therefore difficult to distinguish bin Laden from Islamism especially because his methods and political program have not been systematically condemned or opposed by Islamist movements.[15]

Third, the administration has not entirely understood the Jihadist strategic goal. Essentially, Jihadists aim to reinforce their bases not so much by attacking targets in Arab countries than by aiming at the superpower and other major powers as a means of building their own power.[16] Bin Laden and Zawahiri appear to have understood a lesson learned by Bismarck: if you want to aggrandize your power, you must confront head on principal powers. Al-Qa'eda's attacks in Iraq, Saudi Arabia and Egypt and bin Laden's alliance with Zarqawi in Iraq suggest that he aims to extend his bases in these countries as a step towards gaining a geostrategic foothold. Bin Laden and Zawahiri and their confederates have reason to hope for US defeat in the region. Vietnam demonstrated that if it is impossible to defeat America militarily, it is possible to defeat it politically. If the goal of the United States is to defeat radical Islamists and assist Muslim populations to modernize their societies, Jihadists have only to demonstrate US incapacity to eliminate Jihadist bases and effort to gain new recruits.

A fourth problem for the Bush Administration is the expansion of the war on global terror by opening yet another front, this time in Iraq. Several analysts have imputed Bush to confuse the adversary and the real threats to US national security. According to their views, Saddam Hussein was not a menace, neither imminent nor distant.[17] Was it really necessary to attack and occupy Iraq if the greater threat was to destroy Al-Qa'eda networks and bring bin Laden and Zawahiri to justice? From the standpoint of disarming Saddam Hussein, there was no reason to attack Iraq since he did not possess weapons of mass destruction even though he had the capability to

---

15   Monte Palmer and Princess Palmer, *At The Heart Of Terror: Islam, Jihadists, and America's War on Terrorism*, Lanham, MD, 2005.

16   See Zawahiri's thinking in Gilles Kepel, *Fitna : Guerre au cœur de l'Islam*, Paris, 2004, 99–138. See also Susan B. Glasser and Walter Pincus, 'Seized Letter Outlines Al Qaeda Goals in Iraq', *Washington Post*, October 12, 2005: A13 and the Letter from al-Zawahiri to al-Zarqawi, July 9, 2005, from the Office of the Director of National Intelligence, <http://www.dni.gov/letter_in_english.pdf>.

17   Jeffrey Record, 'Threat Confusion and its Penalties,' *Survival*, 46/2 (Summer 2004): 51–72; Chaim Kaufmann, 'Threat Inflation and the Failure of the Marketplace of Ideas: The Selling of the Iraq War,' *International Security* 29/1, (Summer 2004): 5–48.

build them. Furthermore, no tangible evidence could be found regarding cooperation between Saddam Hussein and bin Laden, even though some contacts had been initiated since at least 1995.[18] But a closer examination of Bush's strategy suggests that the real reason for Iraq's invasion and the subsequent overthrow of Saddam's regime and US occupation was to strike a target in the Arab-Islamic world as a way to demonstrate US resolve to vindicate the loss of American lives on September 11, 2001 and respond to extremist behaviour such as that of suicide bombers who appeared to enjoy the support and understanding of Arab public opinion and the Muslim clergy.[19] Iraq had thus become a suitable target. It was an isolated state both among Arab states and the international community. Iraqis were exhausted by many years of economic sanctions and repression at the hands of the Saddam regime. Iraq seemed to invite a swift military action that could result in establishing the foundations of a democratic political system corresponding to Iraq's level of economic and social development. From the viewpoint of American military commanders, Iraq was a battlefield that could keep several waves of Jihadists busy:[20] a dangerous assumption that could backfire against the United States. Finally, drawing on their experience in rehabilitating defeated powers, the United States were aiming to build a democratic state in Iraq as a way of providing an example to Islamic states as to how to reform their political institutions.

Sources of ambivalence

The Bush Administration remains ambiguous towards the Jihadist adversary. First and foremost, Washington does not have a policy towards Islamism.[21] It appears enthused about the moderate Islamist government led by Erdogan in Turkey because it represents a form of Muslim democracy[22] capable of promoting democratization with the consent of the secular Turkish military establishment. Since the Administration's mind is not made up as to what to do with Islamism, Washington has been trying to

---

18   National Commission on Terrorist Attacks Upon the United States, *The 9/11 Commission Report*, August 2004, <http://www.9-11commission.gov/report/911Report.pdf>, 61.

19   The best representative of this thesis is Thomas L. Friedman, 'Because We Could', *The New York Times*, 4 June 2004.

20   Bruce Hoffman, 'Saddam Is Ours: Does Al Qaeda Care?' *The New York Times*, December 17, 2003: A39/1.

21   Bruce Hoffman, 'Al Qa'eda and the War on Terrorism: An Update,' *Current History* (November 2004): 423–427. For a systematic study of the Carter, Reagan and Bush (senior) Administrations towards Islamism see Fawaz A. Gerges, *America and Political Islam: Clash of Cultures or Clash of Interests?* Cambridge, UK, 1999.

22   Colin Powell, 'U.S., Turkey Resolve Outstanding Issues', Joint press conference in Ankara with Turkish Foreign Minister Gül, April 2, 2003, <http://ankara.usembassy.gov/powell/pow0402.htm>; reiterated by his successor Condoleezza Rice, 'Interview With Metehan Demir of Turkey's Kanal-D TV', February 6, 2005, <http://www.state.gov/secretary/rm/2005/41856.htm>.

converse with Islamist political parties, such as the Muslim Brotherhood, as a way of familiarizing itself with the goals and objectives of traditional and conservative Islamist parties.[23]

But to develop a consistent policy towards Islamism would lead the United States to change its policy towards two allied Muslim states: Saudi Arabia and Pakistan. The alliance with the Saudis and Pakistanis are largely due to the engagement of their top leaders. King Abdallah and Pervez Musharraf are ostensibly close allies of Washington, but both have limited maneuvering space since they are surrounded by political circles pursuing objectives that are not incompatible with Islamism.[24] It is therefore somewhat problematic to exert too much pressure on them lest their regimes become even more fragile and exposed to virulent Islamist influence. It would also lead these two states to switch sides, something which the United States cannot afford as long as it confronts Iran, an Islamist state since 1979.[25]

Furthermore developing too hastily a policy towards Islamism could generate the perception that the United States is at war with Islam. The Bush Administration appears to be walking on a tightrope: namely, how to wage an ideological struggle against a political doctrine that derives from a religion whose origins are closely associated with political action and even methods of state building that may run against US values?[26]

As we shall see below, the Administration does not have as yet a clear view on political and social trends of the Arab and Muslim societies that have given rise to poverty, frustrations and despair. Hence it does not yet fully grasp how to differentiate Islam from Islamism and the implications of this difference in Muslim publics. For

---

23   John Mintz and Douglas Farah, 'In Search of Friends Among the Foes,' *Washington Post*, September 11, 2004: A01. Several commentators consider that Islamism cannot be bypassed; the best expression of this can be found in Graham Fuller and John Esposito, 'Is Islamism a Threat? A Debate', *Middle East Quarterly,* December 1999, VI/4, <http://www.meforum.org/article/447>. For a short but useful outline on Islamism in Egypt and the Ikhwan al-Muslimin see Mustapha Kamel Al-Sayyid, *The Other Face of the Islamist Movement*, Carnegie Endowment for International Peace Working Paper, no. 33, January 2003; see also Youssef H. Aboul-Enein, 'Al-Ikhwan Al-Muslimeen: The Muslim Brotherhood', *Military Review* (July–Aug 2003): 26–31.

24   For Saudi Arabia see International Crisis Group, *Can Saudi Arabia Reform Itself?* Middle East Report, No. 28, 14 July 2004, <http://www.crisisweb.org/home/getfile.cfm?id=1311&tid=2864> and Michael Scott Doran, 'The Saudi Paradox', *Foreign Affairs* (January/February 2004); for Pakistan, see Hassan Abbas, *Pakistan's Drift Into Extremism: Allah, the Army, and America's War on Terror*, London, 2005.

25   James Fallows, 'Will Iran Be Next: Soldiers, Spies, and Diplomats Conduct a Classic Pentagon War Game – With Sobering Results', *The Atlantic* (December 2004); see also Seymour Hersh, 'The Coming Wars: What the Pentagon Can Now Do in Secret', *The New Yorker*, January 24, 2005, 80/44.

26   However, the Bush Administration appeared to be conscious of this problem as it decided to wage an ideological campaign against 'Islamic extremism', see, notably, President Bush's address to the National Endowment of Democracy, October 4, 2005, <http://www.whitehouse.gov/news/releases/2005/10/20051006-3.html>.

example, if it is true that secular Arab nationalist movements have failed, it does not necessarily follow that Muslims would consent to let extremists to use Islam to develop political doctrines that could irreversibly jeopardize Islam as a religion when these doctrines fail to achieve their goals. In many ways, Arab societies are living their 'Weimar moment': they may not find Islamists agreeable but they do also know that secular ideologies have not worked. While Arab and Muslim societies are searching for answers, Islamism has become a vehicle for social identification in the Middle East and in Muslim immigrant communities in Europe. Thus Washington confronts a conundrum: should it promote secular anti-autocratic forces who remain fragmented and weak, and thus contribute to instability in the Middle East or explore the extent to which Islamists groups and parties are ready to participate in democratic political process and promote stability?

Is the Administration ambivalent or simply at loss to explain the complex nature of dealing with Islamism and the extremist threat that arises from within? The more this adversary has been unusual and difficult to grasp, the more Bush has been reluctant to fully identify the real adversary. Explaining the power base of Jihadism to the American public would have been a daunting task and indeed would have distracted the public from supporting the prosecution of the war against global terror. Instead of explaining the real reasons why it was necessary to invade Iraq, Bush preferred to represent it as an operation of dismantling weapons of mass destruction – even when there was little evidence that Saddam Hussein actually had them. Had the Administration developed a policy towards Islamism, the necessity to overthrow Saddam's regime would have been guided by a different set of strategic considerations.

Iraq: Is There an Exit?

If overthrowing Saddam's regime was relatively easy, the occupation and rehabilitation of the Iraqi state turned out to be difficult. The prerequisites of rehabilitation were simply not present. The United States tried hard to reconstitute Iraqi political institutions and processes, but progress was minute and not promising enough. The climate of fear on the eve of the January elections and the refusal of Sunni parties to participate in the electoral process and in drafting the Constitution indicated that the road to democracy remained as sinuous as ever. The American political elites did not wish to see the United States remaining indefinitely in Iraq and expected the Administration to articulate an exit strategy. Washington linked the exit to the success of rehabilitation, which minimally consisted of an Iraqi government capable of ensuring the security of its citizens and denying Jihadists the chance to transform Iraq into a new *qa'eda*. Washington did not appear ready to evacuate Iraq without having accomplished its mission. Nor was it open to internationalizing the rehabilitation process, if it averred to be difficult to achieve through US–led efforts.

A Botched Occupation

The Bush Administration had not planned the occupation of Iraq; it thus found itself confronting numerous tasks that its troops were not prepared for.[27] Washington thought that defeating the Iraqi forces was easy enough, especially when it saw the Iraqi army dissolving into the Mesopotamian countryside. But the problem was not Saddam's utter defeat through a grand 'shock and awe' operation but the difficulty of occupation. If the number of US troops corresponded to the needs of defeating the Iraqi armed forces, the number and quality of US and allied troops needed to rehabilitate Iraq did not. Evidently, Washington ignored the social and psychological state of Iraqis who were exhausted from years of economic sanctions and systematic repression at the hands of the Baathist regime. The Administration's knowledge of Iraq derived almost exclusively from exiled Iraqis. The United States thought that the swift overthrow of the Saddam regime would generate a spontaneous rally reminiscent of those of the velvet revolutions in Eastern Europe.[28]

If the Iraqi forces were easily defeated, those of the Baath party succeeded to survive the downfall of the regime. Washington was at first agnostic regarding the Baath party, heavily dominated by Saddam's own dynasty. Washington at first thought it did not need to co-opt its members to reconstruct the state because it intended to introduce a regime in complete break with its Baathist past. Nor did it have a view as to what to do with the party itself. The US proconsul in Iraq, L. Paul Bremer III, decided otherwise by swiftly proceeding with the destruction of Baath's power, decommissioning the Iraqi armed forces and barring former Baathists from holding public office.[29] But these steps produced soon enough a Baathist insurrection which continues to this day. Thus Saddam is in captivity, and continues his gardening, writes his poems and prose and prepares his defence for crimes he admittedly committed against Iraqis. But his followers under the guidance of Izzat Ibrahim al-Douri[30] continued to pursue a modified version of Stalin's scorched earth policy with the collaboration of the Jihadist Zarqawi promoted to the rank of emir by bin Laden. Facing this insurrection, Washington's response resulted in loss of life and negative perceptions of US occupation in the Arab world.

27　For an overview of occupation problems in Iraq see Anthony Cordesman, 'US Policy in Iraq: A 'Realist' Approach to its Challenges and Opportunities', Center for Strategic and International Studies, August 6, 2004, <http://www.csis.org/features/040806_USPolicyInIraq. pdf>; see also Larry Diamond for a closer look at the issue, 'What Went Wrong in Iraq?', *Foreign Affairs* (September/October 2004).

28　For a short analysis on the assumptions of occupation see Michael E. O'Hanlon, 'Iraq Without a Plan,' *Policy Review*, No. 128 (December 2004).

29　On de-Baathification see Jon Lee Anderson, 'Out on the Street: The United States' de-Baathification Program Fuelled the Insurgency. Is It Too Late for Bush to Change Course?', *The New Yorker*, November 9, 2004.

30　Douglas Jehl, 'U.S. Said to Weigh Sanctions on Syria Over Iraqi Network', *The New York Times*, January 5, 2005, A1/6.

In devising its military campaign and subsequent occupation of Iraq, Washington repeatedly evoked its vast experience in rehabilitating Germany and Japan.[31] But Iraq was certainly no Germany or Japan of 1945. Once at the table of surrender, Germans and Japanese were looking forward to turning the page and reconstituting their state and civil society. Their armed forces accepted defeat, were demobilized and organized no resistance. There were no insurgents in Germany or Japan as both had already used all avenues of violence. There were no outside forces striving to short-circuit the efforts for rehabilitation. The Soviet Union kept its German part and recognized US's prerogative to rule the other with its French and British allies. It conceded to Washington the right to recast Japan and pledged not to stir up civil disobedience in Tokyo or elsewhere in Japan since it kept Eastern Europe. Germany and Japan knew how democratic institutions could work since they had prior experience in this respect and both sought to recast their state according to the rule of law. *Last but not least*, Germany was jointly occupied and well planned. Planning and implementing the renewal of the Japanese state was assigned to General MacArthur who was not exactly a neophyte in occupation matters in Asian conditions. The German state was suspended for four years whereas Japan's was not, due to MacArthur's insistence to ensure continuity in Japan's political development albeit under the aegis of the United States.[32]

In sum, the performance of the Bush Administration in Iraq was minimal, which did not produce maximum results. Despite the high costs in human lives that the United States continues to sustain, this intervention shared a lot of similarities with other ill-fated interventions that the United States undertook in failed states in the wake of the end of the Cold War.[33]

---

31   See the remarks by two prominent members of the US foreign policy establishment on misplaced analogy between US occupation of Iraq with those of Germany and Japan, Henry Kissinger, 'Interview with Zbigniew Brzezinski, Henry Kissinger [et al.]', *CNN Late Edition with Wolf Blitzer*, December 26, 2004, <http://transcripts.cnn.com/TRANSCRIPTS/0412/26/le.01.html>.

32   For a general account of US military occupation of Germany and Japan see Robert Wolfe (ed.), *Americans as Proconsuls: United States Military Government in Germany and Japan, 1944–1952*, Carbondale, IL, 1984; on Japan, see the account of its first post-war prime minister, Shigeru Yoshida, *The Yoshida Memoirs: The Story of Japan in Crisis* (tr. Kenichi Yoshida), London, 1961. Edward Luttwak adds political education as factor in successful reconstruction of post-war German and Japanese states: 'Iraq: the Logic of Disengagement', *Foreign Affairs* (January/February 2005): 25–36.

33   For comparative studies on American rehabilitation and reconstruction experiences see James Dobbins, *America's Role in Nation-Building: From Germany to Iraq*, Santa Monica: RAND, 2003 and his abridged version in 'America's Role in Nation-Building: From Germany to Iraq', *Survival*, 45/4 (Winter 2003–04): 87–110. Dobbins will modify his views in 'Iraq the Unwinnable War', *Foreign Affairs* (January/February 2005): 16–25.

Rebuilding Iraq's Power Structure

The United States sought to reconstitute Iraqi power in insurrectional conditions. The insurrection was far from being spontaneous.[34] First, it was fuelled by members of Saddam's dynasty and diehard and disgruntled members of the Baath party. Second, it was supported by a growing Sunni Jihadist contingent presumably led by Zarqawi. Third, it was also sustained by local militias and tribal groups eager to express a mix of Islamic-nationalist resentment against US occupation.[35] On the ground, all sections of the insurrection appeared to coordinate their strikes against Iraqi government officials, politicians, US occupation forces and Iraqis in general. The reconstitution of the Iraqi power structure was mortgaged by the refusal of the Sunni polity to renounce to its traditional power privileges. Although the January 2005 elections represented a preliminary step towards the reconstitution of the Iraqi state, the remaining obstacles were daunting. Ensconced in their triangle in the centre of Iraq, the Sunnis faced the fact that their capacity to rule Iraq was substantially reduced. The Shi'a hoped to rule Iraq thanks to their demographic weight and control of southern Iraq.[36] The Kurds were looking forward to consolidating their autonomy in the north while waiting for the right moment to declare independence. The end result was that Iraq was heading towards partition.[37] If Iraq was to remain a single country, the three constitutive parts of the nation had to agree on some essential founding principles. If Washington failed to seal a pact between them, partition seemed almost inevitable and its consequences in the Middle East even more dire than Yugoslavia's break-up was in Europe. A quasi-independent Iraqi Kurdistan would generate tremendous tensions with neighbouring states. The United States would thus be amending Sykes-Picot[38] by creating a brand new state in the Middle East; a bad omen for Turkey, Syria and Iran. In the course of drafting a new constitution the Shi'a majority insisted on Islamic principles and obedience to the Shari'a but eventually agreed to complement it with democratic and human rights principles. Furthermore the Shi'a majority lacked state experience and sought to consult Teheran on how to run a country. Washington seemed to take the creeping

---

34   Dexter Filkins and David S. Cloud, 'Defying U.S. Efforts, Guerrillas in Iraq Refocus and Strengthen', *The New York Times*, July 23, 2005: A1/5.

35   See the testimony of Daniel L. Glaser, Acting Assistant Secretary Office of Terrorist Financing and Financial Crimes, US Department of the Treasury, Before the House Financial Services Subcommittee on Oversight and Investigations and the House Armed Services Subcommittee on Terrorism, July 28, 2005, <http://financialservices.house.gov/media/pdf/072805dg.pdf>.

36   Edward Wong, 'Secular Shiites in Iraq Seek Autonomy in Oil-Rich South', *The New York Times*, June 30, 2005: A16/1.

37   See notably Galbraith's thesis on this possible outcome, Peter W. Galbraith, 'How to Get out of Iraq', *New York Review of Books*, 51/8, May 13, 2004 and 'Iraq: The Bungled Transition', *New York Review of Books*, 51/14, September 23, 2004.

38   Efraim Karsh and Inari Karsh, *Empires of the Sand: The Struggle for Mastery in the Middle East, 1789–1923*, Cambridge, 2001, 259–269.

Iranian influence in Iraq's politics in stride[39] and allowed a moderate Islamist Iraqi party supported by the Shi'a clergy to run the state in a secular manner since it had really no other option.

Which Exit Strategy?

During the first year of its second mandate, the Bush Administration had not identified a deadline for a complete withdrawal of US troops from Iraq. Bush believed he could do so only when the United States reached its stated goal: to rebuild the Iraqi state to the extent it could reasonably provide security to its citizens. But with constant losses of American troops and suicide bombings showing no sign of abating, Congress and public opinion appeared to demand an end to occupation. Two problems needed to be addressed in this regard: (1) the consequences of a complete withdrawal before the United States and its allies succeed in rehabilitating Iraq; (2) in the case where such withdrawal remained imperative and a functional Iraqi state failed to appear, the conditions for internationalizing the occupation which would allow the United States to disengage.[40]

Despite optimistic assessments to the effect that Iraqis were on their way to providing for their own security, the United States did not believe it could afford to withdraw from Iraq because withdrawal would expose the country to a certain civil war and the effective partition of Iraq accompanied by the intervention of neighbouring non-Arab and Arab states. The emerging Iraqi government did not have at its disposal efficient armed forces and intelligence capabilities and US military authorities faced a long road to forming a military and security establishment in Iraq.

Nor did the replacement of US military authorities by an international force, as suggested by several observers, seem a viable prospect. For one thing, the majority of principal powers declined to go down that path as long as the United States retained primacy in deciding Iraq's future. In fact the trend among US allies in Iraq was how to reduce their forces. If Europe remained non committal, it was hard to see how other major states could embark into the unknown. None of the Arab states, or Russia, China or India, showed interest in engaging in the Iraqi cauldron without any perceived benefits or national security imperatives. As usual, the response was minimalist and all major powers preferred to pass the buck to the United States and Britain. But the internationalization option remained on the table in the eventuality that the United States would become unable to manage threats to Iraq and the Middle East of a magnitude that major powers would find it intolerable to their own security.[41]

---

39   Not without serious objections, see Edward Wong, 'Iraq Dances with Iran, America seethes' *The New York Times*, July 31, 2005.

40   The option to internationalize was proposed for instance by Kissinger; see note 29.

41   A glimpse of that possibility demonstrated itself at the G8 Summit on July 7th, 2005, when the leaders of all major powers stood solemnly in line behind a visibly shaken Tony

Reform and Democracy in the *Dar Al-Islam*

In reality, the United States was far from having an exit strategy because it intended to build democratic institutions in Iraq and in the broader Middle East. Iraq appeared to be a testing ground for a democratic Islamic area stretching from Morocco to Pakistan. This may have sounded an impossible mission, but the Bush Administration was bent on achieving this program against all odds.[42] The Administration considered that not to take up this mission would be tantamount to inviting yet another Jihadi attack on the United States, this time even more destructive than 9/11. Undeniably, this program for democratic reform required the same bipartisan consensus and a multigenerational investment to those of the Cold War. Compared to other US grand strategies, recasting domestic political structures in the Middle East represented perhaps the most complex and ambitious project because it concerned the transformation of a region that conceives politics as extension of a religious belief, that is not simply personal but a way of life for entire communities.

The Greater Middle East Initiative

Although Bush had alluded to the need for developing democracy in Arab states since 2002, we can see elements of this initiative in his speech of November 5, 2003.[43] The speech buildt on US achievements in rebuilding Germany and Japan as full-fledged democratic states, examined the progress achieved in Russia and China towards democracy and congratulated India for remaining the largest democracy in the world. But the principal subject of the speech was democratization of Islamic societies. After having affirmed that democracy and Islam are not incompatible, Bush chided Western nations, including the United States, for having favoured stability at the expense of freedom in the Middle East:[44] a clear indication that America would no longer remain indifferent to political development in the Arab and Islamic world.

Blair announcing Britain's response to the London suicide bombings. Having timed their bombings with the summit, the Jihadists appeared to remind established powers, including China and India, of the absence of a Muslim global power.

   42   See his second inaugural speech: George W. Bush, 'Second Inaugural Address', January 20, 2005, <http://www.whitehouse.gov/news/releases/2005/01/20050120-1.html>.

   43   George W. Bush, 'Freedom in Iraq and Middle East', Remarks by the President at the 20th Anniversary of the National Endowment for Democracy United States Chamber of Commerce, Washington, DC, November 5, 2003, <http://www.whitehouse.gov/news/releases/2003/11/20031106-2.html>; see also his 'Whitehall' speech, George W. Bush, 'Remarks on Iraq Policy at Whitehall Palace', November 19, 2003, <http://www.whitehouse.gov/news/releases/2003/11/20031119-1.html>; see George W. Bush, 'Importance of Democracy in Middle East; Remarks on Winston Churchill and the War on Terror', February 4, 2004, <http://www.whitehouse.gov/news/releases/2004/02/20040204-4.html>.

   44   'Sixty years of Western nations excusing and accommodating the lack of freedom in the Middle East did nothing to make us safe – because in the long run, stability cannot be purchased at the expense of liberty. As long as the Middle East remains a place where freedom does not flourish, it will remain a place of stagnation, resentment, and violence

The initiative drew from the Arab Human Development Reports prepared by a group of Arab academics and researchers published by the United Nations Development Program (UNDP).[45] US planners intended to submit the initiative to the next G8 Summit at Sea Island in June 2004. Details of the initiative were not published and most Arab governments were not consulted. It was an Arab journal, *Dar Al-Hayat*, published in London, which revealed some of its details in February 2004.[46] Given the early opposition and criticism towards the initiative, Washington quickly modified the scope of the initiative to win the approval of its partners at Sea Island who finally approved a far less ambitious program for reform.

The initiative was devoid of a security dimension. One would have expected that the settlement of Middle Eastern conflicts, such as the Israeli-Palestinian conflict, would have been a starting point for reform. The absence of this dimension was a surprise to most observers and reform architects. The initiative consisted of three features. First, it focused on promoting democratic political processes through the free participation of political parties, the creation of independent electoral commissions, free elections monitored by international bodies, the extension of freedom of expression and association and promotion of a free judiciary. It also comprised the development of secular laws not contradicting the principles of the Shari'a, and improvement of women's participation in elections and their representation at all levels of governance.

The initiative included an economic dimension aiming essentially to improve conditions for investment in the Middle East by encouraging the repatriation of significant capital back to the region. To that end the initiative thought it would be well-advised to create a Middle Eastern development bank and promote micro-financing programs. The initiative called upon Arab-Islamic states to liberalize their trade policies as a condition for be admission to the WTO.

The socio-cultural feature appeared the most problematic from the viewpoint of its implementation. For example, it aimed to promote change in the societal attitude towards women in Islamic civil societies and included a literacy program especially for girls and younger women. In spite of its comprehensive nature, the initiative was silent about Middle Eastern minorities whose number dwindled with the failure of Arab modernization, the conflict with Israel and the emergence of totalitarian

---

ready for export. And with the spread of weapons that can bring catastrophic harm to our country and to our friends, it would be reckless to accept the status quo.' George W. Bush, 'Freedom in Iraq and Middle East: Remarks by the President at the 20th Anniversary of the National Endowment for Democracy', November 5, 2003, <http://www.whitehouse.gov/news/releases/2003/11/20031106-2.html>.

45   United Nations Development Programme, Arab Fund for Economic and Social Development, *Arab Human Development Report 2002: Creating Opportunities for Future Generations*, New York, 2002; and *Ibid., Arab Human Development Report 2003: Building a Knowledge Society*, New York, 2003.

46   *Dar Al-Hayat*, 'U.S. Working Paper For G-8 Sherpas: G-8 Greater Middle East Partnership', February 13, 2003, <http://english.daralhayat.com/Spec/02-2004/Article-20040213-ac40bdaf-c0a8-01ed-004e-5e7ac897d678/story.html>.

behaviour and intolerance in Islamic societies. The initiative did not dwell on how to implement these reforms; it ignored why autocratic regimes would be interested in engaging in the reform process and power relations in Islamic countries that would sustain it in the long run. In sum, the initiative remained a tentative draft whose structure appeared at best underdeveloped.[47]

Negative Reactions

Once revealed, the initiative was opposed by several constituencies. On one hand, Arab states accused the United States of not having consulted them about a project which indeed concerned their countries. Mubarak, amongst others, characterized it as illusory.[48] Most rejected the notion of the 'Greater Middle East'[49] since the Arab world figured in a motley geopolitical space in which one could find traditional allies of the United States (e.g. Turkey and Pakistan) and less traditional ones. The final communiqué of the Arab League's summit in May 2004 suggested that reforms must stem from Arab countries. On the other hand, European states did not seem overly enthused by the initiative because it interfered with the objectives of their Euro-Mediterranean Partnership (the Barcelona process) introduced in 1995. Moreover, Brussels was promoting its newly established European Neighbourhood Policy (ENP), which aimed to create a ring of friendly states around the borders of the new enlarged EU. Nevertheless, Brussels thought there was a need to coordinate European initiatives with the United States at a time when Washington seemed more than ever willing to engage in the future of the Arab and Islamic world.

At first blush, the program to democratize the greater Middle East appeared laudable, but faced daunting obstacles. First, the United States lacked credibility in the Arab world as a result of its pro-Israeli stance, misunderstandings and faulty communication with Arab publics. Washington has long been identified with the policies of autocratic Arab states and the Israeli occupation of Palestine, not to mention its own occupation of Iraq. To reclaim its credibility, the United States needed to establish direct links with Arab civil societies who were tired of their governing elites and mired in a political culture increasingly at odds with present

---

47   For a detailed outline of this initiative, see International Crisis Group, *The Broader Middle East and North Africa Initiative: Imperilled at Birth*, Middle East Briefing, June 7, 2004, <http://www.crisisweb.org/home/getfile.cfm?id=1268&tid=2795>.

48   Joel Brinkley, 'U.S. Slows Bid to Advance Democracy in Arab World', *The New York Times*, December 5, 2004: A28.

49   According to the Bush Administration's geopolitical vision, the Greater Middle East would include not only Arab states, from the Atlantic Ocean to the Persian Gulf, but also Turkey, the Caucasus, Central Asia, Iran, Afghanistan and Pakistan. This vision engulfs the geopolitical range of Europe's own projects of Euro-Mediterranean Partnership and European Neighbourhood Policy (ENP), see Völker Perthes, 'America's 'Greater Middle East' and 'Europe: Key Issues For Dialogue', *Middle East Policy*, XI/3 (Fall 2004): 88; Mona Yacoubian, *Promoting Middle East Democracy: European Initiatives*, United States Institute of Peace Special Report 127, October 2004.

global political trends. Since the Arab opinion seemed outmanoeuvred by Islamist parties and movements, they remained somewhat closed to anything that emanated from the United States. Their change of attitude depended on the willingness of Washington to understand Arab grievances and to make Arab governments accountable for their lack of initiatives for reform. Clearly, Arab publics expected the United States to play an active role in bringing about significant changes that were perceptibly beneficial to Arab and Muslim populations.

Second, the United States did not develop a clear view as to how concretely bring about political, economic and social reforms in a region where the application of Western-style democracies have proven elusive. Basic concepts were relatively easy to articulate, but the greater challenge resided in their implementation. The United States continued to be unconvinced that autocratic leaders needed to be pressured to reform.[50] For instance, as a result of repeated Arab criticism of US plans for reform, Washington modified its stance several times. It first placed emphasis on economic and social reforms in its initiative, but after Rafik Hariri's assassination in February 2005 it supported Georgian-style political changes in Lebanon (including mass demonstration in Beyrouth) to end Syria's grip on Lebanon. Even though Bush and Secretary of State Rice were convinced that democratic reforms represent an indispensable goal, there remained old imperatives which they could not ignore: security, oil and Israel.[51] To advocate reform at the expense of these three imperatives would indeed throw US Middle Eastern policy into disarray. This preoccupation seemed to dictate American ambivalence towards moderate Islamist parties: if political reforms are imperative and autocratic regimes unable to reform, is it necessary to seek agreement with Islamist parties? If contacts with these parties are out of question, as the Secretary of State suggested in a question and answer period in Cairo,[52] what are then the other political parties or forces that can promote reform?

Third, the eyes of the Arab and Islamic world were fixed on the rehabilitation of the Iraqi state and civil society under the aegis of the United States. In the absence of clear signs of rehabilitation, Arab publics tended to believe that American reforms were pipe dreams and perhaps a sinister American plot to keep Arab and Islamic countries in perpetual servitude. Not only had Iraqis to demonstrate that under the US security umbrella relatively free elections were feasible, but also to show that it was possible to develop a political process free of autocratic interference, both of which were not easy to achieve given the prevailing insecurities in Iraq.

---

50   Thomas L. Friedman, 'Holding Up Arab Reform', *The New York Times*, December 16, 2004.

51   See Marina Ottaway, 'United States: Can Its Middle East Policy Serve Democracy?', *Arab Reform Bulletin*, 3/6, July 2005.

52   Question and Answer at the American University in Cairo, Secretary Condoleezza Rice, Cairo, Egypt, June 20, 2005, <http://www.state.gov/secretary/rm/2005/48352.htm>.

Conclusion

Under the Bush Administration, the United States engaged in conflicts to modernize the Arab-Islamic world. To be sure, this was not a project that the United States wanted to undertake. For a long time, it hesitated to engage in the political, economic and social modernization of Arab states and societies. To neoconservative strategists, this engagement was similar to the struggle against communism and the USSR that resulted in the utter defeat of that ideology and state. The United States took up this challenge to radically transform the Arab-Islamic world without relying upon a strategy or long-term policy. Contrary to the policy of containment, the United States has yet to develop a comprehensive policy towards Islamism. Is Islamism an ideology compatible with American values? Would America accept coexistence with Islamist states? If these states decide to coalesce in an Islamist bloc, would the United States oppose the rise of such a global power? [53]

The Administration has thus far not provided a clear answer to these questions which the chief architect of US foreign policy, Condoleezza Rice, must have asked. During its second mandate, the Bush Administration faces an Arab world less inclined to live under autocratic and dynastic regimes with whom the United States continues to maintain close relations. If their replacement means the advent of Islamist parties, Washington may well seek common ground with them. However, the United States does not appear to have found that common ground. The absence of reference to Islamism in the Bush Administration's statements and policies suggests that the United States would not object to interacting with governments led by Islamist majorities. But if Islamist parties decide to challenge US power in the Middle East, Washington may not have any choice but to proceed to destroy their social and political bases.

If results of the January 2005 elections are any indication, the region may have witnessed a turning point where Islamist parties gain power through elections.[54] If we set aside the Islamist performance in Algeria following the refusal of the incumbent government to accept the election results in 1992, it is not clear that Islamist majorities would sustain themselves in power if they accept the rules of the

---

53   Arab states are said to have tried to constitute without success a Middle Eastern power, see for instance, Ian Lustick, 'The Absence of Middle Eastern Great Powers: Political "Backwardness" in Historical Perspective', *International Organization*, 51/4 (Autumn 1997): 653–83. Lustick explains the absence of Middle Eastern great powers in the three failed attempts of Middle Eastern states to build power (1840, 1957–70, 1990–91). If we follow the logic of this study, the bin Laden episode would be the fourth attempt, this time through a Pan-Islamist movement and ideology which appears to be more effective than the Pan-Arab nationalist project promoted essentially by states.

54   See Bush's advice to Egypt and Saudi Arabia in his State of the Union Address, February 2, 2005, <http://www.whitehouse.gov/news/releases/2005/02/20050202-11.html>, which he reiterated before European leaders on February 20, 2005. George W. Bush, 'President Discusses American and European Alliance in Belgium', <http://www.whitehouse.gov/news/releases/2005/02/20050221.html>.

game of democracy. The present constitutional process underway in Iraq suggests that when Islamist parties play by these rules secular groups can check Islamist ambitions for total power. The constant and careful building of democratic political processes in the Arab-Islamic world would eventually strengthen the development of secular movements representing the interests of diverse sections of civil society, provided that Islamist majorities do not resort to violent methods to gain and maintain power.

Chapter 7

The Clash Between Europe and the United States: A New Cold War?

Julien Tourreille and Élisabeth Vallet[1]

> Nations also drift, and their sentiments drift with them. At some times,
> two peoples move closer, drawn together by a movement with complex
> causes; at other times, they move apart, carried by opposing currents.[2]

'The world needs the United States more than the United States needs the world. That is not a definition but a characteristic of hegemony.'[3] Whether it is viewed as model or foil, as a standard-bearer of modernity or of neo-imperialism, the United States provokes both exasperation and fascination. It has nourished an abundant literature, which similarly alternates between Americophilia, Americophobia and Americomania.[4] Described as a 'hyperpower' by former French Minister of Foreign Affairs Hubert Védrine, accused of imperialism,[5] the US is at the centre of a unipolar

---

1   The authors would like to thank Charles-Philippe David and David Grondin for their support and John Detre for his most helpful assistance.

2   René Rémond, *Les États-Unis devant l'opinion française 1815–1852* (Paris: Armand Colin, Cahiers de la fondation nationale des sciences politiques, 1962), Vol. 2, p. 867.

3   Serge Sur, 'L'hégémonie américaine en question', *Annuaire français de relations internationales* 2002, <http://www.dossiersdunet.com>.

4   The term 'américanomanie' was coined by Denis Lacorne and Jacques Rupnik, 'La France saisie par l'Amérique', in Denis Lacorne, Jacques Rupnik, Marie-France Toinet (eds), *L'Amérique dans les têtes – Un siècle de fascinations et d'aversions* (Paris: Hachette, 1986), p. 12.

5   Daniel Vernet, 'Impérialisme post-moderne', *Le Monde*, 25 April 2003. The US is charged with dominating everything from legal culture and plea bargaining practices to freedom of the skies, accounting standards and copyright rules. See *Le Monde*, 'Globalisation, américanisation?' *Thématique*, 10 November 2004, <www.lemonde.fr>. See also Élisabeth Vallet, 'L'empire américain et ses nouveaux barbares : Discussions autour de la qualification du rôle des États-Unis dans le monde', bibliographic study, *Études internationales*, 36/4 (December 2005).

historic moment[6] characterized by a widely decried unilateralism[7] that appears to have prevailed since the end of the Cold War. *Transatlantic Trends 2004*, a series of surveys commissioned by the German Marshall Fund, confirms the decline of the United States' image in Europe. And this is a snapshot of European public opinion taken before the Abu Ghraib scandal, Jimmy Carter's statements about Guantanamo and the revelations about CIA 'black sites'.

However, while they are negative, European perceptions of the US are not uniform, as is evident in the cacophony of diplomatic voices raised in the lead-up to the Iraq war. Indeed, the very notion of 'European public opinion' is being questioned.[8] Moreover, most pollsters operate through the prism of EU member states, entrenching the national dimension in their analysis,[9] even though the EU recognizes the existence of a 'European people'.[10]

Divergences and common points in European public opinion about the United States in general and US hegemony in particular are of historic origin. The American mirage has never been viewed dispassionately.[11] The US was born of a rupture with the Old World, as an 'antidote to Europe'[12] far removed from European politics, from which George Washington was determined to separate the new nation.[13] This may be seen as the beginning of what Robert Kagan has described as the Mars/Venus split between the US and Europe. That discussion, which Kagan casts in caricatured terms, has provided fodder for editorials, analyses and academic polemics, lending

---

6   See Charles Krauthammer, 'The Unipolar Moment', *Foreign Affairs* (Winter 1990–1991): 23–33. Samuel P. Huntington, 'The Lonely Superpower', *Foreign Affairs* (March–April 1999). This unipolar moment may even be a unipolar 'era': Joseph Nye, 'Limits of American Power', *Political Science Quarterly*, 117/4 (Winter 2002–2003): 545.

7   See Jürgen Habermas, 'Letter to America', *The Nation*, 16 December 2002; James Wirtz, James Russell, 'US Policy on Preventive War and Preemption', *The Non-proliferation Review* (Spring 2003): 113; Charles W. Kegley Jr, 'Preventive War and Permissive Normative Order', *International Studies Perspectives* 4 (2003): 385–394; Michael Byers, 'Preemptive Self-defense: Hegemony, Equality and Strategies of Legal Change', *The Journal of Political Philosophy*, 11/2 (2003): 171–190; Michael Byer, 'Jumping the Gun', *London Review of Books*, 25 July 2002.

8   Robert Graham, 'A European Public Opinion Is Just an EU Pipe Dream', *Europe's World* (Fall 2005): 70–75.

9   Claes H. de Vreese, 'How Europe's Media Report the EU Through National Prisms', *Europe's World* (Fall 2005): 71–73.

10   See Florence Chaltiel, *Manuel de droit de l'Union européenne* (Paris: PUF, Droit fondamental, 2005), pp. 62–64.

11   Gilbert Chinard, 'Le mirage américain', in *Les réfugiés huguenots en Amérique* (Paris: Les Belles Lettres, 1925), p. XXIX; Bruno Tertrais, 'L'Amérique qu'on aime détester', *Le Figaro*, 22 July 2004.

12   Michael Kelly, 'The Divided States of Europe', *The Washington Post*, 13 June 2001.

13   Louis Balthazar, 'Aux sources de l'antiaméricanisme', in Charles-Philippe David (ed.), *Nous antiaméricains? Les États-Unis et le Monde*, Les Cahiers Raoul-Dandurand (March 2003): 25.

the debate breadth if not sense.[14] Here, the contrast between the two cultures is seen as a confrontation between two Messianic visions,[15] the city on the hill versus a EU-topia[16] founded on the values of Schuman and Monnet.[17]

Without embracing the clash of civilizations between Europe and the US predicted by Charles Kupchan,[18] we might be able to agree with René Rémond that there is a civilization gap.[19] Naturally, every nation views others through the prism of its own values and culture[20] and this is the basis for the European view of US hegemony. But while Kagan stresses the irreconcilable mythologies, there is clearly a degree of mutual dependence.[21] Continental drift would appear to be a near-inescapable feature of the new international disorder. However, we cannot ignore the community of values between the US and Europe, which transcends the recent chill in transatlantic relations.

Continental Drift in the Age of US Hegemony

The image of the United States in the rest of the world is deteriorating due to the widening chasm between the way Americans see themselves and how they are seen by others.[22] Two varieties of anti-Americanism spring from this soil: one assails Americans for what they do and the other for what they are.[23] Both views have a

---

14 See Timothy Garton Ash, 'Anti-Europeanism in America', *Hoover Digest* 2 (2003), <www.hooverdigest.org>.

15 Andrew Moravcsik, 'The World Is Bipolar After All', *Newsweek*, 5 May 2004; Charles Kupchan, 'The End of the West', *The Atlantic Monthly* (November 2002). René Rémond makes the same point in his discussion of mid-19th century perspectives: 'Regarding the United States, two societies, two moral conceptions, two forms of civilization stood in opposition.' René Rémond, p. 649.

16 Timothy Garton Ash, <www.hooverdigest.org>.

17 'The contribution which an organized and living Europe can bring to civilization is indispensable to the maintenance of peaceful relations. [...] A united Europe was not achieved and we had war.' Schuman Declaration, 9 May 1950. For behind European messianism lies the idea that 'the impact of American preponderance is softened when it is embodied in a web of multilateral institutions'. Joseph Nye, 'Limits of American Power', *Political Science Quarterly* 17/4, (Winter 2002–2003): 553.

18 Charles Kupchan, 'The End of the America Era: U.S. Foreign Policy and the Geopolitics of the Twenty-first Century' (New York: Alfred A. Knopf, 2002).

19 See René Rémond, pp. 864–865.

20 Christian Deblock, 'Le côté obscur de la force', in Charles-Philippe David (ed.), *Nous antiaméricains?* p. 33.

21 Julian Lindley-French, 'Les termes de l'engagement : le paradoxe de la puissance américaine et le dilemme transatlantique après le 11 septembre', *Cahiers de Chaillot* 52 (May 2002): 5–91.

22 *Ibid.*

23 Stanley Hoffman, 'Why Don't They Like Us?' *The American Prospect* 19 (November 2001).

long history and cool transatlantic relations are by no means a new phenomenon: 'Anti-Americanism isn't back; it never went away.'[24] But while anti-Americanism arose in the mid-19th century,[25] the war in Iraq[26] has lent it unprecedented 'scope and legitimacy'.[27]

Cycles in European Perceptions of the US

The idea that things have changed is sometimes couched in dramatic terms; it has been argued that 'Europeans have never held so low an opinion of America as they do today'[28] and that 'never again will transatlantic relations be what they were'.[29]

Salience of Anti-Americanism in Public Opinion Cycles

The fiery speeches and editorials denouncing US imperialism and arrogance during George W. Bush's first term echo some of the books and articles published during the Reagan presidency. To be fair, however, it must also be said that 'Reagan-mania' flourished during Ronald Reagan's first term; so much so that on November 10, 1984, *Le Figaro* headlined 'The Decline of Anti-Americanism in France' and in September 1984 *Le Nouvel Observateur* published a special report on 'Life in America'. President Mitterrand contended that the American model was applicable in France[30] and Marie-France Toinet claimed that Americophiles were morphing into Americoworhippers.[31] It was only later, as Reagan's gaffes and unqualified statements accumulated, that public opinion turned and became fiercely anti-American. The Reagan period therefore demonstrates the cyclical nature of European perceptions of American doings. Waves of Americomania have alternated with anti-Americanism since the creation of the American Republic.[32]

Perceptions of the US in France are a distorting mirror of European perceptions in three ways. First, because for the past two centuries, France has been a great

---

24   Gilles Finchelstein, 'France-États-Unis : regards croisés', *Le Banquet* 21 (October 2004): 19.

25   See Philippe Roger, *L'ennemi américain. Généalogie de l'antiaméricanisme français* (Paris: Seuil, 2002), p. 10.

26   See Michel Gueldry, *Les États-Unis et l'Europe face à la guerre d'Irak* (Paris: L'Harmattan, 2005).

27   For this argument, see *Le Débat* 125 (May–August 2003): 291.

28   Fraser Cameron, 'Comment l'Europe voit les États-Unis', *Le Banquet* 21 (October 2004): 239.

29   Édouard Balladur, Axel Poniatowski, 'Les relations entre l'Europe et les États-Unis', Rapport d'information, Commission des Affaires étrangères, Assemblée nationale, 11 October 2005: 5.

30   Jean Boissonnat, 'Mitterrand parle', *L'Expansion*, 16 November 1984.

31   Marie-France Toinet, 'L'antiaméricanisme existe-t-il', in Denis Lacorne, Jacques Rupnik, Marie-France Toinet, p. 268.

32   See Alain Duhamel, *Le complexe d'Astérix* (Paris: Gallimard, 1985).

power and then a middle power in Europe, distinct from the great power Britain, a traditional ally of the American Republic. The case of France is particularly relevant here because 'what was specific to France – the obsession with American power – has become a more widely shared concern in western Europe'.[33] Second, because it is in France that the pendulum of public opinion swings back and forth the farthest, while the relative stability of the French state gives us a constant sample over time. Third, because until quite recently Franco-American relations were an extensively studied barometer of transatlantic relations.[34]

The Obsession with the US in French Public Opinion

The US has had its detractors and its admirers since Lafayette, and later the creation of the *Revue américaine* in 1826.[35] 'At the end of the Restoration, political sympathy for the United States was at its acme' and it would have been difficult to foresee 'the reversal of public opinion that was the most salient feature of the July Monarchy.'[36] French opinion grew hostile to the US (in 1832, it was possible to speak of 'a general assault on American institutions'[37]) and it was only at the end of World War I, with the American intervention in late 1917, that the anti-American currents subsided and pro-American sentiment revived.[38] Marie-France Toinet notes 'the importance [...] and high calibre of French studies of American political institutions in the early 20th century'. She lists some thirty works on the topic produced between 1900 and 1940.[39] But the French did not necessarily understand Wilson's goals[40] and the enthusiasm in popular opinion and on the editorial pages declined.[41] With no agreement on debt

---

33   Jacques Rupnik, 'Les meilleurs amis de l'Amérique en Europe – Les perceptions et les politiques de l'Europe centrale et de l'Est à l'égard des États-Unis', *Le Banquet* 21 (October 2004): 42.

34   However, times have changed. In 2004, the Brookings Institution changed the name of its Center on the United States and France to the Center on the United States and Europe, indicating a change or at least a new perspective on the degree of France's representativeness in Europe.

35   René Rémond, pp. 626–627.

36   *Ibid.*, pp. 655 and 659.

37   *Ibid.*, p. 696.

38   On this point, see Jean-Baptiste Duroselle, *La France et les États-Unis – Des origines à nos jours* (Paris: Seuil, 1976), pp. 108–109.

39   Marie France Toinet, 'Le jugement des jurists', in Denis Lacorne, Jacques Rupnik, Marie-France Toinet, p. 231.

40   See Yves-Henri Nouailhat, *France et États-Unis, août 1914 – avril 1917* (Paris: Publications de la Sorbonne, 1979), pp. 392–398.

41   André Kaspi, *Le temps des Américains. Le concours américain à la France, 1917– 1918* (Paris: Publications de la Sorbonne, 1976).

repayment, anti-Americanism gained ground again[42] and there was a proliferation of books castigating American power.[43]

Prior to European unity, anti-Americanism was primarily nationalist in nature.[44] Thus, at the end of the Second World War, French anti-Americanism identified itself with anti-Germanism.[45] The ground shifted as Gaullist nationalism became the spearhead of European anti-Americanism,[46] upholding a non-aligned policy in the Northern hemisphere.[47] It was not until the decline of the Soviet myth in the 1980s, which had been tarnished by events in Kabul and revelations from Solzhenitsyn, that the American model became saleable again,[48] which did not however prevent 'the resurgence of a neo-Gaullist variant of anti-Americanism.[49] At the end of Ronald Reagan's second term, the editorials grew radical again and anti-Americanism appeared to reach new heights. France's most prominent experts on the US felt impelled to produce a rigorous study of anti-Americanism.[50]

Contemporary European Perceptions

When a coalition assembled around the United States for the first Gulf War, the criticisms of the US were toned down. Subsequently, President Clinton occasionally sparked polemics but his style eased the tensions: he was able to 'maintain good relations between an America that had to some extent lost contact with Europe and a

---

42   Jean-Baptiste Duroselle, p. 137.

43   For example: Robert Aron, Arnaud Dandieu, *Le cancer américain* (Paris: Rieder, 1931), 246 p.; Henri Hauser, *L'impérialisme américain* (Paris: Pages libres, 1905), 127 p.; Lucien Romier, *Qui sera le maître, Europe ou Amérique?* (Paris: Hachette, 1927), 244 p.; Charles Pomaret, *L'Amérique à la conquête de l'Europe* (Paris: Armand Colin, 1931), 287 p.; Émile Boutmy, *Les États-Unis et l'impérialisme* (Paris: Félix Alcan, 1902) – all titles that are eerily similar to some contemporary bestsellers.

44   Marie-France Toinet notes that while the word 'antiaméricanisme' has been in use in France since the 19th century, it was not enshrined in the *Petit Robert* dictionary until 1968, in Denis Lacorne, Jacques Rupnik, Marie-France Toinet, p. 269.

45   Denis Lacorne, Jacques Rupnik, 'La France saisie par l'Amérique', in Denis Lacorne, Jacques Rupnik, Marie-France Toinet, p. 26.

46   See Jean-Baptiste Duroselle, p. 182.

47   See Jean Touchard, *Le gaullisme*, (Paris: Poche, Points histoire, 1978) and Serge Bernstein, *Histoire du gaullisme* (Paris: Poche, Tempus, 2002).

48   See for example Umberto Eco, 'Il mito americano di tre generazioni anti-americane', *Comunicazione di massa* 3 (1980): 133–149. Thierry Chopin, 'L'héritage du fédéralisme – Europe/États-Unis', *Note de la Fondation Robert Schuman* 8, 89 p.; Justin Vaïsse, *Le modèle américain* (Paris: Armand Colin, Synthèses Histoire, 1998), 96 p.

49   Denis Lacorne, Jacques Rupnik, 'La France saisie par l'Amérique', p. 31. The authors cite Régis Debray, *Les Empires contre l'Europe* (Paris: Gallimard, 1985) and Jacques Thibau, *La France colonisée* (Paris: Flammarion, 1980).

50   Denis Lacorne, Jacques Rupnik, Marie-France Toinet, *L'Amérique dans les têtes – Un siècle de fascinations et d'aversions* (Paris: Hachette, 1986).

Europe that was beginning to have little ideological affinity with the United States'.[51] The election of George W. Bush in November 2000, at a time when European public opinion was starting to converge with American opinion, led some to think that the United States would disengage from the international arena.[52] Then September 11 united the countries of the EU around a wounded America. However, European public opinion shifted sharply in response to the second Gulf War. By 2003, the perception of the US in Europe was sharply negative, the editorials had grown trenchant again, and pundits were again predicting the demise of the transatlantic relationship. (See Figure 7.1.)

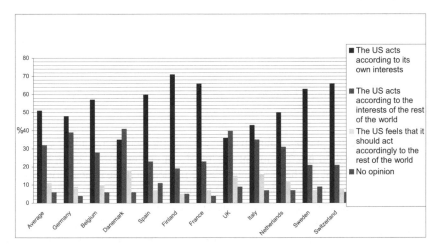

Figure 7.1 In Your Opinion, What are the Core Objectives of US Action in the World?

Source: 'Europeans believe US foreign policy is destabilizing the world.' Survey conducted by TNS Sofres between September 17 and October 7, 2003 for CNN and *Time* magazine with a sample of 1,000 people in Belgium, Denmark, Finland, France, Germany, Great Britain, Italy, the Netherlands, Spain, Sweden and Switzerland, using representative samples in each country <http://www.tns-sofres.com/presse_communique.php?id=228>.

As can be seen, anti-American cycles have been recurrent in French public opinion, which provides a prism through which we can observe European perceptions of US hegemony. We need to place today's anti-Americanism in perspective and look beyond the 'seasonal variations' if we wish to understand it.[53] Between Jean-Baptiste Duroselle, who spoke of a 'hereditary enemy', and Philippe Roger, who speaks of the 'American enemy', there have been multiple cycles of love and hate which the simple Mars/Venus duality cannot account for. We need to distinguish

---

51   See Michael Cox, 'Qu'est-il arrivé à la relation transatlantique? L'Amérique vue par l'Europe : de la guerre froide à la guerre contre le terrorisme', *Le Banquet* 21 (October 2004): 89.

52   See Elisabeth Vallet in *L'année stratégique 2002* (Paris: IRIS, 2002).

53   Philippe Roger, p. 10.

anti-Americanism as an oppositional stance by a cultural minority from criticism of US hegemony based on foreign policy positions.[54] European perceptions of US hegemony are not absolute, still less immutable, and they sometimes stem from 'lack of understanding of American diversity, which is veiled by inopportune statements by the United States' official representatives'.[55] It is in this light that we should view the intensity of transatlantic differences during the second Gulf War.

Transatlantic Differences During the Second Gulf War

'The transatlantic differences over the war in Iraq undermined America's relationship with Europeans to some extent', concluded the analysts who produced *Transatlantic Trends 2003*.[56] But this overlooks the state of affairs prior to September 11. A Pew Center poll conducted in August 2001 found considerable hostility to the US administration's policies.[57]

The Paradoxical Contrast Between Perceptions of US Hegemony and the
Importance of the Transatlantic Relationship

It has been suggested that the antagonism to US hegemony lessened after September 11,[58] which marked an interruption in the history of contemporary European anti-Americanism, and that this helps account for the sudden increase in hostility towards the US afterwards. For example, Anand Menon and Jonathan Lipkin discuss the 'temporary change in attitude towards the United States'[59] in platitudinous terms. In fact, the transatlantic crisis reflects a deeper 'double disjunction':[60] on the one hand, the linkage between European security and US intervention has been broken

---

54   Ben Tonra, *Misperception, Asymmetry and Desequilibrium – Addressing Challenges to the Transatlantic Relationship, Transatlantic Divide*, International Conference, University of Victoria, 11–13 June 2004.

55   Louis Balthazar, 'Aux sources de l'antiaméricanisme', in Charles-Philippe David (ed.), *Nous antiaméricains?* p. 27.

56   'Europeans Question the Role of U.S. as Superpower, While Americans Support U.S. Involvement Overseas in Record Numbers', *Transatlantic Trends* 2003, p. 1, <http://www.transatlantictrends.org>.

57   The Pew Research Center for the People and the Press, 'Bush Unpopular in Europe, Seen As Unilateralist', Survey Report, 15 August 2001, <http://people-press.org/reports/display.php3?ReportID=5>.

58   See The Pew Research Center for the People and the Press, 'America Admired, yet its New Vulnerability Seen as Good Thing, Say Opinion Leaders', *Survey Report*, 19 December 2001, <http://people-press.org/reports/display.php3?ReportID=145>.

59   See Anand Menon, Jonathan Lipkin, 'Les attitudes européennes et reations transatlantiques entre 2000 et 2003 : une vision analytique', Rhodes and Kastellorizo, Groupement d'études et de recherches Notre Europe, *Études et Recherches*, 26 (May 2003): 7.

60   Stephen Klimczuk, 'The Transatlantic Yin and Yang', *The Globalist*, 19 January 2005.

(as evidenced by the Europeanization of Balkan conflicts) and, on the other, the Atlantic alliance no longer appears as important for the defence of US interests (hence the US refusal to invoke Article 5 of the NATO Charter).[61] Nevertheless, the transatlantic bond is vital.[62] According to Colin Powell, the 'transatlantic marriage is intact, remains strong, will weather any differences that come along'.[63] It accounts for 70% of world trade:[64]

> [T]he EU and the US both account for around one fifth of each other's bilateral trade, a matter of €1 billion a day. In 2003, exports of EU goods to the US amounted to € 226 billion (25.8% of total EU exports), while imports from the US amounted to € 157.2 billion (16.8% of total EU imports).[65]

In all, 12 million jobs depend on US–EU trade.[66] Therefore, 'the transatlantic community of values and interests has no equal'[67] and 'the forces supporting the transatlantic edifice are more powerful than those trying to pull it down'.[68] This is probably why there is talk of '*contestation partenariale*' [challenging hegemony to replace it with partnership],[69] for while they do not wish a final break,[70] 'a growing number of Europeans want to play a more independent role in a world where U.S. leadership is less omnipresent'.[71]

---

61   Édouard Balladur, Axel Poniatowski, p. 15.

62   Pierre-Louis Malfatto, *Le processus de consultation et de coopération entre l'Union européenne et les États-Unis*, Grenoble, M.A. thesis, Séminaire Grands problèmes européens, manuscript (2000).

63   Colin Powell, 'Remarks at the Davos Economic Forum', Davos, 26 January 2003, <http://www.state.gov/secretary/rm/2003/16869.htm>.

64   Andrew Moravcsik, 'Striking a New Transatlantic Bargain', *Foreign Affairs* 82/4 (2003): 82–84. 'Every working day, nearly $1 billion in commercial transactions take place between the US and France': Ambassador Leach, 'Les relations économiques franco-américaines : une affaire qui marche', *Les Echos*, 1 February 2005.

65   European Commission, *Bilateral Trade Relations*, September 2004, <http://europa. eu.int/comm/trade/issues/bilateral/countries/usa/index_en.htm> 'The Last EU-US Summit of June 2004 adopted a joint declaration on strengthening our bilateral economic partnership', <http://europa.eu.int/comm/external_relations/us/intro/summit.htm>.

66   Édouard Balladur, Axel Poniatowski, p. 5.

67   *Ibid*, p. 31. See Philip H. Gordon, 'Bridging the Atlantic Divide', *Foreign Affairs* 82/1 (January–February 2003): 70.

68   Michael Cox, p. 84.

69   Serge Sur, online.

70   See Anthony Blinken, 'The False Crisis over the Atlantic', *Foreign Affairs*, 80/3 (May–June 2001).

71   The German Marshall Fund, 'The Transatlantic Relationship One Year After Iraq', *Transatlantic Trends 2004*: <http://www.transatlantictrends.org>.

Paradoxical Coexistence of Transatlantic Cooperation and Diplomatic Tension

All conditions would appear to be in place for the differences of opinion between Colin Powell and Dominique de Villepin, which came to a head at the Security Council, to be smoothed over. Despite the deep disagreements over Iraq, the transatlantic relationship is working relatively well through NATO. For example, NATO added seven new members at its Prague Summit in November 2002 and accepted the principle of a NATO Response Force. Since then, the European Defence and Security Policy (EDSP) has been strengthened, first with four missions in Bosnia, the Former Yugoslav Republic of Macedonia and Congo, and then with the Berlin Plus Permanent Agreement of March 2003, which increased the linkages between European security and NATO capabilities. Finally, the European Council in Brussels bolstered the ties between the EU and NATO through extensive planning procedures. The purpose of the NATO reform launched at the Prague Summit was 'not only to enhance NATO's freedom of action, but make it more European at the same time'.[72] And, in June 2004, when President Bush was in Normandy with Jacques Chirac at his side, transatlantic differences seemed to melt away as they spoke.

So why then did the transatlantic crisis reach such intensity that it seems likely to have serious historic consequences? First, the perceived meaning of September 11 differed on the two sides of the Atlantic. Despite clear demonstrations of sympathy after September 11 (NATO invoked Article 5 of its Charter and offered its support; the countries of Europe unanimously assured the US of their backing[73] and supported the intervention in Afghanistan[74]), Europe did not feel it was 'at war', at least not until the March 11, 2004 attack in Spain. For Europe, the watershed event of recent history has been not September 11 but 'the collapse of the Soviet empire, symbolized by the fall of the Berlin Wall'.[75] As well, the US President's style certainly had some impact on the tenor of the European response.[76] The fact that key EU nations directly challenged the core tenets of US foreign policy shook the

---

72   Michael Schaefer, *NATO and ESDP: Shaping the European Pillar of a Transformed Alliance*, Keynote speech by Dr. Michael Schaefer, 'NATO, ESDP & OSCE: Synergy in Progress' conference, organized by the German Federal Foreign Office and the George C. Marshall Center on 15 March 2004, Berlin, <http://www.diplo.de/www/en/archiv_print?archiv_id=5500>.

73   'The celebrated *Le Monde* headline on September 13 proclaiming 'Nous sommes tous Américains' and Schröder's simultaneous pledge of 'unconditional solidarity' were not just rhetoric.' Andrew Moravcsik (2003), p. 82.

74   See Jeremy Shapiro, *The Role of France in the War on Terrorism* (Washington, DC: Brookings Institution, 2002).

75   Andrew Moravcsik (2003), p. 83.

76   Charles-Philippe David, *Au sein de la Maison-Blanche – La formulation de la politique étrangère des États-Unis* (Sainte Foy, Québec: Presses de l'université Laval, 2004).

transatlantic relationship.[77] One article published in April 2003 even asked, 'Should we fear the United States?'[78]

Do Tardieu's comments, made in 1908, to the effect that 'American interventionism is the long-awaited evidence that the United States has finally become aware that it is a great power and is conducting itself as a great power',[79] apply today? It should be noted that as early as October 2002, the Dutch government, while asserting its support for the US, withheld full backing for American policies and maintained that any military action must be based on sufficient evidence – in the event, evidence concerning Bin Laden and Al Qaeda.[80] France, whose head of state had been the first to visit the ruins of the World Trade Center and pay tribute to the victims, spearheaded the challenge, long after Hubert Védrine, known for his creeping anti-Americanism, had left office. In so doing, President Chirac was keeping French foreign policy on a Gaullist course: 'Chirac was keen to accept praise for constraining the United States to act against Iraq only through the UN and for preventing the passage of a Security Council resolution that could automatically trigger war.'[81] Meanwhile, in 2002, Chancellor Schröder won re-election by appealing to anti-American sentiment. He succeeded in diverting public attention from domestic issues, on which his record was spotty, to international issues.[82] His comments comparing Bush to Hitler deepened the emerging rift.[83] The diplomatic exchanges toughened. The US suggested it might push for the EU to take France's permanent seat on the UN Security Council. Having been stymied in its multilateral efforts, the US hinted it would turn away from multilateralism and towards bilateral initiatives. 'We will want to make sure that the United States never gets caught again in a diplomatic choke point in the Security Council or in NATO' said an American

---

77   Meanwhile, British public opinion favoured the EU as a 'parallel, competing superpower to the US' and opposed the war in Iraq: Mark F. Proudman, 'Soft Power Meets Hard: The Ideological Consequences of Weakness', in *Canada Among Nations: Coping with the American Colossus* (Toronto: Oxford University Press, 2003), pp. 332–54. See also Jacques Beltran and Frédéric Bozo (eds), 'États-Unis – Europe : Réinventer l'alliance', *Travaux et recherches de l'Ifri*, 2001, 184 p.

78   Jean-Michel Demetz, 'Faut-il avoir peur des Etats-Unis', *L'Express*, 24 April 2003.

79   André Tardieu, *Notes sur les États-Unis : la société, la politique, la diplomatie* (Paris: Calmann-Lévy, 1908), pp. 116–117, cited in Marie France Toinet, 'Le point de vue des juristes', p. 234.

80   Monica Den Boer, Joerg Monar, '11 September and the Challenge of Global Terrorism to the EU as a Security Actor', *Journal of Common Market Studies* 40 (2002): 13.

81   Mark F. Proudman, p. 154.

82   See Mark Kesselman et al., *European Politics in Transition* (Boston: Houghton Mifflin, 2002), p. 137.

83   See Ulrike Guérot, 'Les États-Unis vus d'Allemagne depuis cent ans : une histoire de l'ambivalence. De l'adoration au septicisme?' *Le Banquet* 21 (October 2004): 78.

official.[84] 'Old Europe' – and France in particular – became the scapegoats[85] for the inability of US diplomacy to garner the required nine votes in the Security Council.

Impact of European Differences in Radicalizing Perceptions of US Hegemony

Finally, the discord was amplified by an unexpected factor: intra-European disagreements.[86] European identity, which until then had been promoted by the Franco-German duo or sometimes by an Anglo-Franco-German triumvirate, was staked out by the new members of the EU. It began when 'EU foreign ministers decided to hand over the Iraq affair to the UN without addressing the strategic case. [...] Not surprisingly London and Paris decided to focus on UN legitimacy, ignoring the European Framework. In this configuration, the Union became irrelevant.'[87] When eight European leaders (José María Aznar, José-Manuel Durão Barroso, Silvio Berlusconi, Tony Blair, Vaclav Havel, Peter Medgyessy, Leszek Miller and Anders Fogh Rasmussen) asserted the strength of the transatlantic link in the *Wall Street Journal* ('the trans-Atlantic bond is a guarantee of our freedom') and claimed European identity (speaking of 'we Europeans'), the break was out in the open.[88]

It stemmed from different perceptions of the roles of Europe and the US: 'We dreamt, without too much hope, that we would one day get the chance to enjoy western values. But when we said West, it never crossed our minds that France is one thing and Germany is another, that Western Europe and Northern America are divergent entities.'[89] Particularly since the European Union is 'viewed as a soft security institution, by no means capable of taking the place of American power.'[90] Therefore, to reduce their strategic marginalization in the wake of September 11,[91] and given that the US is seen as 'a balancing force in the European arena, correcting the imbalance with France and Germany',[92] 'the NATO newcomers [promoted] ever

---

84   Joseph Fitchett, 'France Likely to Suffer Reprisals from America', International Herald Tribune, 15 March 2003. That is in fact what the US did, starting with the campaign in Afghanistan, to which states generally contributed concrete aid on the basis of bilateral agreements.

85   See Justin Vaisse, 'American Francophobia Takes a New Turn', *French Politics Culture and Society* 21/2 (Summer 2003): 17–31.

86   Nicolas de Boisgrollier, 'The European Disunion', *Survival* 47/3 (Fall 2005). Jacques Rupnik, 'Les meilleurs amis de l'Amérique en Europe', p. 39.

87   Jean-Yves Haine, 'The EU's Soft Power', *Conflict & Security* (Winter/Spring 2004).

88   'United We Stand – Eight European Leaders Are as One with President Bush', *The Wall Street Journal*, 30 January 2003.

89   Andrei Plesu, 'Who Do You Love The Most?' *Transregional Center for Democratic Studies Bulletin* 13/2 (Issue 44, June 2003), <http://www.newschool.edu/centers/tcds/bulletinbackissues.htm>.

90   Jacques Rupnik, 'Les meilleurs amis de l'Amérique en Europe', p. 46.

91   See Helga Haftendorn, 'NATO III', *Internationale Politik* (Summer 2002): 29–34.

92   Jacques Rupnik, 'Les meilleurs amis de l'Amérique en Europe', p. 59.

closer alignment with US positions'.[93] This split had a significant impact on the image of the European Union among the future member states, taking some of the sheen off EU membership.[94]

The transatlantic divide therefore mirrors an opposition between two models, 'in which the debate about the identity of the European Union is readily recognizable'.[95] In this sense, the war in Iraq laid bare deep pre-existing divisions.[96] However, despite the cacophony of European voices and the differences at the governmental level, it remains that the majority of Europeans were 'united in diversity',in the words of the EU's motto, and 'saw a certain consistency in the EU's critical position towards the US, despite its contradictions and divergences'.[97] The disconnect between Europe's political elites and public opinion was striking, leading to the electoral defeat of several governments that were in office during the war in Iraq. The European Union now has its own fault lines, which reproduce the opposed interpretations of transatlantic differences: 'Pessimists maintain that differences in power, threat perceptions, and values are forcing an inexorable divergence in European and American interests. Optimists see recent troubles as the product of rigid ideologies, domestic politics, and missed diplomatic opportunities.'[98]

Even as it is struggling to come up with a federal constitutional charter, the EU is defining itself in relation to the US on the basis of tenacious constructs, but this process is not entirely eclipsing the importance of the transatlantic relationship. The redefinition of the transatlantic partnership depends on the acceptance of intra-European and transatlantic differences.

Accepting Differences in Order to Renew the Transatlantic Partnership

The arrival of George W. Bush at the White House in January 2001 and his administration's unilateralist tendencies, illustrated by the rejection of international constraints and the doctrine of pre-emption set forth in September 2002, had created transatlantic tensions. These grew to crisis proportions following the US intervention in Iraq. Despite signs of good will on both sides since January 2005,[99]

---

93   *Ibid.*, p. 47.

94   Richard Gowan, 'Waiting for Europe, Wanting America', *The Globalist*, 24 October 2005, <http://www.theglobalist.com>.

95   Édouard Balladur, Axel Poniatowski, p. 11.

96   See Anand Menon, Jonathan Lipkin, p. 4.

97   Dominique David, 'Puissance dominante, puissance référente ou hyperpuissance? Une vue européenne sur les stratégies américaines et l'antiaméricanisme européen', in Charles-Philippe David (ed.), *Nous antiaméricains?* p. 7.

98   Andrew Moravcsik (2003), p. 83.

99   George W. Bush's first official visit to Europe in his second term, during which he used the term 'European Union' for the first time, recognized the EU's importance as an actor on the international stage. For their part, European countries made a good will gesture by offering their aid to the US after Hurricane Katrina ravaged Mississippi and Louisiana.

some argue that the magnitude of the Iraqi crisis has opened an inexorably widening gulf between the two sides of the Atlantic, which have become potential rivals. As a result, the view that a united Europe must be built as a counterweight to US power has made significant inroads in public opinion and some European governments since 2003.[100]

However, the prospect of rivalry between Europe and the US must be treated with caution. For one thing, Europeans appear too divided amongst themselves about the direction of European construction and Europe's relations with the US. Therefore, the idea of the EU as a counterweight to US hegemony only seems to throw up obstacles to creating a Europe that is a political power and not just a free trade area and zone of economic prosperity. For another, the real differences of opinion between Europeans and Americans about how to deal with the main threats of the early 21st century (terrorism and the proliferation of weapons of mass destruction) cannot overshadow the broad consensus about the seriousness of these threats nor the continued existence of common values between the two shores of the West.

Intra-European Differences: Obstacles to Building a European Counterweight to US Hegemony in the International Arena

The transatlantic crisis over Iraq seems to have revealed the existence of a current of public opinion in Europe that could provide the foundation for the construction of a strong European political entity. Opposition to US intervention against Saddam Hussein's regime was demonstrated by millions in France, Germany, Italy, Great Britain and Spain, although the governments of the latter three countries backed the US action. Now, two years after the public outcry in Europe against the Bush administration's policies on Iraq, the European Union is at loggerheads. The constitution that was to have equipped the EU with some of the means to express its power, including a European Ministry of Foreign Affairs, is dead and buried after the 'No' victories in the referenda held on the new constitution in France and the Netherlands in early 2005. The divisions among Europeans on the form and direction of European construction and on Europe's relations with the US are therefore the two major obstacles to the emergence of a European entity that can counterbalance US hegemony.

---

100 A June 2005 survey found support for the proposition that Europe should be more independent of the US running at 50% in Spain, 53% in Great Britain, 59% in the Netherlands and Germany, and 73% in France; 85% of the French even said that the emergence of a military rival to the US would be beneficial: 'American Character Gets Mixed Reviews; U.S. Image Up Slightly, but Still Negative', *The Pew Global Attitudes Project*, 23 June 2005: 30 and 3.

Europeans and the Building of the Europe of the Future

The rejection of the proposed European constitution by the French and the Dutch has clearly interrupted the process of building Europe. At the same time, it exposed deep differences on sensitive subjects. During the British EU presidency in the second half of 2005, British Prime Minister Tony Blair and French President Jacques Chirac were consistently at odds on how to restart European construction and hence on budget priorities for the 2007–2013 period. Tony Blair wanted to focus on the so-called Lisbon goals, which call for increased European investment in education, high-tech and innovation, areas considered vital to future economic growth and in which the EU is clearly lagging behind the US in particular. However, since the European budget is limited to 1% of the GDP of member states, these new priorities would mean redirecting spending, and most contentiously diverting it away from the Common Agricultural Policy (CAP), which is the EU's largest budget item (accounting for 40% of expenditures) and to which France, as the prime beneficiary, is very attached. These rifts are paralyzing European construction and have led to a French veto threat at the WTO if the Doha round negotiations now under way should jeopardize the CAP. In addition to these quarrels between the governments of two of the most important European states, France and Great Britain, two other major players in the building of Europe, Germany and Italy, face political uncertainties. The tight victory of the centre-right in the former and the centre-left in the latter at the last general elections (Fall 2005 in Germany and Spring 2006 in Italy) weaken – at least in the short run – the positions of those two founding states within the EU as well as the European construction process itself.

2005 was therefore a bleak year for European construction (see Figure 7.2). The draft constitution is buried, at least for now, economic growth in the euro zone is sluggish, unemployment high, there are sharp disagreements between the political leaders of the member states, and the opening of talks on Turkish membership in the EU in October 2005 promises to fuel future disputes about the borders and the nature of the EU. But the glum mood does not mean that public opinion in the member countries is turning away from Europe. The reasons commonly advanced for the defeat of the referenda in France and the Netherlands – fear of unemployment, fear of immigration, the prospect of Turkish membership – have not caused public opinion to sour on the idea of European construction *per se*.

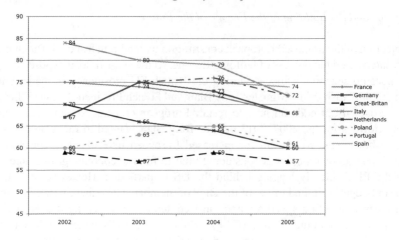

Figure 7.2 Sympathies Toward the European Union
Source: *Transatlantic Trends*, Key Findings 2005.

Europeans and the Role of the EU in the International Arena

Europe's political crisis is being played out at the governmental level. Governments do not appear to agree on the direction of European construction while public opinion is solidly behind a strong Europe. More than two years after the US intervention in Iraq, Europeans seem to have come to the conclusion that Europe must again become a major player in international relations, clearly independent of the US: 70% believe that the EU should become a 'superpower' in the image of the United States.[101] Going further still, certainly beyond what European governments are willing to contemplate, European public opinion is favourable to a single permanent seat for the EU on the UN Security Council. Overall, 60% of Europeans support the idea: in France, 62% are for it; in Germany, 64%. Only in Britain is the majority (55%) opposed.[102]

The apparent consensus on an active role for the EU on the international stage cannot however conceal deep differences on how this goal is to be realized. The 'superpower' concept is quite vague. While 36% of Europeans agree that the EU would have to increase military expenditures in order to exercise power, compared with 26% who would prefer a superpower wielding 'soft power,'[103] only 22% are actually in favour of spending more on defence.[104] Most Europeans, therefore, support a pragmatic approach to international relations in which the use of force is a

---

101 *Transatlantic Trends 2005: Key Findings*, p. 10: <www.transatlantictrends.org/doc/TTKeyFindings2005.pdf>.

102 *Ibid.*

103 *Ibid.*

104 *Transatlantic Trends 2004: Key Findings*: <www.transatlantictrends.org/doc/2004_english_key.pdf>.

last resort, strictly governed by international law. The 'doves', defined as those who look to economics rather than the use of force as the main driver of contemporary international relations, exercise dominant political influence in Europe, out of all proportion to their influence in the United States.[105]

While these empirical data seem to confirm Robert Kagan's thesis that Europeans are from Venus and Americans are from Mars, Europeans are divided on the form the EU should take, its role in the world and its relations with the US. Crossing views on Europe's relations with the US with preferences as to the use of hard power versus soft power yields four ideal types for a European model:[106]

1. a 'Blair Europe' based on the Atlantic alliance and military force;
2. a 'Schröder Europe' closely allied with the US but using non-military soft power;
3. a 'Chirac Europe' independent of the US and capable of military action;
4. a 'Swiss Europe' independent of the US and relying on soft power alone.

The centre of gravity in Europe appears to be a 'neither-nor' model that reflects a fundamental indecision and deep cleavages about the EU's international role and place. This centre of gravity is not too close to the US and not too independent, leaning towards the civil dimension of power without neglecting the military side. The EU would thus be a mute, disoriented player at the centre of the international stage.

Europeans and Relations with the US

The clear, massive opposition in European countries to the intervention in Iraq has developed into a sharply negative view of US influence in the world (see Figure 7.3). (So much so that China now has a more positive image in Europe than does the US![107])

---

105   Ronald Asmus, Philip P. Everts and Pierangelo Isernia, 'Across the Atlantic and the Political Aisle: The Double Divide in U.S–European Relations', *Transatlantic Trends 2004: Analytical Paper*, p. 5: <www.transatlantictrends.org/doc/2004_english_analytical.pdf>.

106   For a detailed analysis of political differences and similarities between Europeans and Americans, broken down by Republicans and Democrats in the case of Americans, see Ronald Asmus, Philip P. Everts and Pierangelo Isernia, *op. cit.*

107   'American Character Gets Mixed Reviews: U.S Image Up Slightly, but Still Negative', *op. cit.*, p. 2.

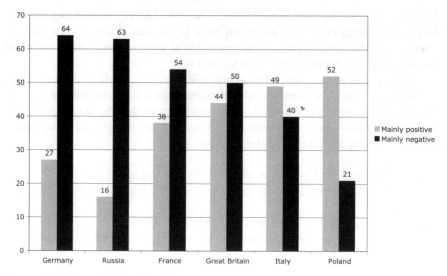

Figure 7.3 View of U.S. Influence in the World
Source: BBC/PIPA Poll, January 20, 2005.

This negative perception of the US generally translates into a desire for Europe to acquire strategic independence so it can pursue its own approach to security and diplomatic issues. However, European attitudes in this area are far from homogenous. Though Defense Secretary Donald Rumsfeld's comments on 'old Europe' and 'new Europe' may have been caricatured, it is true that the Iraq crisis exposed deep differences among the EU's 25 member states on relations with the US. While they are not opposed to the emergence of an independent EU, Great Britain and the eastern European countries, particularly Poland, do not want this independence to be achieved against the wishes of the US, which remains in their eyes the main guarantor of their security.

The disappearance of the common threat posed by the USSR during the Cold War created the systemic conditions for frank and open expression of transatlantic disagreements.[108] This was demonstrated by the Iraqi crisis in the winter of 2003. Tensions rose to such a pitch and the misgivings, indeed distrust, remain so acute that they seem to support the thesis of an emerging rivalry between the US and Europe.[109] To be sure, the Iraq crisis provided an opportunity for 'European public opinion' to

---

108 Philip Gordon, Jeremy Shapiro, *Allies at War: America, Europe, and the Crisis over Iraq* (New York: McGraw-Hill, 2004).

109 John Mearsheimer, *The Tragedy of Great Power Politics* (New York: 2001); Charles Kupchan (2002). See also the debate on 'soft-balancing', the idea that Europe in particular could use soft power to counterbalance American hegemony: Robert A. Pape, 'Soft Balancing Against the United States', *International Security* 30/1 (2005): 7–45; T.V. Paul, 'Soft Balancing in the Age of U.S. Primacy', *International Security*, 30/1 (2005): 46–71; Stephen G. Brooks and William C. Wohlforth, 'Hard Times for Soft Balancing', *International Security*, 30/1

take shape and express its opposition to the war. Also – and most importantly – it laid bare fundamental issues concerning the EU's identity and future.[110] The divisions and roadblocks to the creation of a European counterweight to US hegemony are such that the independent, autonomous Europe to which most European governments and peoples aspire cannot be built in opposition to the US. While the differences between the two sides of the Atlantic are numerous and run deep, the existence of a common core of shared values and interests argues for renewal of the Atlantic alliance.

Beyond the Disagreements, the Existence of Points in Common Supports Renewal of the Atlantic Alliance

After his re-election on November 2, 2004, George W. Bush made rapprochement with Europe a foreign policy priority for his second term. There were a number of signals and decisions in this direction: President Bush made his first official visit to Europe,[111] during which he used the term 'European Union' for the first time.[112] He named his former communications counsellor, Karen Hughes, to head 'public diplomacy' at the State Department. Condoleezza Rice was appointed Secretary of State, signalling that US foreign policy would steered by diplomats, not by Pentagon hawks. These moves did not, however, help thaw transatlantic relations (see Figure 7.4).

While it may not be accurate to speak of a new flare-up of anti-American sentiment, the re-election of George W. Bush did little to improve European perceptions of the US. Public opinion in the United States' traditional European allies responded negatively to Bush's re-election by wide margins: 77% in Germany, 75% in France, 64% in Great Britain, 54% in Italy.[113] This response has also translated into a more negative view of the American people, which is seen as 'greedy' and 'violent',in addition to positive attributes such as 'inventive', 'honest' and 'hard-working'.[114]

(2005): 72–108; and Keir A. Lieber and Gerard Alexander, 'Waiting for Balancing: Why the World Is Not Pushing Back', *International Security* 30/1 (2005): 109–139.

110   Édouard Balladur, Axel Poniatowski, p. 22.

111   The European trip was officially the first of George W. Bush's second term since it took place after the swearing-in ceremony in January 2005.

112   George W. Bush thereby acknowledged the EU's importance as a player on the international stage for the first time since he took office in January 2001.

113   According to a BBC World Service Poll, 20 January, 2005: <www.pipa.org/OnlineReports/Views_US/BushReelect_Jan05/BushReelect_Jan05_rpt.pdf>.

114   'American Character Gets Mixed Reviews: U.S. Image Up Slightly, but Still Negative', p. 5.

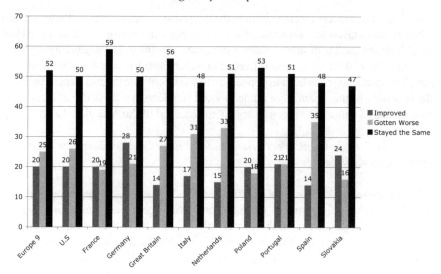

Figure 7.4 U.S.-Europe Relations in the Aftermath of Bush's Reelection
Source: *Transatlantic Trends*, Key Findings 2005.

Iraq, a Subject of Continuing Controversy Between Europe and the US

More than two years after the US intervention, Iraq remains the main bone of contention between the two sides of the Atlantic. In June 2005, a solid majority of Europeans – both in the countries that sent troops to fight alongside the Americans and those that refused to do so – believed that the use of force against Saddam Hussein's regime had been a mistake.[115] The opposition to the war has certainly been strengthened by the difficulties the US has encountered in post-war Iraq. By the beginning of November 2005, when the number of US combat deaths in Iraq passed the 2,000 mark, a majority of Americans had also come to the view that the war had been unnecessary.[116] However, the agreement between Americans and Europeans about the war ends there. While most Americans believe the world is safer without Saddam Hussein, the majority of Europeans think the opposite (see Figure 7.5).[117] One important consequence of European disagreement with the intervention in Iraq is that the US cannot count on the support of its traditional allies to help it improve

---

115 In June 2005, the level of opposition to the war in Iraq was as follows: 41% in the Netherlands, 61% in Great Britain, 76% in Spain and Poland, 87% in Germany and 92% in France, according to 'American Character Gets Mixed Reviews: U.S. Image Up Slightly, but Still Negative', p. 27.

116 According to a *Washington Post* – ABC News Poll conducted between 31 October and 2 November 2005, 60% of Americans believe the war in Iraq was a mistake: <www.washingtonpost.com/wp-srv/politics/polls/postpoll110305.htm>.

117 'American Character Gets Mixed Reviews: U.S. Image Up Slightly, but Still Negative', p. 27.

the situation on the ground. A survey conducted by the University of Maryland's Program on International Policy Attitudes in early October 2005 in the European countries that had committed troops to Iraq found that most people wanted their soldiers withdrawn: 57% in Great Britain, 60% in Italy, 59% in Poland, 48% in Denmark.[118]

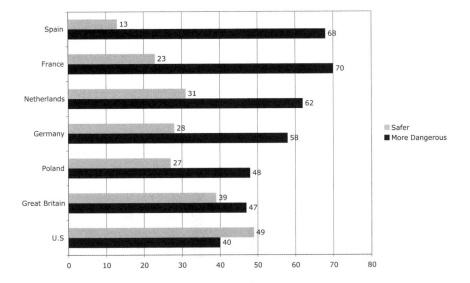

Figure 7.5 Is the World Safer Without Saddam?
Source: 'American Character Gets Mixed Reviews. U.S. Image Up Slightly, but Still Negative', *The Pew Global Attitudes Project*, 23 June 2005, p.27.

Democracy, a Common Principle on Both Sides of the Atlantic

The transatlantic divisions on Iraq reflect recurring differences between Americans and Europeans which raise the possibility that the US and Europe may inexorably drift apart. European political leaders (especially in France) have consistently opposed the Anglo-Saxon (i.e. American) and European (particularly French) models, suggesting that the US and Europe subscribe to radically different social models and even that they hold opposed values. While they certainly have different conceptions of the role of the state, social responsibility and the place of religion, Americans and Europeans do share the same liberal values. They support a market economy, free trade, human rights and democracy.

---

118 'Among Key Iraq Partners, Weak Public Support for Troop Presence', *Program on International Policy Attitudes*, 14 October, 2005: <www.pipa.org/templates/fullPage.php?typ e=analysis&visit=1&id=1#resume>.

Defending human rights and promoting democracy appear to be common principles that should figure prominently in the foreign policies of states on both sides of the Atlantic. Europeans are even more committed to promoting democracy than are Americans (74% versus 52%).[119] Not only do Europeans and Americans agree on the importance of promoting democracy as part of their foreign policy, they also agree on the means to be used (see Figure 7.6). A survey conducted by the Chicago Council on Foreign Relations and the Program on International Policy Attitudes, released at the end of September 2005, showed that a majority of Americans reject the use of military force to promote democracy and support the use of diplomatic approaches within a multilateral framework such as the UN.[120]

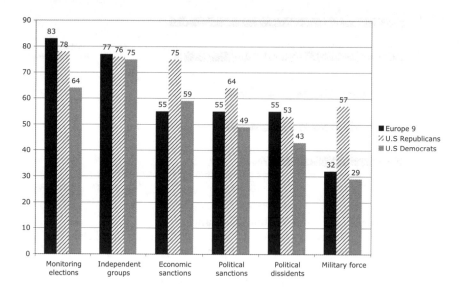

Figure 7.6 Support for the Following as a Means to Promote Democracy
Source: Transatlantic Trends 2005, Key Findings, p. 13.

Possible Cooperation on International Issues

The data from the *Transatlantic Trends 2004* survey shows that the 'hawks' are a leading force in the US, a fundamental difference between Americans and Europeans which supports Robert Kagan's thesis that the two do not share the same

---

119 *Transatlantic Trends 2005: Key Findings*, p. 11.

120 'Americans on Promoting Democracy', *Chicago Council on Foreign Relations* and *Program on International Policy Attitudes*, 29 September, 2005: <www.pipa.org/OnlineReports/AmRole_World/Democratization_Sep05/Democratization_Sep09_rpt_revised.pdf>.

view of the use of force as a tool in international relations.[121] While this discrepancy certainly gives rise to disputes in specific cases, Iraq being only the latest (other recent examples include the lively discussions between the Allies on the need for armed intervention in Kosovo in 1999 and Bosnia in 1995), it does not amount to an irreconcilable difference in perceptions of the international situation and its main issues and threats.

Despite the impact of September 11, 2001, which helped make the twin threats of terrorism and Islamic fundamentalism appear more urgent to Americans than to Europeans, both share a largely similar analysis of the main international issues of the early 21st century. A major economic crisis, international terrorism, nuclear weapons and global warming are the four main threats listed by respondents on both sides of the Atlantic (see Figure 7.7). Europeans and Americans even agree that NATO, undermined by Donald Rumsfeld's 'coalition of the willing' doctrine, is still the best tool for US–European cooperation on these issues.[122]

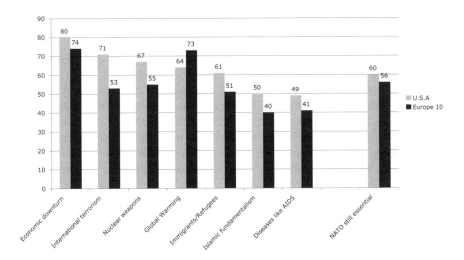

Figure 7.7 Identification of Main Threats and Role of NATO
Source: Transatlantic Trends 2005, Key Findings.

If the Atlantic alliance, which has been the linchpin of international peace, stability and prosperity since the end of the Second World War,[123] is to be renewed, four key points that emerge from our analysis of European perceptions of US hegemony must be considered:

121 Ronald Asmus, Philip P. Everts and Pierangelo Isernia, pp. 2–5.

122 *Transatlantic Trends 2005: Key Findings*, pp. 17–18.

123 Zbigniew Brzezinski, *The Choice: Global Domination or Global Leadership* (New York: Basic Books 2004), pp. 89–106.

1. In Europe, negative perceptions of US power appear to be deeply entrenched. Contrary to certain American advocates of intervention in Iraq, they have not faded away since the easy victory over Saddam Hussein's regime. Given the continuing troubles in Iraq, this is bad news for the US, which cannot count on the support of its allies to maintain order in the country.
2. This negative perception is fostering European aspirations to build an EU independent of the US that could be a global power on the international stage. However, independence does not necessarily mean rivalry or competition. There are too many obstacles to building the EU in opposition to the US and the attempt would create too many divisions among member states.
3. To be sure, the Iraq crisis has deepened and widened the transatlantic gulf, but fundamentally the divorce between the US and Europe was made possible by the end of the Cold War. The beginning of the separation does not date from March 2003 but from December 1991 and the dissolution of the USSR.
4. In view of their differences and common points, Europeans and Americans need to develop a new partnership based on their complementary features.

Conclusion: Complementary Characteristics, the Cornerstone of a Renewed Atlantic Alliance

The war in Iraq has increased the likelihood that Europe will try to become a counterweight to the American empire rather than a partner.[124] There are some signs that suggest that Washington and Brussels may go the way of Rome and Constantinople in terms of geopolitical rivalry.[125] European heads of state who are obsessed with creating a multipolar world welcome this prospect. It may also be attractive to the majority of public opinion in Europe, which now regards the US as more a threat to than a guarantor of international peace.[126] However, obstacles such as the difficulties European governments are experiencing in defining the borders and nature of the Union, an aging population, economic performance that lags well behind the US, and a culture based on leisure rather than international competitiveness are absorbing the energies of the EU as it strives to maintain an internal balance, and are diverting attention away from the exercise of European power beyond its borders. The EU's introverted power, in relation to the US, might make an analogy with Switzerland more appropriate than the comparison with Constantinople.[127]

Not only does European construction face internal difficulties, but in the final analysis the proposition that increasing Europe's military power would promote more balanced relations with the US is a dangerous illusion.[128] First of all, this thesis

---

124 Niall Ferguson, *Colossus: The Price of America's Empire* (New York: Norton & Company, 2004), p. 227.

125 *Ibid.*, p. 225.

126 William Drozdiak, 'The North Atlantic Drift', *Foreign Affairs* 84/1 (2005): 92.

127 Niall Ferguson, pp. 239–256.

128 Andrew Moravcsik (2003), pp. 82–84.

is unrealistic, given the magnitude of US military spending and the predictable reluctance of Europeans to take money out of social programs in order to significantly increase military capabilities. Second, striking a new balance of power with the US by launching an arms race would create frictions within the Atlantic alliance and more broadly in the international community. Complementary efforts, not a new balance of power, must be the guiding principle of a renewed Atlantic alliance.

The US and Europe are closely complementary in three areas.[129] First, they are the engines of the global economy. As leading economic and trading partners, they account for more than 50% of the flow of global trade and investment. And the potential of the relationship has yet to be fully realized.[130] Second, European countries already have military forces that can coordinate their actions with US forces and are capable of stepping into the breach. In the Balkans, for example, the EU assumed responsibility for maintaining stability, making it possible to redeploy US forces to Iraq and Afghanistan. Third, at the diplomatic level, the combination of a credible US threat to use force and the EU's preference for negotiation can produce positive outcomes in delicate situations, such as the Balkans, the Israeli-Palestinian conflict and Iran's nuclear ambitions.

In the economic, commercial, diplomatic and even military spheres, the potential for complementary actions by Europeans and Americans is clear and holds great promise. To realize this potential, a sustained dialogue must be opened on matters of common interest, which would in a sense take the place of the Soviet threat. This transatlantic agenda would include the following key points:[131]

- Step up the fight against terrorism and against the proliferation of weapons of mass destruction;
- Set forth an agenda of political and economic reforms for the Middle East: stabilization in Iraq and resolution of the Israeli-Palestinian conflict would be key stages;
- Prevent instability in the Caucasus and Central Asia, which would pose a threat to both Europe and the US;
- Redefine NATO missions and facilitate the development of an independent European defence identity;
- Develop new international (specifically UN) standards that define when force may or may not be used.

Europe and the US must draw lessons from the Iraq crisis and put in place these common structures and a shared agenda that reflects the community of values and interests that remains a central element of international relations. Renewal of the

---

129 Drozdiak, pp. 89–95.

130 *Ibid.*, pp. 89–91.

131 These points are summarized from articles by Ronald Asmus, 'Rebuilding the Atlantic Alliance', *Foreign Affairs* 82/5 (2003): 20–31; Drozdiak, *op. cit.*; Robert Hunter, 'A Forward-Looking Partnership', *Foreign Affairs*, 83/5 (2004): 14–18; Moravcsik, *op. cit.*

Atlantic alliance demands a return to diplomacy, which is to say acceptance of differences and responsiveness on each side to the other's concerns. In the short term, this means George W. Bush must consider the EU a full partner in dealing with the international issues confronting the alliance as a whole. His administration needs to stop playing off the 'old Europe' against the 'new Europe' and reaffirm the United States' support for European unification. Explicitly renouncing any intention of overthrowing the Teheran regime from the outside and active engagement in resolving the Israeli-Palestinian conflict would help the Bush administration restore a relationship of trust with Europe.[132] For their part, Europeans need to realize that trying to build the EU on an anti-American basis will only increase the divisions within the Union. They must stop regarding US power as a problem rather than an opportunity.[133] The complementary characteristics of the two sides of the Atlantic make it possible to contemplate an international division of labour that could serve as an effective lever for promoting international peace, security and prosperity.

132 Hunter, *op. cit.*
133 Asmus, *op. cit.*, p. 29.

Chapter 8

The Limits to American Hegemony in Asia

André Laliberté[1]

There is no question in Asia that the United States is going to remain for a few decades the predominant power in the region. The Bush administration has never concealed its intent to preserve a strong American presence in the region, regardless of the wishes and fears of states in the region.[2] Yet, there is also no question that this predominance in Asia is going to have to come to term with the emergence of two other powers: the People's Republic of China and the Indian Union. If current trends of high-growth rate in both countries continue, these two emerging economies are likely to surpass the United States' performance by the middle of the twenty-first century. Many of those who believe that economic prowess necessarily leads to claims for political power often argue that the growth of the Chinese and Indian economies is going to give rise to turbulent times ahead for the US.[3] Yet there is nothing inexorable about the political consequences of economic growth: the emergence of Japan in the 1970s or the recovery of Europe after World War Two did not threaten American supremacy. The rise of India, in particular, is often met with acceptance rather than anxiety. However, there are many who believe that the rise of China poses a significantly different challenge.[4] Managing this regional hegemonic transition and its global consequences in the realm of the economy and the environment is likely to be the most important geo-strategic challenge of the twenty-first century bar none.

'Hegemony', as the international relations theory literature uses this term, makes reference to the Gramscian notion of domination through consent. In China, 'hegemonism' (*baquanzhuyi*) refers to mere bullying. Discussion about American hegemony in Asia, therefore, is highly likely to be marred by misunderstanding from the start. In its discussion of American hegemony in Asia, this chapter broadly refers

1   The author would like to thank the Fonds québécois pour la recherche sur la société et la culture for the financial support of the research leading to the writing of this chapter, and Ulric Couture, for his research assistance. The author remains responsible for any omission or errors.
2   Condoleezza Rice, 'Our Asia Strategy', *The Wall Street Journal* (October 24, 2003): A15.
3   National Intelligence Council, *Mapping the Global Future: Report of the NIC's 2020 Project* (Washington, DC, 2004), pp. 54–55.
4   For a recent statement, see Robert D. Kaplan, 'How We Would Fight China', *Atlantic Monthly*, 295/5 (June 2005): 49–64.

to 'hegemony' from a Gramscian perspective. However, it is not using it with the same lenses as the ones used in the anti-globalization literature.[5] Rather, the notion of hegemonic stability used here borrows from that which has been developed by Robert Gilpin and other students of the international political economy (IPE),[6] who argue that any global order depends on the capacity of a state to take responsibility for ensuring a world-wide economic and political stability. One central argument that can be made on the basis of this school of thought is that if China and other Asian states oppose *baquanzhuyi* and the use of force, for example in the war against terrorism, they still accept American hegemony in the region because they agree with the neo-liberal economic order that is buttressed by existing international institutions. The question that this chapter discusses is the extent to which American domination in the region is going to be accepted in the foreseeable future. To discuss this issue, the chapter is divided as follows. It discusses first the Asian security architecture that underpins American hegemonic stability in that part of the world. Second, it will discuss the implications of the rise of China, the actor most likely to drive an eventual hegemonic transition. The third section, finally, will look at the 'Achilles' heel' of American hegemony in Asia, by briefly reviewing the strains of its security alliances.

The American Security Architecture in Asia

If the current period of hegemonic stability is going to be challenged in the economic or military-strategic spheres, there is little question that the impetus will emerge from Asia.[7] Yet an eventual transition towards a different regional order in Asia would be difficult because the region, contrary to Europe, has no 'stability-enhancing' international institution that can mitigate conflicts comparable in scope to NATO or the EU.[8] The concept of Asia itself represents something of an artificial construct that is just too vast and too complex to be compared to Europe or even the broader North Atlantic security community. Asia encompasses a variety of cultures that have distinct and separate historical trajectories, with different models of state

---

5   A classical statement of which is found in Robert W. Cox, 'Social Forces, States, and World Orders', in Robert O. Keohane (ed.), *Neorealism and Its Critics* (Columbia, 1986), pp. 204–54. See also Robert W. Cox, *Approaches to World Order* (London: Cambridge University Press, 1996); 'Gramsci, Hegemony, and International Relations: An Essay in Method', in Stephen Gill (ed.), *Gramsci, Historical Materialism, and International Relations* (Cambridge University Press, 1993), pp. 49–66.

6   Robert Gilpin and Jean Gilpin, *Global Political Economy: Understanding the International Economic Order* (Princeton, NJ: Princeton University Press, 2001); Robert Gilpin, *The Political Economy of International Relations* (Princeton, NJ: Princeton University Press, 1987).

7   Kaplan, 'How We Would Fight China'.

8   Aaron L. Friedberg, 'Ripe for Rivalry: Prospects for Peace in a Multipolar Asia', *International Security*, 18/3 (Winter 1993/94): 5–33.

organizations. Even with respect to the global phenomenon of colonialism at the end of the nineteenth century, Asia has experienced this trend both as victim and as aggressor. Most of South and Southeast Asia were colonized by Western powers, but Japan was itself a colonial power.

Asia is far too diverse to compare to any other regional entity and the idea of an overarching security structure encompassing its dazzling diversity is problematic. The area falling under the responsibilities of the US forces Pacific Command conveys the magnitude of the challenges faced by American hegemony. The territories that fall within the scope of the Pacific Command – which also covers the Indian Ocean – covers almost 60 percent of the world's population, faces the other five largest armed forces on the planet, and is the most dynamic part of the global economy.[9] Analytically, it is more appropriate to divide this area in three distinct regions, each defined by Barry Buzan as three distinct security complexes. Each of these security complexes is defined by a major enduring rivalry, a regional balance of power and a regional hegemon. Although they all relate to the global international system, the dynamics within each of these regional security complexes is *sui generis*. These three complexes were defined as follows during the Cold War:[10]

1. The Northeast Asian security complex is defined primarily by the emergence of China, a major power whose leaders have asserted claims to annex Taiwan if this state, which is *de facto* sovereign, seeks to affirm this status *de jure*. This enduring rivalry, which conflates conflicting claims of nationhood (unification for China, independence for Taiwan), meshes with the complex web of economic relations between China and Japan that has developed in the shadow of a century-long enduring rivalry for regional supremacy. Finally, in the shadow of this rivalry persists the division of the Korean peninsula. The economic potential of the region makes it one of the three cores of the global economy. This economic growth, however, also fosters growth of military expenditures that could intensify existing rivalries.

2. The South Asian security complex is defined by the regional hegemony of India, which has been contested by Pakistan since the onset of both countries' emergence in 1947. The Pakistani authorities have often sought to link the South Asian security complex to the East Asian one through their security cooperation with China. Another defining structure of this region is the numerous governance problems faced by the states surrounding India, which have often triggered military interventions reinforcing the perception that India seeks to assert regional hegemony. Although the economic growth of the

---

9   They are the armed forces of China, Russia, India, North and South Korea. The area covered by the Pacific command represents 34 percent of the gross world production (the US represents 21 percent) <http://www.pacom.mil/about/pacom.shtml>.

10   Barry Buzan and Ole Waever, *Regions and Powers: The Structure of International Security*, Cambridge Studies in International Relations no. 91 (Cambridge University Press, 2004), pp. 98–99.

region is impressive, it has yet to rival that of the Northeast Asian complex.
On the other hand, sources of instability abound.

3. The Southeast Asian security complex is not defined by any major interstate
    rivalry, and it is not influenced by a regional hegemony. An economic
    regrouping thanks to the Association of Southeast Asian Nations (ASEAN),
    it has yet to be a security community comparable to the European Union:
    differences between regimes and enormous discrepancies in terms of economic
    development prevent a deepening of cooperation. The main challenges that
    beset the region are not rivalries between sovereign states, but rather problems
    of weak states, domestic insurgencies, and major threats coming from piracy
    and transnational organizations that could disrupt trade routes. The region has
    also experienced considerable growth but the profound social inequities that
    have remained despite these progresses ensure that the stability of the region's
    states remains fragile.

Since the end of the Cold War, a hierarchical order has emerged among these
three regional security complexes. Buzan and Waever consider that the Northeast
Asian security complex since the end of the Cold War and the Southeast Asian
security complex have been intertwined through the ASEAN regional forum (ARF)
process to such an extent that they represent now two regional subcomplexes in a
broader East Asian regional security complex.[11] The East Asian and South Asian
regional complexes, in turn, are constituting an emerging and expanding Asian
security super-complex. Two developments are likely to shape its future: the rise
of China, and the American decision to remain in the region or to start a gradual
disengagement.[12]

There is little question that in the long run, the basis for a sustainable hegemonic
stability under the leadership of the US in Asia is eroding. The current hegemonic
stability, which depends on the economic performance of the US, is going to have
to cope with the rise of the Chinese and Indian economies. Although debates remain
about the speed and the scope of these two major states' emergence, few dispute
the likelihood that the global economy is going to depend increasingly on the
prosperity of these two important Asian societies.[13] The pressing political question
for American decision-makers is whether the leaders of these states will accept the
global institutional framework put in place by the US. This issue, however, is beyond
the scope of this chapter. The following will focus more narrowly on the existing
arrangements whereby the US can maintain its presence and its hegemony in Asia.

Three tools help maintain US hegemony in Asia: the convergence of interest
among all Asian states about regional stability, the maintenance of existing security

---

11   *Ibid.*, pp. 155–164.

12   *Ibid.*, pp. 164–165.

13   Pranab Bardhan, 'China, India Superpower? Not so Fast!', *Yale Global* (25 October
2005); Robert Samuelson, 'US Shouldn't Fear Rise of China, India', *The Business Times* (26
May 2005), <http://yaleglobal.yale.edu/display.article?id=5762>.

relations, and the enmeshing of China in a relation of interdependence to reassure other states and increase the price of military adventure. This section will briefly address the first argument about the convergence of interests among Asian states about the US contribution to regional stability, and then elaborate on the maintenance of American security arrangements in Asia. The enmeshing of China in a relation of interdependence will be discussed in a subsequent section.

The convergence of interest about regional stability suggests a preference for the status quo, and therefore leads to the acceptance of American presence in the region. Such an international order propped up by a distant foreign power may also appear preferable to a regional order imposed by a neighbour. Illustrative of this view was the statement of a Burmese delegate at a 1947 conference who expressed then why Asian small and middle powers prefer such a type of status quo, when he said that 'It is terrible to be ruled by a western power, but it was even more so to be ruled by an Asian power.' The experience of Japanese aggression was still fresh in the memory, but the concern expressed then was about Chinese or Indian regional hegemony. There are no reasons to believe that Asian small and middle powers would have changed views on this matter.[14] Perhaps more significant, even Beijing welcomes the American presence in the Asia-Pacific region as a stabilizing factor.[15]

The regional US hegemony rests on a structure known as the 'San Francisco System'. Contrary to the large assemblage of nations joined together in NATO, it is defined by a set of bilateral agreements linking the US with one state. In the mind of those who have build it, the 'spider web' generated by these mutual defence treaties tries to compensate for the absence of multilateral security cooperation in the Asia-Pacific region.[16] Hemmer and Katzenstein have argued that attitudes of cultural superiority explain why American strategists preferred to use a network of bilateral treaties instead of an overarching multilateral organization such as NATO.[17] Although this argument is convincing, especially in light of recent discussions by Huntington and other conservatives about the 'European-ness' of American identity, another obstacle to the constitution of a multilateral structure in Asia is the absence of a common regional identity encompassing the entire Asia-Pacific region.[18] A cursory look at the different components of the San Francisco system, along the geographical divisions suggested by Buzan's regional security complexes, illustrates these divisions.

---

14   Amitav Acharya, 'Will Asia's Past Be Its Future?', *International Security*, 28/3 (Winter 2003/04): 149–164.

15   David Shambaugh, 'China Engages Asia: Reshaping the Regional World Order', *International Security*, 29/3 (Winter 2004–2005): 64–99.

16   Peter J. Katzenstein and Nubuo Okawara, 'Japan, Asian-Pacific Security and the Case for Analytical Eclecticism', *International Security*, 26/3 (Winter 2001/02): 156.

17   Christopher Hemmer and Peter J. Katzenstein, 'Why is there no NATO in Asia? Collective Identity, Regionalism, and the Origins of Multilateralism', *International Organization*, 56/3 (Summer 2002): 576.

18   Samuel P. Huntington, *Who Are We? – The Challenges to America's National Identity* (New York: Simon & Schuster, 2004).

At the core of the San Francisco system lie two major mutual defence treaties: the US–Japan Mutual Defence Treaty and the Mutual Defence Treaty between the US and the Republic of Korea. Derived from a mutual security assistance pact signed in 1952, the US–Japan treaty has been the basis for Japan's security relations with the US. The pact was upgraded into a more formal treaty in 1960 to be in force for 30 years, and renewed in 1996. It is the main element for US hegemonic power in Asia: Japan's self-defence forces consume one of the largest military budgets in the world, and its economy is second only to the United States'.[19] Together, the US armed forces and the Japanese self-defence forces have undertaken the Keen Sword/Keen Edge Joint/bilateral training exercises to increase combat readiness and interoperability of their forces for the defence of Japan. The mutual defence treaty with South Korea represents the second major component of the US presence in East Asia. Signed in 1954, this treaty still represents a valued component of South Korean security, in light of the uncertainties surrounding DPRK nuclear ambitions.[20] Along with Japan, the UK, Australia, Canada and Chile, South Korea is one of the participants of the RIMPAC exercises (Rim of the Pacific), a biennial large-scale multinational power projection and sea control exercise undertaken with the US forces.

A third, much more controversial, component of the US security structure in Northeast Asia is defined by the Taiwan Relations Act. Not per se a mutually binding international agreement, it supersedes a mutual defence treaty that was signed between the US and the Republic of China in 1954 and that was abrogated in 1979, when the US shifted diplomatic recognition to the PRC. The TRA declares that US policy is: 'to provide Taiwan with arms of a defensive character; and to maintain the capacity of the US to resist any resort to force or other forms of coercion that would jeopardize the security, or the social or economic system, of the people on Taiwan'. This piece of legislation was adopted by Congress and does not represent a component of US diplomacy nor are US forces officially committed to joint operations with ROC forces. Yet, despite this low-key status, it is routinely denounced by the PRC as interference in its 'domestic affairs'.

The 'southern rim' of the San Francisco system, which extends into Southeast Asia and Australia, does not carry the same weight as the 'northern rim' of Northeast Asia, although the current 'war on terrorism' invites a reconsideration of its

---

19   Measured in Purchasing Power Parity, Japan's GDP is third, with 3,778 billion USD, but using market exchange rates, Japan's economy ranks as the second largest with 4,666 billion USD. See OECD in figures 2005 edition. Available at the following URL: <http://ocde. p4.siteinternet.com/publications/doifiles/012005061T004.xls>. In 2004, Japan's military expenditures ranked fifth, with spending of 45 billion USD, immediately slightly less than China's, which spent in 2003 56 billion USD. See the 'U.S. Military Spending vs. the World', Center for Arms Control and Non-Proliferation, February 7, 2005. Available at the following URL: <http://www.armscontrolcenter.org/archives/001221.php>.

20   See Nicholas Eberstadt, *The End of North Korea* (Washington, DC: American Enterprise Institute, 1999); Scott Snyder, 'North Korea's Decline and China's Strategic Dilemmas', *United States Institute of Peace*, October 1997 <http://www.usip.org/pubs/ specialreports/early/snyder/China-NK-pt1.html>.

importance. Two bilateral mutual defence treaties and one collective defence system underline this structure. The first of these mutual defence pacts, with Australia and New Zealand, was signed in 1952, but New Zealand was left out of that structure over the issue of nuclear weapons in 1986. The second mutual defence treaty, also signed in 1952, links the US with the Philippines. Although it does not have the same importance as the Japan–US, the ROK–US, or the Australian–US treaties, the country has been designated in 2003 a 'major non-NATO military ally'. Another major non-NATO military ally, Thailand, has no treaty with the US, while Singapore is exploring concluding with the US a strategic framework agreement.[21] The Southeast Asia Collective Defence system, signed in 1955, is the only multilateral defence arrangement in the region. It includes three states that are, or were, party to existing mutual defence treaties (e.g., Australia, the Philippines and New Zealand), one outsider to the region (France), as well as Thailand.[22]

Although the South Asian regional security complex falls within the ambit of the Pacific Command, it is not included in the 'San Francisco System' and as such represents the weak link in the Asian component of US hegemony. Yet the region also stands as a pivot in any strategy that would seek to counter-balance an emerging China. The two main military powers in the region, India and Pakistan, have developed uneasy but important relations with the US. The relationship between Washington and New Delhi is based on mutual interests including the development of trade, the enhancement of maritime security, the fight against terrorism, and the reinforcing of shared democratic values.[23] Although the US would like to see India counterbalance China, and even if Indian leaders have abandoned the most strident components of their rhetoric against the US presence in the Indian Ocean, the policy of non-alignment policy has not yet been shelved. Although some Indian security planners think that China is a threat to their country's security, most believe that the main challenge to India remains the development of a strong economy capable of sustaining its military and the increase of its diplomatic profile.[24] The other important bilateral relationship in South Asia, the US relationship with Pakistan, focuses on the war on terrorism. The defence pact between the US and Pakistan that was signed in 1954 was abrogated as a result of the 1965 Indo-Pakistani war and was never revived, even if close military cooperation has been re-established in the aftermath of September 11.[25]

---

21   Statement by Adm. William J. Fallon before the House Committee on US Pacific Command Posture (March 9, 2005), p. 21.

22   James F. Hoge, 'A Global Power Shift in the Making', *Foreign Affairs*, 83/4 (July/August 2004): 2–64.

23   Mohan Malik, 'High Hopes: India's Response to U.S. Security Policies', *Asian Affairs*, 30/2 (Summer 2003): 104–112.

24   A.Z. Hilali, 'India's Strategic Thinking and Its National Security Policy', *Asian Survey*, 41/5 (September/October 2001): 737–764.

25   Bokhari Farhan, 'US and Pakistan in Pact on Defence', *Financial Times* (February 11, 2002): 10.

Despite its impressive scope and the depth of the commitments offered by its allies, the security architecture established by the US in Asia remains fragile because of two trends. Firstly, changes in the global economy which are increasingly defined by the rise of China, and to a lesser degree, India, are redefining the interests and preferences of many states in the region. The rise of China's economy, in particular, elicits much more concern than India's. Although, paradoxically, China adheres more than India to the strictures of neo-classical economic policies, uncertainties about its political system and the intents of its leaders cast doubts about the consequences of an hegemonic stability under the aegis of China, and thus, about the likelihood that the US would accept with equanimity this hegemonic transition the way the UK supported the US rise to prominence in the global economy at the end of World War II. Secondly, the stability of the existing security arrangements depends on the ability of many governments to preserve the unity and enhance the prosperity of their own countries. In the 'northern rim' of the 'San Francisco' system, it is the risk of regime collapse in North Korea, as well as tensions within and between Japan and South Korea that renders the security architecture vulnerable. In the 'southern rim', it is the frailty of young democracies, prone to fall under the sway of populist authoritarian regimes, or the weakness of societies beset by poverty, social inequities, ethnic or communal unrest, that threaten the regional order. The next two sections will examine these two issues in turn.

Coping with the Rise of China

The Chinese leaders remain very cautious about the possibility that their country may assume in the long run the role of pivot for a new global hegemonic stability. When they admit this possibility, they profess that 'China's rise' will not lead to the destructive wars for hegemonic transitions triggered during the first half of the twentieth century by Germany and Japan. In their view, the process of China's emergence as a great power is underway, but they also believe that this achievement needs not lead to conflict. This view had received official support when Zheng Bijian, a close collaborator of the Chinese President Hu Jintao, had asserted it in 2003. There were concerns in early 2004 that the foreign policy of 'peaceful rise' could embolden Taiwanese separatists, and it was briefly abandoned. But after this brief eclipse, it has been reasserted in 2005.[26] Throughout the year, new developments in cross-strait relations, including a historic visit by Taiwanese opposition leaders, have apparently encouraged the Chinese government to renew its support for that policy.

One of the intellectual lines of argument that proponents of China's 'peaceful rise' advance to contradict the 'China threat' view is the claim that China does not seek hegemony, and that even the emergence of a new great power need not incur a military confrontation: the historical experience of the transition from British to American hegemony suggests that if the actor buttressing the international system

---

26   Zheng Bijian, 'China's Peaceful Rise to Great Power Status', *Foreign Affairs*, 84/5 (September/October 2005): 18–24.

agrees with the institutional structure put in place by the incumbent hegemon, conflicts need not unfold. Wars of hegemonic transition happen only when the aspiring hegemon seeks to change the international order: German and Japanese powers, which upheld nationalist commercial and economic policies, the theory argues, were bound to clash with the Anglo-Saxon powers, who supported liberal policies. So far, China demonstrates a willingness to accept the rules of the current international institutions. In fact, China represents one of the staunchest defenders of the current global economic status quo.

This attitude should not surprise since the PRC is likely to improve its standing by abiding by the rules of the current hegemonic stability. From being suspicious of international organisations, China has changed its perspective rapidly in the past decade.[27] Throughout the 1990s, it has increased its influence and power in the Asia-Pacific region simply by joining international organizations, creating new institutions (such as the Shanghai Cooperation Organisation), or taking initiatives for the founding of new ones (ASEAN plus three, the Boao Forum, etc.). Furthermore, it is moving pro-actively in regional diplomacy, with the organization of the Six-Party Talks. Chinese leaders realize that acceding to international and regional organizations based on rules and agreements, far from undermining the autonomy of their country, enhances its sovereignty.[28] They therefore see international organizations as mechanisms that help promote trade and security for China, and even see its accession into the World Trade Organisation and its presence at the United Nation's Security Council as mechanisms that help advance its national interest.

China's policy of 'peaceful rise' may be recent, but one could argue that it is not an opportunistic, short-term tactic: after all, since 1978, China harbours no claim to change the international order the way it did under Mao, and since the 1980s, it has adhered to the formula of 'peace and development' (*heping yu fazhan*), developed by Hu Yaobang and Zhao Ziyang, and which remained endorsed by Deng Xiaoping, even after the latter ordered the demise of the two leaders. This policy proclaims the economic development of the nation as its highest priority and peace as the essential condition for this development.[29]

The policy of China's 'peaceful rise' has been cautiously received in Asia. Some hold the benign view that Asians generally welcome rather than oppose Chinese regional emergence. Illustrative of this view is David Kang's claim that China may eventually achieve an hegemonic transition at the regional level by revitalizing the Sino-centric order that prevailed during the beginning of the Qing dynasty (1644–1911).[30] This regional order would 'fit' the neo-Gramscian concept of hegemony

---

27   David Shambaugh, 'China Engages Asia', p. 68.

28   Jean A Garrison, 'China's Prudent Cultivation of "Soft" Power and Implications for U.S. Policy', *Asian Affairs*, 32/1 (Spring 2005): 25–30.

29   Albert Legault, André Laliberté et Frédérick Bastien, *Le triangle Russie/États-Unis/ Chine : un seul lit pour trois?* (Sainte-Foy, Quebec : Les presses de l'Université Laval, 2004), p. 109.

30   David C. Kang, 'Getting Asia Wrong: The Need for New Analytic Frameworks', *International Security*, 27/4 (Summer 2003): 57–85.

as domination through consent because China would exercise its leadership simply through the demonstration effect of its economic prowess and would serve as a model for achieving wealth, independence and security. Using the logic of the realist approach to international theory, Kang argues that in their quest for security, Asian nations, far from balancing against China, prefer band-wagoning.[31] David Shambaugh sees that unfolding when he suggests that states close to China are starting to see it as a good neighbour: although he admits that not every country is persuaded by China's charm offensive, he argues that the perception of a 'China threat' increasingly reflects a minority view.[32]

However, other Asian states feel uneasy about any assertion of Chinese counter-hegemony: whether it is the Japanese, who have their own disputes with China, or South Koreans' opposition to irredentist claims suggested by China when its history books stated that a former Korean kingdom was part of China. With the exception of embattled and isolated states such as Burma and North Korea, other Asian powers do not look kindly at China's assertion of regional hegemony. In a rebuttal to David Kang, Amitav Acharya wrote that 'suspicions of China remain sufficiently strong to prevent opportunistic band-wagoning in which a state's political and military alignments would correspond closely with its economic linkages with China'.[33] Japan represents the most obvious example. Despite massive flows of Japanese foreign direct investment in China, and an intense trade between the two Asian giants, the density of their economic interaction has not altered the deep suspicions that mar their relationship at the political level. Chinese leaders remain incensed by the inability of the Japanese government to atone for the crimes of the imperial army during World War Two, and Japanese leaders believe that behind the rhetoric of 'China's peaceful rise' lies an agenda of regional domination.

Although it is true the Sino-Japanese relationship may represent an extreme case of mistrust, other Asian states such as South Korea, Thailand and the Philippines, while openly welcoming China's influence, do not intend to relinquish their security agreements with the US. Not only do these states seek to maintain their arrangements, but new patterns of security cooperation are quietly emerging. Hence India's initiatives for a rapprochement with the US, combined with the beginning of a détente between India and Pakistan, conforms with the US position that India represents an important counter-balance to China's influence in Asia. The resilience of the existing security arrangements and the emergence of new ones suggest that China's regional emergence does not lead to band-wagoning.[34]

Although conservative-leaning strategic studies experts in the US routinely claim that China is the only credible contender to American hegemony in Asia, they are far from expressing a consensus within the epistemic community involved in the

---

31   David C. Kang, quoted by Acharya, 'Will Asia's Past Be Its Future?', p. 149.
32   David Shambaugh, 'China Engages Asia', p. 64.
33   Acharya, 'Will Asia's Past Be Its Future?', p. 149.
34   *Ibid.*, p. 150.

making of the US–China policy.[35] Many not only dismiss the 'China threat' view as unnecessary and alarmist scare-mongering, but would go as far as questioning the idea that the 'rise of China' represents an irresistible juggernaut. In their opinion, not only does China lack the military capability to act as credible counter-hegemon in the near future, but they believe that its economy is hampered by serious flaws that prevent future expansion.[36] Other opponents to the 'China threat' hypothesis, who believe that hegemony rests on a good amount of persuasive power, argue that China still lacks the soft power that could help it assume the responsibilities underpinning the establishment of a regional, or even global, hegemonic stability.[37]

Given China's current military capability and the limits to its economy, many analysts argue that it will probably take China 25 years before it becomes a sophisticated geopolitical actor in East Asia and in the Western Pacific capable of rivalling the US.[38] At the beginning of the twenty-first century, the US still maintains an enormous technological advantage that makes it difficult for China to achieve its ambition to close the gap with the US.[39] A credible challenge to US hegemony in Asia would require from China a far more sophisticated military force than the one it can muster currently. The US Navy still maintains complete naval supremacy, preventing the Chinese People's Liberation Army's Navy from representing a threat: simulations demonstrate that the Chinese Navy would be most likely to lose a battle in the neighbouring waters of Singapore or Malaysia.[40] Moreover, China remains so beset by domestic conflicts that military adventurism abroad may pose serious risks to regime survival. If diversionary theories of war argue that domestic instability can push embattled leaders to instigate international crises, other historical evidences point to a causal links in the opposite direction: military adventurism may precipitate a regime collapse.[41]

The same limitations hold with respect to other dimensions of power. Hence, there is little question that China's soft power has yet to match the United States'. If

---

35   Colin Dueck, 'New perspective on American Grand Strategy', *International Security*, 28/4 (Spring 2004): 204.

36   A well-known statement of this view that generated considerable controversy was Gerald Segal, 'Does China Matter?', *Foreign Affairs*, 78/5 (September/October 1999): 24–36; George J. Gilboy, 'The Myth Behind China's Miracle', *Foreign Affairs*, 83/4 (July/August 2004): 33–47.

37   Pei Minxin, 'Beijing's Closed Politics Hinders "New Diplomacy"' *Financial Times* (12 September 2004): <http://www.carnegieendowment.org/publications/index.cfm?fa=view&id=15836>.

38   John Gershman, 'Is Southeast Asia the Second Front?', *Foreign Affairs*, 81/4 (July/August 2002): 60–74.

39   Thomas J. Christensen, 'Posing Problems Without Catching Up: China's Rise and Challenges for U.S. Security Policy', *International Security*, 25/4 (Spring 2001): 5–40.

40   Benjamin Schwarz, 'Managing China's Rise', *Atlantic Monthly*, 295/5 (June 2005): 27–28.

41   See for example the outcome of the Malvinas' War between Argentina and the UK, or the fallout from the loss of Bangladesh after the Indo-Pakistan War of 1971.

one considers participation in the United Nations' peacekeeping mission as a form of soft power, China does not yet represent a major actor. Despite the size of its huge armed forces, its contribution to peacekeeping mission represents a drop in the ocean: in 2005, China sent only 1,026 military personnel, civilian police and troops serving for twelve missions. As of June 2005, India, a country with a population comparable to China's, and an economy that has received far less international investments than China, had dispatched 6,176 people in peacekeeping missions. Two other Asian countries with less than a tenth of China's population, Pakistan and Bangladesh, have sent 9,914 and 8,208, and Nepal, a country with only 25 million people, had sent 3,565.[42]

Economists and international relations specialists adhering to a liberal perspective also question the 'China threat' thesis, but they do so for different reasons. Many of them believe that China represents a source of opportunities for sustained growth in the US itself, in China, and in the world generally. These more optimist analysts believe that China does not pose any threat to the region or to US hegemony because it depends too much on the maintenance of the status quo to meet its own domestic goals.[43] Both the US and China are enmeshed in a complex relationship whose central component is a far-reaching economic partnership.[44] China is more than an exporter of goods: it also stands as a major importer in northeast Asia. Hence, although Beijing had a $124 billion trade surplus with the US in 2003, it had significant trade deficits with its Asian neighbours: $15 billion with Japan, $23 billion with South Korea, $40 billion with Taiwan and $16 billion with the members of the Association of Southeast Asian Nations (ASEAN).[45] American business tends to view this trend rather positively: the current enthusiasm for international organizations expressed by China represents precisely the kind of outcome that previous administrations have tried to achieve: ensure that China has a stake in the liberal, rule-based international structure that the US had established during World War Two.[46] In other words, China is becoming a pillar of the existing hegemonic stability.

Yet, recent trends have made American policy-makers nervous about China's real intent, and whether the policy of 'peace and development' is as resilient as

---

42   United Nations, 'Contributors to United Nations Peacekeeping Operations' (June 2005) <http://www.un.org/Depts/dpko/dpko/contributors/>.

43   Hongying Wang, 'Multilateralism in Chinese Foreign Policy: The Limits of Socialization', *Asian Survey*, 40/3 (May/June 2000): 475–491.

44   See Brad Setser, 'How Scary is the Deficit?', *Foreign Affairs*, 84/4 (July/August 2005): 194–200; US Government, *2005 Report to Congress of the U.S-China Economic and Security Review Commission*, 109th Congress (1st session, November 2005) <http://www.uscc. gov/annual_report/2005/annual _report_full_ 05.pdf>; Board of Governors of the Federal Reserve System, *Report on Foreign Portfolio Holdings of U.S. Securities as of June 30, 2004*, Department of the Treasury Federal Reserve: Bank of New York (June 2005), <http://www. treas.gov/tic/shl2004r.pdf>.

45   George J. Gilboy, 'The Myth Behind China's Miracle', *Foreign Affairs*, 83/4 (July/August 2004): 33–49.

46   *Ibid.*

its proponents claim. Besides the periodic bouts of tension between the PRC and the ROC (1995–1996, 1999), which the Chinese government considers 'domestic affairs', the recent deterioration of relations between China and Japan undermines the progress towards greater regional integration achieved during the 1990s. The Sino-Japanese enmity results from an unsolved legacy inherited from World War Two, competition for resources, and a host of domestic considerations. One of the most important unresolved issues between China on the one hand, and the US and Japan on the other, remains the thorny question of Taiwan's status. If a pro-independence government would proclaim Taiwanese sovereignty, it is most likely to provoke immediate military intervention from China.[47] If the likely response of the US to such an eventuality is the use of military force, the attitude of other Asian countries remains unknown: an American conflict with China over Taiwan may very well threaten the delicate fabric of the security structure buttressed by the 'San Francisco system" The next section looks into this.

The American Security Architecture in Asia under Strain

The San Francisco System's 'Northern Rim': a Declining Anchor of Stability in the East Asian Regional Security Complex

The three bilateral agreements that define this component of America's hegemony in Asia are facing strains that result from the rise of China and the end of the Cold War. Although the 'rise of China' may not necessarily lead to band-wagoning, it does affect the calculations of Japan, South Korea and Taiwan in their relations with their giant neighbour, and it inevitably affects their relations with the US. The 'rise of China' represents a tremendous opportunity for business in all three countries, and a hostile posture towards China by their respective governments represents a serious liability for them. Furthermore, many politicians in Japan, South Korea and Taiwan are sensitive to the arguments of their respective business communities when they argue that the prosperity of their own polity depends increasingly on good relations with China. In sum, pressures from within for better relations with China weaken the case for maintaining a defence treaty with the US. Conditions specific to the three polities make it even more complicated to maintain the existing bilateral arrangements intact.

(1) The domestic pressure in Japan for a more moderate policy towards China and the assertion of a more independent policy towards the US have been an important feature of Japanese politics throughout the Cold War, but the domination of the conservative-leaning Liberal Democratic Party (LDP) during most of the period prevailed, ensuring that the presence of US troops in Japan would remain the bedrock of the alliance between the two countries. This policy was sustainable because Japan

---

47   James F. Hoge, 'A Global Power Shift in the Making'.

benefited from it economically. Defence expenditures were capped and the resulting savings were re-allocated to help Japan recover from the destruction of World War II. This arrangement was gradually undermined during the last decade of the Cold War, however, when the rising economic prominence of Japan coincided with difficulties in the American economy, leading to accusations that Japan was a 'free rider' unwilling to contribute its fair share in military cooperation with the US and its allies.[48] Backed by a domestic public opinion overwhelmingly supportive of a pacifist posture for its foreign policy, the LDP government has weathered throughout the Cold War calls for more robust participation in the enforcement of collective security.[49]

Yet despite the attachment of many Japanese to the 'pacifist constitution', the country has developed one of the most powerful military forces in the world, with significant offensive and defensive capabilities: Tokyo's military budget ranks has the second or third biggest in the world.[50] Furthermore, recent trends have generated a shift in popular support for more assertive Japanese foreign and defence policies. The nuclear ambitions of the DPRK, and in particular the Taepodong missile tests that have intruded into Japanese airspace in 1998, have invigorated revisionist currents in Japan who want to amend a Constitution which they consider too constraining. More recently, the rise of anti-Japanese sentiments expressed in popular demonstrations in Chinese large cities and in the rejection of Japan's claim to have a permanent seat at the UN Security Council have offered opportunities to Japanese conservative politicians who favour a more hard-line attitude towards China.

Assuming that the Japanese people remain attached to the values and the policies they have supported for over half a century, a more important participation by Japan in Asia geopolitics, far from challenging US hegemony in Asia, would strengthen it. Its eventual military build-up and the willingness to contemplate the use of military force abroad are occurring within the context of US demands to strengthen the alliance of democracies.[51] A more assertive Japan, which generated some anxiety in the 1980s, represents the linchpin of the US security strategy in East Asia at the beginning of the twenty-first century.[52] The economic clout of Japan, reviving after more than ten years of stagflation, may ensure that in the post-Cold War era, the Japan–US alliance is more likely to represent a partnership between equals rather than a rivalry.[53] Yet major trends in Japanese demography, and shifts in the regional

---

48   Jennifer M. Lind, 'Pacifism or Passing the Buck?: Testing Theories of Japanese Security Policy', *International Security*, 29/1 (summer 2004): 92–121.

49   Frank Langdon, 'American Northeast Asian Strategy', *Pacific Affairs*, 74/2 (Summer 2001): 167–185.

50   Peter J. Katzenstein and Nubuo Okawara, 'Japan, Asian-Pacific Security'. p. 156.

51   Zalmay Khalilzad, *et al.*, *The United States and Asia: Toward a New U.S. Strategy and Force Posture* (Rand Corporation, 2001), p. 13.

52   Derek J. Mitchell, 'US Security Strategy for the Asia-Pacific Region', *Asian Affairs*, 28/3 (Fall 2001): 159–166.

53   Francis Fukuyama, 'Re-envisioning Asia', *Foreign Affairs*, 84/1 (January/February 2005): 75–87.

economy, make the regional supremacy unsustainable in the middle run. The effect of Japan's ageing population on the willingness of the public to invest heavily for defence is unknown, but there is little doubt that spending for social welfare is going to represent an increasingly important share of the national budget. In this context, the US–Japan pillar of the American hegemony remains frail.

(2) The ROK–US defence treaty represents the second pillar of the 'San Francisco system'. Its strains are more severe than those that affect the US–Japan defence treaty. Two threats loom large over the resilience of this security agreement: the uncertainties that loom over the DPRK, and the increasing hostility felt by many South Koreans over a continued US presence in the peninsula. The first threat may have for years cemented the US–South Korea alliance. The fear of a military invasion, concerns over a regime collapse and a flood of refugees pouring across the border as a consequence, and lately, the announcement that Pyongyang wanted to develop a nuclear weapons programme, provided important motivations for the South Koreans who wanted to maintain the defence treaty in force. Many of their compatriots, however, believe it is the very intransigence of the US in its relations with the DPRK, if not their military in the peninsula, which exacerbates the DPRK's posture of hostility towards the ROK. It is this negative perception of the US that represents the second threat to the American presence in Korea.

The six-party talks convened to defuse the tension in the Korean peninsula have brought their share of tension between the US and South Korea. These tensions often pit the government against a substantial proportion of the population: the former opposes a weakening of the US–South Korea alliance, but many South Koreans wish the US presence in their country diminished. Conservative politicians support a strong presence of US troops in South Korea and even the democratically elected president Roh Moo-yun had to admit in 2003 after the first meeting of the 'Future of the ROK–US Alliance Policy Initiative' that the reduction of US troops could not be discussed before the resolution of the crisis with the DPRK over its nuclear programme.[54] Yet many South Koreans are upset that the American government devotes most of its attention to Iraq and does not seem interested in negotiations with the DPRK.[55] In addition, tensions between US military forces in South Korea and the local population have led to the realization that this once-strong alliance can be fragile. The June 2002 incident involving two US soldiers who accidentally killed two young Korean schoolgirls and the Korean casualties from the war in Iraq have generated uneasiness from a good section of the Korean population, leading many young Koreans to believe that the US is a greater threat to their security than the

---

54   Xinhua News, 'Reduction of US troops in S. Korea Long Term Matter: Roh Moo-hyun', (April 10, 2003).
55   Scott Snyder, 'The Fire Last Time', *Foreign Affairs*, 83/4 (July/August 2004): 144–149.

regime of Kim Jong Il.[56] It remains to be seen how future elected governments can refuse to yield to demands from many Koreans.

(3) The third component of the US regional hegemony in Northeast Asia, the Taiwan Relations Act, represents an even more serious liability. Viewed from the Chinese perspective, its resilience represents one of the most important irritants in Sino-American relations, proof that the US cannot be relied upon as a sincere partner and a demonstration that successive American administrations have all conspired to keep China weak and divided. As such, it poisons relations between the two countries. Yet successive American administrations from both parties have reiterated their resolve to act according to the prescription of this law, and to help defend Taiwan if it is subjected to an armed intervention by China. For them, it is a matter of credibility. But the prospect of a conflict between the US and China over a Taiwanese declaration of independence represents a major source of concern, and in recent years the Americans have signalled that they will not encourage such a declaration. Should that happen, the US would be faced with a very difficult dilemma: if its troops avoid intervening on Taiwan's side, this would undermine the trust of US allies; but the alternative may be even more difficult to contemplate: a major conflict with the PLA. Since 1979, the US has managed to avoid such a dangerous escalation in the Taiwan Strait through a policy of 'strategic ambiguity' ensuring that China, Taiwan and the US can reach face-saving compromises.[57] This policy has withstood the challenges of a pro-independence President being elected in 2000, and the renewal of his mandate in 2004, only because the Democratic Progressive Party and its ally, the Taiwan Solidarity Union, do not control the legislature. In the event that political parties favouring the cross-strait status quo lose their fragile parliamentary supremacy, the dynamic of Taiwanese domestic politics may become unpredictable and have serious consequences for the stability of the entire region and seriously undermine the American hegemony.

The San Francisco System's 'Southern Rim': The Challenges of the Southeast Asian Regional Security Sub-Complex's Fragmentation

The challenges faced by the US in Southeast Asia differ from those encountered in Northeast Asia. Unstable regimes beset by serious problems of governance, inadequate cooperation between governments in the region, weak or stagnant economies, social inequalities and fragile political institutions make the creation of a

---

56   Fukuyama, 'Re-envisioning Asia'.

57   See Roy Pinsker, 'Drawing a Line in the Taiwan Strait: "Strategic Ambiguity" and its Discontents', *Australian Journal of International Affairs*, 57/2 (July 2003): 353–368; Steven M. Goldstein and Randall Schriver, 'An Uncertain Relationship: The United States, Taiwan and the Taiwan Relations Act', *The China Quarterly*, 165 (March 2001): 147–172.

reliable collective security structure very problematic.[58] The fact that the Americans and their Australian allies have determined that the region is becoming another front in the global war on terrorism does not simplify matters.[59] Many states in the region, who were reluctant to get too involved with the US in security matters during the Cold War because of their posture as non-aligned states, find that allying too closely with the US would not help them meet the challenge of extremism. For instance, the invasion of Iraq has been badly received by the people of Indonesia and Malaysia, who saw it as an attack against fellow Muslims.[60] The other concern about the American approach to terrorism for many Southeast Asian governments is the lack of attention levelled against the social and economic sources of popular discontent on which Islamic fundamentalist and other extremists feed on.[61]

One of the few exceptions in the region is the Philippines, where US troops were redeployed in 2002 in order to help counter home-grown insurgencies.[62] Besides this old alliance and the partnership with Australia, however, the US cannot expect to expand its security network furthermore in the region. Thailand and Singapore, two states contemplating free trade agreements with the US and the maintenance of robust security cooperation with the US, refrain from going further for fear this would upset China.[63] Vietnam has increased its cooperation with the US in recent years, including in security-related matters, and its trade with the US, the most important component of this bilateral relation, has expanded significantly. Yet Vietnam cultivates an omni-directional foreign policy and therefore does not seek a rapprochement with the US at the expense of improving relations with China.[64] The economic dimension of the US hegemony in the region is also weakened by the uncertainties of governance in most states of the region. The causes of the financial crisis of 1997–1998 have yet to be addressed for Indonesia and Thailand, two of the most dynamic economies in the region, while states like Myanmar, Cambodia and Laos remain beset with more fundamental problems typical of failed states.[65]

---

58   Renato Cruz De Castro, 'US War on Terror in East Asia: The Perils of Preemptive Defense in Waging a War of the Third Kind', *Asian Affairs*, 31/4 (Winter 2005): 212–231.

59   According to Renato Cruz de Castro the term 'global terrorism' is far from being proper to SEA because most radical or militant Islamist groups in SEA cannot be considered international terrorist groups (with the exception of Jemaah Islamiyah in Malaysia and Indonesia). See 'US War on Terror in East Asia', p. 216.

60   Gershman, 'Is Southeast Asia the Second Front?'.

61   Renato Cruz De Castro, 'US War on Terror in East Asia', p. 225.

62   Gershman, 'Is Southeast Asia the Second Front?'.

63   Emma Chanlett-Avery, *Thailand: Background and US Relations*, US Congressional Research Services (CRS), Report 18 (September 6, 2005), p. 21.

64   Thomas Lum, *The Vietnam–U.S. Normalization Process*, Federation of American Scientists: CRS Issue Brief for Congress, June 17, 2005.

65   Thomas Lum, *Cambodia: Background and U.S Relations*, Federation of American Scientists: CRS Report for Congress, July 8, 2005, p. 14; *Laos: Background and U.S Relations*, Federation of American Scientists: CRS Report for Congress, November 22, 2004.

A Turbulent Periphery of the San Francisco System: The South Asian Regional Security Complex

South Asia presents American strategic planners with an even more daunting dilemma: the region represents an important component of the Asian security super-complex and another theatre in the war against terrorism, but this time the two most important allies on which the US relies to achieve its objectives, India and Pakistan, have a long history of mutual enmity and confrontation preventing the establishment of a stable regional security structure. In stark contrast to the security architecture of Northeast Asia, which relies on prosperous and stable democracies, and much in common with the states of Southeast Asian states, the states of the South Asian regional security complex are themselves bests by serious economic difficulties and unstable regimes, and because of domestic political sensitivities, they must avoid too close an entanglement with the American-centred security architecture. The US has traditionally been allied with Pakistan, a state that has periodically represented a security liability, but it has never entered into a formal treaty or military alliance with India, despite the fact that it represents the largest democracy in the world. India's adherence to a non-aligned foreign policy during the Cold War and in its aftermath explains this situation.

Concerns over the rise of China and a convergence of interest over the war on terrorism have provided incentives for closer cooperation between India and the US. In addition, since the beginning of the 1990, economic growth has enabled India to expand its military and geopolitical ambition in Asia,[66] and as a result, the US has expressed an increasing interest for closer security cooperation with India.[67] Although nuclear testing on the subcontinent at the end of the 1990s had briefly compromised US relations with both major powers in the region, the September 11 attack has forced a rethinking of this policy. If the recent detente between India and Pakistan facilitates a rapprochement with both states and the US, the thaw remains fragile and rest on the ability of General Musharraf to hold together Pakistan in the face of ethnic unrest, Islamic fundamentalist agitation and the problems of poverty that foster both.[68] The states surrounding India and Pakistan all face similar problems of poor governance and domestic instability, making them all unlikely partners for the US. This is the case of Nepal, afflicted by a Maoist insurgency that has spilled across the border to merge with similar movements throughout North India,[69] as well

---

66   Sorpong Peou, 'Whitering Realism? A Review of Recent Security Studies on the Asia-Pacific Region', *Pacific Affairs*, 75/4 (Winter 2002–2003): 575–585.

67   Rollie Lal and Rajesh Rajagopalan, *U.S.–India Strategic Dialogue* (Rand Corporation, Center for Asia Pacific Policy, 2004); Mohan Malik, 'High Hopes: India's Response to U.S. Security Policies', *Asian Affairs*, 30/2 (Summer 2003): 104–112.

68   Aarish Ullah Khan, *The Terrorist Threat and the Policy Response in Pakistan*, Stockholm International Peace Research Institute (SPIRI), policy paper no. 11 (Stockholm: SPIRI, September 2005).

69   Brad Adams, 'Nepal at the Precipice', *Foreign Affairs*, 84/5 (September/October 2005): 121–134.

as Sri Lanka, whose peace accord with Tamil Tiger secessionist guerrillas remains fragile.

Conclusion

The US maintains an important network of bilateral security agreements ensuring that the emerging Asian security super-complex remains tied closely to its global hegemony. Yet frictions within some key bilateral agreements, and the unlikelihood that this structure can be consolidated or expanded further raises uncertainties about its sustainability in the long run, especially in the face of a changing distribution of economic, political and military power. In particular, the rise of China already undermines American hegemony to the extent that even Asian states traditionally close to the US such as Japan and South Korea are growing increasingly worried about deepening their strategic cooperation with China, lest it undermine the foundation of their economic prosperity, which is increasingly tied up with China's economic prominence. A final note: to the extent that Chinese leaders believe that the current architecture of the global economy and that adherence to greater standards of transparency suit their national interest, there is no reason to believe that a transition to a global hegemony under Chinese leadership would represent a catastrophic change in the global order, or a threat to the prosperity of the American people. The consequences of such a transition hinges upon the willingness of American leaders to accept such a change, as much as on the political changes Chinese leaders undertake within their own polity.

Chapter 9

The Role of the United States in Western Africa: Tying Terrorism to Electoral Democracy and Strategic Resources

Cédric Jourde

Political actors act upon their representations of political reality. In the specific case of US–Africa relations, this argument implies that the United States government's relations with African states are defined by its decision-makers' representations of Africa. These representations circumscribe the range of policies towards Africa's fifty-three states, making certain policies possible while precluding others from even becoming imaginable options. This chapter analyzes the development of three major American representations of Africa in the post–Cold War era, with a special focus on the Bush administration and West Africa. I argue that these representations are significant because they have made possible the administration's political, economic and security policies toward Africa, while excluding alternative policy paths. With the fall of the Soviet Union, the US government's understanding of politics in the developing world has somehow changed. Issues such as Anti-Americanism expressed in the language of Islam, major civil wars, humanitarian crises, democratization and the provision of new natural resources constitute the new language through which US foreign policy-makers talk about and interpret political events in Africa (and in the rest of the Third World). In turn, the focus put on such issues shaped the evolution of US–Africa relations, as seen in the implementation of a more robust military cooperation with African states deemed to be threatened by terrorists, support to elections, as well as the financial and institutional support for US companies investing in oil producing countries. In brief, since the early 1990s, and more clearly since the Bush administration came to power, American governments have resorted to three important representations, closely connected to one another, through which they have interpreted African politics and, consequently, designed policies towards that continent: Africa as a new battlefield in the 'global war on terror'; Africa as a provider of strategic natural resources; and Africa as a democratically weak region in need of external support.

Given that Africa is made of many states, fifty-three, this chapter limits its analysis to the case of West Africa's sixteen states.[1] Methodologically, this chapter investigates the discourses held by various agencies of the Bush administration to reveal key American representations of West Africa. It then links these representations with the foreign policies that the US government has implemented in West African states.

The next section of this chapter spells out the theoretical framework upon which the analysis is based, explaining why an analytical focus on the role of representations in foreign policy and international relations helps to understand the recent evolution of US policy in West Africa. Then, the chapter analyzes in more details each of the three major US representations through which its decision-makers interpret and conceive of West African politics. The chapter then shows how these representations have made thinkable and possible the set of policies adopted by the American administration towards that region. The argument does not consist here in explaining why one specific policy has been adopted at the expense of another, but rather how representations provide the conditions for the emergence of a certain number of policies, that is, how representations make certain policies conceivable and imaginable in the first place. Finally, the concluding section offers a critical analysis of the three representations, highlighting alternative ways to conceive and imagine West African politics, thus revealing the political and ideological assumptions upon which the Bush administration's representations are founded.

Theoretical Framework: Hegemony, Representations, and Foreign Policy

Relations between states are, at least in part, constructed upon representations. Representations are *interpretative* prisms through which decision-makers make sense of a political reality, through which they define and assign a subjective value to the other states and non-state actors of the international system, and through which they determine what are significant international political issues.[2] For instance, officials of a given state will represent other states as 'allies', 'rivals', or simply 'insignificant', thus assigning a subjective value to these states. Such subjective categorizations often derive from representations of these states' domestic politics, which can for instance be perceived as 'unstable', 'prosperous', or 'ethnically divided'. It must be clear that representations are not objective or truthful depictions of reality;

---

1   Though defining regional boundaries is an arbitrary endeavor, I nonetheless define West Africa as including the following sixteen countries: Bénin, Burkina Faso, Cape Verde, Côte d'Ivoire, The Gambia, Ghana, Guinea-Bissau, Guinée, Liberia, Mali, Mauritania, Niger, Nigeria, Sénégal, Sierra Leone and Togo.

2   See Roxanne Lynn Doty, *Imperial Encounters: The Politics of Representation in North-South Relations* (Minneapolis: University of Minnesota Press, 1996); Donald A. Sylvan and James F. Voss (eds), *Problem Representation in Foreign Policy Decision Making* (Cambridge: Cambridge University Press, 1998); Jean-Pascal Daloz, *Élites et représentations politiques: la culture de l'échange inégal au Nigéria* (Bordeaux: Presses universitaires de Bordeaux, 2002).

rather they are subjective and political ways of seeing the world, making certain things 'seen' by and significant for an actor while making other things 'unseen' and 'insignificant'.[3] In other words, they are founded on each actor's and group of actors' cognitive, cultural-social, and emotional standpoints. Being fundamentally political, representations are the object of tense struggles and tensions, as some actors or groups of actors can impose on others their own representations of the world, of what they consider to be appropriate political orders, or appropriate economic relations, while others may in turn accept, subvert or contest these representations.

Representations of a foreign political reality influence how decision-making actors will act upon that reality. In other words, as subjective and politically infused interpretations of reality, representations constrain and enable the *policies* that decision-makers will adopt vis-à-vis other states; they limit the courses of action that are politically thinkable and imaginable, making certain policies conceivable while relegating other policies to the realm of the unthinkable.[4] Accordingly, identifying how a state represents another state or non-state actor helps to understand how and why certain foreign policies have been adopted while other policies have been excluded. To take a now famous example, if a transnational organization is represented as a group of 'freedom fighters', such as the multi-national *mujahideen* in Afghanistan in the 1980s, then military cooperation is conceivable with that organization; if on the other hand the same organization is represented as a 'terrorist network', such as Al-Qaida, then military cooperation as a policy is simply not an option. In sum, the way in which one sees, interprets and imagines the 'other' delineates the course of action one will adopt in order to deal with this 'other'.

American Representations of West Africa

This chapter undertakes a discourse analysis of the Bush government. It identifies and analyzes three important American representations of West Africa and, consequently, it identifies the policies that stem from such representations. In effect, US governmental agencies represent West Africa as a new significant site in what they call the 'global war on terror'; as a new provider of strategic natural resources; and as a democratically weak region. In turn, these representations shape US policies in West Africa, making certain policies conceivable while excluding others: military cooperation with any regime thought to be facing 'terrorists'; democracy promotion with an exclusive focus on electoral support and legal reforms; and pressures in favor of the liberalization of natural resources markets, mainly oil and gas markets. The governmental agencies this chapter investigates are those located at the center of US foreign policy towards West Africa: the White House, the State Department,

---

3   Neta Crawford, *Argument and Change in World Politics: Ethics, Decolonization, and Humanitarian Intervention* (Cambridge: Cambridge University Press, 2002), pp. 20–21.

4   Michael Schatzberg, *Political Legitimacy in Middle Africa: Father, Family, Food* (Bloomington: Indiana University Press, 2001), pp. 31–33.

the Department of Defense, the Department of Energy, and the US Agency for International Aid.

Representing West Africa as an Emerging Frontline in the 'Global War on Terrorism'

Since the end of the Cold War, Western decision-makers have increasingly interpreted world politics through the representation of global terrorism. Islamic fundamentalism 'has replaced Communism as the *different*' in the view of US foreign policy-makers.[5] The emergence and consolidation of this global representation impacted how American decision-makers have interpreted and classified political events in African states. To be sure, they applied the interpretative grid of terrorism to some regions of Africa more than others: the Horn of Africa and its southern fringe (Kenya and Tanzania), North Africa, and more recently West Africa. Specific events certainly contributed to the growth of this representation: the first attack against New York City's World Trade Center, in 1993, saw the participation of Egyptian activists. Though Egypt has always been defined as a Middle Eastern state more than an African state, despite it being on the African continent, the country's borders with and proximity to other African states, notably Sudan, Libya, Kenya and Tanzania, made these states parts of the Islamic terrorism problem. Terrorist attacks in France in the mid-1990s by Algerian groups, though not against American targets, strengthened the idea that Western states' interests were targeted by African Islamists. Like Egypt, Algeria is also often represented as being more connected to the Middle East than to Sub-Saharan Africa; but its shared borders with the later clearly brought the issue of terrorism into Western states' foreign policy toward Africa. The representation of Africa as a fertile ground for anti-American terrorism consolidated significantly following the bombings of the American embassies in Kenya and Tanzania in 1998. Following the 9/11 attacks, the emergence of a new concept, the global war on terror, helped to weave together various local and regional acts of terrorism into a single narrative, thereby giving additional weight to the representation of Africa as a fertile ground for terrorism. Hence, the kidnapping of European tourists by the Algerian *Jamaa'at as-Salafiyyat lil-Da'wat wa al-Qital* (known in French as the *Groupe salafiste de prêche et de combat*; GSPC) in the winter of 2003, was interpreted by the American administration as a significant event, mainly so because representatives of the GSPC had publicly claimed allegiance to Al-Qaida. This public act of allegiance to the United States' public enemy, as well as the alleged presence of the GSPC in most of the Sahelian countries (from Mauritania to Chad) and the military clashes between the GSPC and the Chadian army consolidated this representation of Africa.

More generally, the American representation of West Africa as a significant site in the global war on terror rests on three main ideas. First, US policy-makers

---

5   Nizar Messari, 'Identity and Foreign Policy: The Case of Islam in US Foreign Policy', in Vendulka Kubalkova (ed.), *Foreign Policy in a Constructed World* (Armonk, NY: M.E. Sharpe), p. 237.

emphasize continuously one particular sociological dimension of West African states: their large Muslim populations. In the words of the acting Coordinator of the Counter-Terrorism Office at the State Department, 'Islamist terrorist groups pose a terrorist threat to a region that is home to more than 100 million Muslims.'[6] For instance, of the innumerable facts one can use to describe Nigeria, governmental documents on Nigeria often chose to draw the attention on one fact: about half of Nigeria's population is Muslim. Hence the State Department explains that 'Nigeria's 140 million people represent 20 percent of sub-Saharan Africa's total population and the country's *increasingly restive* 60 million Muslim population is about the same size as the Muslim populations in Egypt and Turkey.'[7] Once the number of Muslims is highlighted, as well as its 'increasingly restive' nature, the following warning usually follows, as argued by a former US ambassador to Nigeria and his co-author to their *Foreign Affairs* readers: 'in Nigeria ... a potent mix of communal tensions, radical Islamism, and anti-Americanism has produced a fertile breeding ground for militancy and threatens to tear the country apart.'[8] The social fabric of Nigeria's small and poor neighbor, Niger, is interpreted through the same prism: 'Niger is the poorest Muslim country on earth, and it is ringed by unstable neighbors making its territory difficult to police. Its impoverished people are a ready target for anti-Western radical extremists, but the Government of Niger considers extremism a threat and supports the coalition against terror.'[9] And in Niger's neighbor, Mali, a former US Ambassador explains that 'What you see is fundamentalist preachers coming through trying to seduce a peace-loving region in Mali and the Sahel into a more fundamentalist branch of the religion.'[10] The American administration also considers as a significant fact the presence of an old Lebanese and Syrian diaspora in West African countries, seen as 'importers' of Islamic radicalism to West Africa from the Middle East. For instance, the State Department notices that in Côte d'Ivoire, 'Abidjan is host to a large community of overseas Lebanese, some of whom support organizations with terrorist links, including Hezbollah.'[11] In sum, West African states' Muslim populations, both native and immigrants, constitute a central pillar

---

6   William P. Pope, 'Eliminating Terrorist Sanctuaries: The Role of Security Assistance', Testimony Before the House International Relations Committee, Subcommittee on International Terrorism and Nonproliferation, March 10, 2005. Available at: <wwwc. house.gov/international_relations/109/pop031005.htm>.

7   *US State Department*, 'FY 2006 Congressional Budget Justification for Foreign Operations', p. 287. Emphasis added. Available at: <www.state.gov/s/d/rm/rls/cbj/2006>.

8   Princeton N. Lyman and J. Stephen Morrison, 'The Terrorist Threat in Africa', *Foreign Affairs*, 83/1 (January–February 2004): 75.

9   *US State Department*, 'FY 2005 Congressional Budget Justification for Foreign Operations', p. 270. Available at: <www.state.gov/s/d/rm/rls/cbj/2005/>.

10   Former Ambassador Vicky Huddleston, quoted in 'US fears Islamic militants in Mauritania, Algeria', *Reuters*, March 18, 2004.

11   *US State Department*, 'FY 2006 Congressional Budget Justification for Foreign Operations', p. 249.

in US policy-makers' representation of West Africa as a significant site of global terrorism.

Two other inter-related ideas also feed into this representation of West Africa: these countries share international boundaries with North African countries, and they have large inhabited areas that are badly controlled by what US officials (and many political scientists alike) consider to be 'weak' and 'unstable' states. As a result of their international borders and weakly controlled areas, US officials conclude that Islamist movements can easily cross international boundaries, threaten US interests in sub-Saharan countries, and smuggle weapons and money between the southern and northern shores of the Sahara. As a spokesperson at the Department of Defense explains, 'Vast, relatively unpopulated areas and a lack of strong government controls make parts of Africa particularly attractive to terrorists. Traditional caravan routes in this area [the southern shore of the Sahara, called the Sahel] can provide hideouts and staging areas for international and regional terrorists and criminals who move goods and money to support their operations without detection or interference.'[12] According to the US Agency for International Aid (USAID), in one of these countries, Mali, 'the vast open territory in the north ... presents potential troubling security threats. Armed gangs have the ability to roam through the porous borders with Algeria, Niger, and Mauritania virtually unchecked. These conditions have the potential to facilitate increased terrorist activities in the north.'[13]

Finally, the representation of West Africa as a significant site for the Global War on Terror is nurtured by an important rhetorical practice: 'analogical reasoning'.[14] Analogical reasoning is a key rhetorical device used frequently by American foreign policy-makers to interpret new political situations and to design a policy to deal with these events. As a new political development unfolds, decision-makers often draw an analogy with previous situations, thereby creating a correspondence between them and calling for a specific response to deal with the new situation in the light of the previous events. And in the case of US representation of West Africa, this rhetorical practice can be seen in the increasingly frequent use of an analogy between Afghanistan politics (or Central Asia more generally) and West Africa. This analogical reasoning leads US officials to conclude that the conditions that led to the emergence of an Islamic and rogue state in Afghanistan could be replicated in West Africa. For instance, Marine General James Jones, commander of the US European Command (EUCOM), told American congressional leaders that, as a consequence of the US military invasions of Afghanistan and Iraq, 'we are seeing indications of [the terrorists'] willingness to move to Africa to start to develop their footholds and to

---

12   New Counterterrorism Initiative to Focus on Saharan Africa, May 17, 2005. Available at: <http://usinfo.state.gov/af/Archive/2005/May/19-888364.html>.

13   Quoted from USAID's Mali country page, <www.usaid.gov/locations/sub-saharan_africa/countries/mali>.

14   Yuen Foong Khong, *Analogies at War: Korea, Munich, Dien Bien Phu, and the Vietnam Decisions of 1965* (Princeton: Princeton University Press, 1992).

export their particular brand of terrorism and instability'.[15] A US Navy officer made a similar comment, arguing that 'With a long history of being a center through which arms and other illicit trade flow, it is becoming increasingly important as terrorists now seek to use these routes for logistical support, recruiting grounds, and safe haven. We have indications of extremist groups with experience in Afghanistan and Iraq operating in the Sahel.'[16] A former coordinator at the State Department's Counter-Terrorism Office makes a similar point, drawing a sociological correspondence between the two regions: 'Those [Islamic fundamentalism] adherents are in places where we aren't fighting yet. Think about the Sahel. Think about the Madrasas [Islamic schools] in the Sahel and what's being taught in those Madrasas. The same people who were teaching in Pakistan are teaching in the Sahel today. Think about the children and the generation who are learning about the worldview that says the West threatens Islam and therefore the only way to defend the faith is to take up arms against the West.'[17] In sum, the representation of West Africa as a new hot spot for the war on terror is predicated upon analogies between Afghanistan and West Africa. For American decision-makers, West African politics is better understood, interpreted and made sense of when compared to Central Asian states, with which they see cultural (i.e., Islamic), geographic and political similarities.

US Security and Counter-Terrorism Policies in West Africa

The representation of West Africa as an emerging site of global terrorism, like any representation, made possible certain courses of action while precluding others. This representation circumscribed a narrow range of policies that the Bush administration could implement to deal specifically with its understanding and definition of a 'terrorist threat' in West African states. The policies made possible by this representation included the creation and consolidation of military training programs with West African states, the provision of lethal and non-lethal military equipment, the financing of and technical support for counter-terrorism legal reforms, the organization of joint military exercises, and the support of regional peace-keeping operations.

15　Quoted in 'EUCOM-based troops training Mali, Mauritania militaries for border patrols', March 17, 2004, *Stars and Stripes*. Available at: <www.stripes.com/article.asp?section=104&article=20295&archive=true>.

16　Statement of Rear Admiral Hamlin B. Tallent, US Navy, Director, European Plans and Operations Center, United States European Command, before the House International Relations Committee, Subcommittee on International Terrorism and Nonproliferation, on March 10, 2005. Available at: <http://www.eucom.mil/english/Transcripts/20050310.asp>.

17　Francis X. Taylor, 'Counterterrorism and Homeland Security: The International Perspective', Remarks to the Defense Worldwide Combating Terrorism Conference, US Department of Defense, Alexandria, VA, October 5, 2004, <www.state.gov/m/ds/rls/rm/36796.htm>.

One of the best examples of a recent policy that derives from the representation of West Africa as a fertile ground for terrorism is the creation of the Pan-Sahel Initiative (PSI) and its successor program, the Trans-Sahara Counter Terrorism Initiative (TSCTI), still in progress at the time of writing. According to the State Department's Counter-Terrorism Office, the Pan-Sahel Initiative is a program that assists Mauritania, Mali, Niger and Chad 'to counter known terrorist operations and border incursions, as well as trafficking of people, illicit materials, and other goods'.[18] The program was created and funded in 2002 by the State Department, and operated by the Department of Defense. In March and June of 2004, Special Forces trainers from the US European Command's Special Operations Command and the Marine Corps trained and equipped military units from the four West African states. The PSI budget however, was relatively small, approximately $US 7 million. For about six weeks, they trained infantry units in a variety of functions, including 'basic rifle marksmanship', 'first aid', 'navigation', 'communication', 'combat drills', and 'patrolling'.[19]

This program not only helps to train and equip West African military units, it also seeks to foster counter-terrorist cooperation among West African and North African states, and to gather information from a region that the US administration has little knowledge about. For instance, just as the PSI training programs on the field ended, a meeting was convened in March 2004 at the US EUCOM center in Stuttgart with the chiefs of staff of Sahelian states (Chad, Mali, Mauritania, Niger and Senegal) and North African states (Morocco and Tunisia). The objective was to bring together security leaders from both North and Sub-Saharan Africa to discuss military cooperation and information exchange, under the aegis of the United States.

The Pan-Sahel Initiative is now being transformed into the Trans-Saharan Counter Terrorism Initiative (TSCTI), and includes more states from both 'shores' of the Sahara, adding three North Africa states (Morocco, Algeria and Tunisia) and two West Africa states (Senegal and Nigeria) to the original four countries. As the Commander of US European Command stated, TSCTI aims to 'build indigenous capacity and facilitate cooperation among governments in the region that are willing partners … in the struggle with Islamic extremism in the Sahel region.'[20] With the creation of TSCTI, West and North Africa now have a program similar to the 'East Africa Counter-Terrorism Initiative' (EACTI), founded in 2003, which 'includes both border and coastal security programs for key countries in East Africa

---

18   See the website of Department of State's Counter-Terrorism Office. Available at: <www.state.gov/s/ct>.

19   C.D. Smith, 'Pan-Sahel Initiative', paper presented at the 'Conference on terrorism and counter-terrorism in Africa', Center for International Political Studies, University of Pretoria, March 23, 2004, p. 4. Available at: <www.up.ac.za/academic/cips/terrorism-conf. htm>.

20   General James L. Jones, 'Statement before the Senate Foreign Relations Committee', September 28, 2005, p. 17. Available at:<www.senate.gov/~foreign/testimony/2005/ JonesTestimony050928.pdf>.

to include Kenya, Djibouti, Tanzania, Uganda, Ethiopia and Eritrea'.[21] The first training program of TSCTI, called Flintlock 2005, took place in June 2005. About one thousand US soldiers were brought into the region and trained military units from the different West and North African countries.[22] In the words of a Department of Defense spokesperson, 'US special operations forces will train their counterparts in seven Saharan countries, teaching military tactics critical in enhancing regional security and stability. At the same time, they will encourage the participating nations to work collaboratively toward confronting regional issues.'[23] The new TSCTI is set to receive about US$100 million.[24]

In addition to these military training programs, the US has channeled money to West African governments and their security apparatus through various funding programs, such as the Foreign Military Financing program (FMF), the International Military Education and Training (IMET) and the Africa Contingency Operations Training Assistance program (ACOTA), which was established under the Bush administration in 2002 to replace a previous program (ACRI) created under the Clinton administration. The Bush administration considered that ACRI was not aggressive enough, and thus decided that ACOTA would, among many things, include 'preparation for *higher threat* peacekeeping operations',[25] a euphemism to say that the program now includes more 'offensive training'.[26]

Other programs which were officially dedicated to development objectives are being geared towards security and military considerations, such as the Economic Support Fund (ESF). Though ESF has traditionally been used to support the establishment of electoral commissions, support to opposition political parties, or the building of educational and health facilities among many things, parts of that fund now serve new functions: 'roughly one quarter of the FY 2006 Africa Regional ESF will be used to support counter-terrorism training and assistance not otherwise provided through other programs, including projects to help countries draft counter-terrorism

---

21   *US State Department*, 'FY 2006 Congressional Budget Justification for Foreign Operations', p. 316.

22   For a revealing day-to-day account of the Flintlock 2005 training program, from the perspective of the US soldiers involved in the operation, see the reports published in the Department of Defense' daily newspaper, *Stars and Stripes* (<www.stripes.com>), who sent a reporter in Tahoua, Niger. These reports are an excellent source for the study of American representations of African security and politics.

23   'New Counterterrorism Initiative to Focus on Saharan Africa', American Forces Press Service, May 17, 2005. Available at: <http://usinfo.state.gov/af/Archive/2005/May/19-888364.html>.

24   *Ibid.*

25   *US State Department*, 'FY 2006 Congressional Budget Justification for Foreign Operations', p. 298. Emphasis added.

26   Pierre Abramovici, 'United States: the New Scramble for Africa', *Review of African Political Economy*, 102 (2004): 688.

legislation, improve administration of borders, and combat money laundering'.[27] Though the amount of resources that support the various policies dedicated to West Africa, and Africa in general are much less important than those channeled to regions such as the Middle East or East Asia, one clearly notes a 'securitization' of these resources and policies.[28] In sum, as West Africa is increasingly represented as a significant site in the war on terror, as its various political features are interpreted through the prism of global terrorism, the US administration designs and implements policies that reflect and act upon this representation.

West Africa as a Supplier of Strategic Resources

The representation of West Africa as a new significant site for global terrorism is closely related to a second representation: West Africa as an emerging supplier of strategic natural resources, notably oil and natural gas. Two bodies of discourses sustain this second representation: national security and neoliberal economics. Access to oil and gas is defined in security terms. As the Middle East continues to be a risky region for the US, its government seeks other oil and gas producing regions. The meaning of West Africa, mainly Nigeria and some emerging oil producing countries, thus acquires a new significance in the national security frame of US government officials. Yet the means to reach that imperative are defined in neoliberal terms. The US government has been pressuring West African states to implement neoliberal economic reforms to ease up and expand access to these strategic resources.

The representation of West Africa as a provider of strategic natural resources has gained considerable importance under the Bush administration. In effect, as the new government came to power in January 2001, it put greater focus on the issue of energy resources. The founding text of the new administration, the National Energy Policy, was produced by a group chaired by Vice President Richard Cheney.[29] Published in May 2001, the 'Cheney Report', as it became known, highlighted both America's dependence on foreign oil and the perceived threats on these foreign sources. It defined oil and gas supplies as matters of national security. The 9/11 attacks and the political turmoil in the Middle East which erupted after the publication of the Cheney Report increased the administration's interest in oil supplies outside the Middle East.

This renewed concern for global oil and gas supply thus helped to re-represent and re-imagine Africa. As Volman explains, the Cheney Report helped to bring

27 *US State Department*, 'FY 2006 Congressional Budget Justification for Foreign Operations', p. 317.

28 Michael C. Williams, 'Words, Images, Enemies: Securitization and International Politics', *International Studies Quarterly*, 47/4 (2003): 511–31.

29 See Daniel Volman, 'The Bush Administration & African Oil: The Security Implications of US Energy Policy', *Review of African Political Economy*, 98 (2003): 573–84; National Energy Policy Development Group, 'National Energy Policy', 2001. Available at: <www.whitehouse.gov/energy>.

Africa back at the center of attention by looking at this continent through the prism of oil production: 'African countries provided 14 per cent of total US oil imports' (equivalent to the per cent provided by Saudi Arabia); but by 2015, according to the US Central Intelligence Agency, West Africa[30] alone will supply 25 per cent of America's imported oil.'[31] The Report indeed systematically defines Africa as a strategic provider of oil: 'Along with Latin America, West Africa is expected to be one of fastest-growing sources of oil and gas for the American market. African oil tends to be of high quality and low in sulfur, making it suitable for stringent refined product requirements, and giving it a growing market share for refining centers on the East Coast of the United States.'[32] The West African nation of Nigeria is Africa's top oil producer and top oil exporter to the US. It is also a growing producer of natural liquefied gas. The State Department's most recent Congressional Budget Justification underscores that dimension to justify its budget spending in Africa's giant state: 'Nigeria is the fifth largest source of US oil imports, and disruption of supply from Nigeria would represent a major blow to the oil security strategy of the US'.[33] President Bush understood quite well the importance of Nigeria; in his only tour of Africa to date (in July of 2003), he told his host, Nigerian President Olusegun Obasanjo: 'I appreciate very much your commitment to trade and markets, and we look forward to being an active trading partner with Nigeria.'[34] Nigeria, however, could soon be accompanied by smaller yet increasingly numerous West African producers, mostly those along the Atlantic shores, from Mauritania to Benin, including Côte d'Ivoire and Ghana. Though this chapter focuses on West Africa, it must be noticed that growing major oil producers are also to be found in Central Africa and Southern Africa, mainly Angola, Chad, Congo-Brazzaville, Equatorial Guinea and Sao Tome e Principe.[35] In sum, though a neglected region in US foreign policy, West Africa now gets more attention as the issue of alternative oil and other energy resources moves up on the national security agenda of the US government.

This national security discourse is closely connected to a neoliberal conception of oil and other natural resources: if the objective of American foreign policy in West Africa is both to improve access to already existing oil and gas fields and to open up new fields, the means to do so are conceived in neoliberal terms. West Africa is thus represented as a region in dire need to both liberalize its trade barriers (open up and

---

30   Note that the US administration's definition of 'West Africa' differs from mine and most analysts in general, as it includes all African states of the Atlantic shore.

31   Volman, 'The Bush Administration & African Oil', p. 574.

32   National Energy Policy Development Group, 'National Energy Policy', 2001, p. 8/11.

33   *US State Department*, 'FY 2006 Congressional Budget Justification for Foreign Operations', p. 287.

34   President Bush, Abuja, Nigeria, 12 July 2003. See <www.whitehouse.gov/news/releases/2003/07/20030712-10.html>.

35   See, for instance, the country analyses of the US Department of Energy, which analyzes both the current and potential oil producing activities in West Africa: <http://www.eia.doe.gov/emeu/cabs/ecowas.html>.

widen access) and harmonize its business practices with those of the United States (ease up and standardize access). Practically, doing so would facilitate and expand American energy companies' activities in West Africa, allow these companies to occupy larger portions of the energy sector, and therefore both guarantee and increase oil exports to the US.

Statements produced by the different agencies of the American administration insist persistently on the gap between the American conception of business and the current state of business relations in West Africa. Key words and concepts frequently appear in such a discourse, such as 'good governance', 'transparency', 'property rights enforcement', and 'anti-corruption laws'. For instance, President Bush's National Energy Policy Development Group 'recommends that the President directs the Secretaries of State, Commerce and Energy to continue supporting American energy firms competing in markets abroad and use our membership in multilateral organizations ... to implement a system of clear, open, and transparent rules and procedures governing foreign investment; to level the playing field for US companies overseas; and to reduce barriers to trade and investment'.[36] The authors of the policy thus argue that the US government should 'deepen bilateral and multilateral engagement to promote a more receptive environment for US oil and gas trade, investment, and operations; and promote geographic diversification of energy supplies, addressing such issues as transparency, sanctity of contracts, and security'.[37] Business relations in Nigeria are depicted in similar terms, as the country is defined as one that 'ranks high among the countries most affected by corruption' and which therefore needs US support to 'root out corruption at all levels ... [T]he United States will contribute to G8 support for Nigerian programs focused on increasing budget transparency and improved fiscal performance'.[38]

In sum, West Africa has been reimagined by US foreign policy-makers, now seen as a provider of strategic natural resources. But it also conceives of this region as one in which the nature of business relations is too distant from the American practice of doing business, and thus needs to be remodeled in accordance with the US business archetype.

US Neoliberal Policies in West Africa

The American representation of West Africa as a provider of strategic natural resources made possible a set of policies, while eliminating or marginalizing other. These policies reflect the representation's two main foundational ideas: national security and neoliberal economics. As West Africa's natural resources are defined in security terms, the US government seeks to implement policies that secure

---

36   National Energy Policy Development Group, 'National Energy Policy', 2001, p. 8/6.

37   *Ibid.*, p. 8/17.

38   *US State Department*, 'FY 2006 Congressional Budget Justification for Foreign Operations', p. 288.

access to these resources. Interestingly, there is here a close connection with the representation of West Africa as a potential site for terrorism. Access to 'strategic' resources must be secured from sources of threat, including terrorism, as well as other domestic sources of instability, be they civil wars, ethnic tensions, or criminal networks. Accordingly, a major aspect of American policies consists in providing support to West African security forces. As Volman nicely puts it, the Department of Defense seeks to 'strengthen the security forces of oil-producing countries and enhance their ability to ensure that their oil continues to flow to the United States.'[39] A good example is a recent policy designed by the State Department: the 'Africa Coastal/Border Security Program'. This program

> seeks to enhance Africa's ability to defend and monitor its vast coastal and border regions from terrorist and criminal activities, as well as to better protect fisheries, oil and environmental resources ... All these countries need better coastal/border security to support the long-term objectives of the global war on terrorism. *Additionally, many of these countries have valuable resources, and require credible security forces to protect their territorial integrity and prevent them from becoming lucrative havens for terrorists and criminals.*[40]

In sum, as both representations of West Africa as a target for global terrorism and as a provider of strategic resources merge one with another, these representations' respective repertoires of policies also increasingly amalgamate to form a coherent set of policies.

The representation of West Africa as a provider of strategic resources also hinges upon a neoliberal conception of international political economy. Hence, US policies aim at compelling West African states to adopt, sustain and deepen neoliberal reforms in order to facilitate and improve American companies' access to energy resources. As explained above, this not only means pushing for the liberalization of trade barriers, but also ensuring that West African business practices are in tune with the American ones. More concretely, US policies press for the privatization of state-owned companies, the liberalization of foreign investment laws, as well as the reform of the judicial system with respect to the protection of private property and the security of contracts. As stated explicitly by the National Energy Report, 'Overall US policies in each of these high-priority regions [the Western Hemisphere, the Caspian, and Africa] will focus on improving the investment climate and facilitating the flow of needed investment and technology.'[41] Another significant example of such policies is the decision by the US Agency for International Aid (USAID) to fund and support an energy consortium, the West Africa Regional Pool (WARP). This initiative provides the institutional basis for the 'investments that will be made by the private sector and

---

39   Volman, 'The Bush Administration & African Oil', p. 577.

40   *US State Department*, 'FY 2006 Congressional Budget Justification for Foreign Operations', p. 316. Emphasis added.

41   National Energy Policy Development Group, 'National Energy Policy', 2001, p. 8/7.

multilateral banks in power lines, power stations, and the like for the ultimate benefit of West African power consumers'.[42] USAID, and through it WARP, is channeling funds to the West African Gas Pipeline project, a '678 km onshore and offshore trans-national pipeline that will deliver Nigerian gas to Ghana, Benin and Togo',[43] and possibly Côte d'Ivoire as well.[44] In this USAID-funded project, the American company Chevron-Texaco is the largest shareholder (42%), while the British-Dutch company Shell is the third largest shareholder (16.5%).[45]

In addition, the US government also adopted two other significant policies that induce neoliberal reforms in West Africa: the African Growth and Opportunity Act (AGOA) and the Millennium Challenge Account (MCA). The African Growth and Opportunity Act (AGOA), created by the Clinton administration in 2000, provides incentives to African countries to reform their economies in exchange for duty-free access to the American market: 'AGOA provides reforming African countries with the most liberal access to the US market available to any country or region with which the United States does not have a Free Trade Agreement. It supports US business by encouraging reform of Africa's economic and commercial regimes, which will build stronger markets and more effective partners for US firms.'[46] In order to gain such a preferential access to the American market, African countries must first become eligible, that is meet certain criteria, most of which relate to the implementation of neoliberal reforms. 'Continual progress' in the following activities must be seen: market-based economies; elimination of barriers to US trade and investment; protection of intellectual property and efforts to combat corruption. Progress must also be seen in the following social and political domains: implementation of the rule of law and political pluralism; policies to reduce poverty, increasing availability of health care and educational opportunities; protection of human rights and worker rights; and elimination of certain child labor practices.[47] In her review of AGOA's fifth anniversary, the official in charge of supervising AGOA at the US Trade Representative Office explicitly conveyed the American administration's conception of what constitutes a good trade policy towards Africa: AGOA countries have liberalized trade, strengthened market-based economic systems, privatized state-

---

42   Quoted on USAID's webpage. Available at: <www.usaid.gov/missions/warp/ecintegration/wapp/index.htm>.

43   *Ibid.*

44   As stated in US Department of Energy, Energy Information Administration, 'Côte d'Ivoire Country Analysis Brief', March 2004. Available at: <www.eia.doe.gov/emeu/cabs/cdivoire.html>.

45   Available at: <www.usaid.gov/missions/warp/ecintegration/wapp>; see also the website of the West Africa Gas Pipeline Company Limited, available at: <www.wagpco.com>.

46   As stated in <www.agoa.gov/agoa_legislation/agoa_legislation.html>.

47   *Ibid.*

owned companies, and deregulated their economies. These changes have improved market access for US companies and benefited African economies.'[48]

For its part, the Millennium Challenge Account (MCA) was established under the Bush administration and intends to provide aid to developing countries on the condition that they meet three main conditions, 'governing justly', 'investing in people', and 'promoting economic freedom'.[49] Sixteen criteria help to measure progress in each of these three conditions. The latter, 'promoting economic freedom', seeks to push countries to adopt neoliberal reforms and is thus predicated on the idea that 'sound economic policies ... foster enterprise and entrepreneurship. More open markets, sustainable budget policies and strong support for individual entrepreneurship unleash the enterprise and creativity for lasting growth and prosperity.'[50] Data to measure the pace of these economic reforms are provided by four major US and international institutions with an explicit neoliberal orientation: the International Monetary Fund, the World Bank, the Heritage Foundation, and the Institutional Investor magazine.[51] In the same vein, the Bush administration established the African Global Competitiveness Initiative in July 2005. With a budget of $200 million, this program reinforces the neoliberal policy towards Africa; its four objectives consist in 'improving the ... environment for private sector-led trade and investment; improving the market knowledge, skills, and abilities of workers and private sector enterprises; increasing access to financial services for trade and investment; and facilitating investments in infrastructure'.[52] Interestingly, among the four 'regional hubs' for 'global competitiveness', whose main task is to implement US trade policies in Africa, two are located in West Africa, one in Accra (Ghana) and one in Dakar (Senegal).[53]

In short, the National Energy Policies, as well as AGOA and MCA, constitute a set of policies through which the American administration attempts to induce West African countries to undertake neoliberal reforms. These reforms are expected to facilitate access to West Africa's natural resources, including resources considered to be 'strategic' such as oil and gas.

---

48   Florizelle B. Liser, 'AGOA: A Five Year Assessment', Statement before the House Committee on International Relations Subcommittee on Africa, Global Human Rights and International Operations, October 20, 2005, p. 4. Available at: <wwwc.house.gov/ international_relations/109/lis102005.pdf>.

49   See the Millennium Challenge Account website : <www.mca.gov>.

50   Quoted in 'MCA update', June 3, 2002, <www.usaid.gov/press/releases/2002/fs_ mca.html>.

51   For a critical analysis of the MCA, see Susan Soederberg, 'American Empire and 'Excluded States': The Millennium Challenge Account and the Shift to Pre-emptive Development', *Third World Quarterly*, 25/2 (2004): 279–302.

52   As reported in <www.usaid.gov/locations/sub-saharan_africa/initiatives/agci. html>.

53   See <africatradehubs.org>.

The Representation of Electoral Democracy

Finally, a third significant American representation of West Africa is that of a region where democracy is fragile. Consistent with a long tradition in US foreign policy, this representation defines the United States ('the self') as 'as an instrument of democratic change in the international system',[54] and the other regions of the world ('the other') as beneficiaries of American enlightenment. According to Monten, this tradition of democracy promotion has at least two faces: '*exemplarism*', which promotes democracy not by intervening in other countries but by setting the example; and '*vindicationism*', best illustrated by the Bush administration, 'in which the active – and even coercive – promotion of democracy is a central component of US grand strategy.'[55] Democracy promotion, however, is not only a goal in itself; it is also a means by which other goals are advanced. Hence, with respect to Africa in general, the State Department underscores clearly how weak and fragile democracies can undermine other US interests:

> Democracy promotion in Africa is not only a reflection of American ideals but represents the bedrock supporting all key U.S. interests on the continent. Democracy represents a stabilizing force capable of alleviating humanitarian crises resulting from armed political power struggles that cost the United States billions of dollars each year. U.S. economic prosperity flourishes through partnerships with stable governments that strive to enforce the rule of law and create suitable investment climates. Like-minded democracies also make the best partners in our global efforts to address international concerns ranging from terrorism, crime, and drug trafficking to weapons proliferation, environmental degradation, and the spread of infectious diseases.[56]

More generally, The Bush administration's representation of West Africa as a region where democracy if fragile and in need of external support is founded on three ideas. First, a close analysis of the different American government agencies' interpretations of West African politics suggests that democracy is mostly defined in 'electoralist' terms. The discourses put much emphasis on the adoption of liberal constitutions and the holding of free and fair multi-party elections as the most important way to measure the quality of democracy in West Africa.

Second, and in close connection with the previous point, there is a strong belief that democratization follows a pre-determined path. This teleological and universalist perspective, which sees America's liberal democracy as the natural model to follow, does not make much room for alternative definitions and understandings of democracy. Though this universalist aspect is still imprecise and nebulous, certain discourses suggest that it takes its roots in the belief that US democracy is universal because it is, above all, a divine gift to humanity. Consequently, the belief is that the

---

54   Jonathan Monten, 'The Roots of the Bush Doctrine: Power, Nationalism, and Democracy Promotion in US Strategy', *International Security*, 29/4 (2004): 114.

55   Monten, 'The Roots of the Bush Doctrine', p. 114.

56   *US State Department*, 'FY 2006 Congressional Budget Justification for Foreign Operations', p. 317.

United States has been chosen to convey that gift to other regions and countries. For instance, speaking in the West African nation of Senegal, during his African tour in 2003, President Bush declared: 'And one of the things that we've always got to know about America is that we love freedom, that we love people to be free, *that freedom is God's gift to each and every individual*. That's what we believe in our country. I'm here [in Senegal and in Africa] to spread that message of freedom and peace ... We're here not only on a mission of mercy, we're also here on a mission of alliance ... May God bless you all. And may God continue to bless Senegal and America.'[57]

Third, US government interprets the fragility of West African democracy by the emergence of a few key threats. Paradoxically, none of these threats are seen as consequences of democracy's antithesis: authoritarian rule. Rather, the antitheses of democracy, that is, the conditions into which democracy could fall are civil war, terrorism and state failure. As compared with these threats, authoritarian rule seems to be democracy's second-best option. The threats to West Africa's fragile democracy call for American support, a support that relates closely to the representation of West Africa as a new site for the global war on terror. In sum, terrorism, civil wars, and instability more generally are said to be inimical to democratizing regimes. For instance, as he ended his first African tour in 2003, President Bush told his Nigerian audience that the African leaders he met throughout his tour 'are committed to the spread of democratic institution and democratic values throughout Africa. Yet those institutions and values are threatened in some parts of Africa by terrorism and chaos and civil war. To extend liberty on this continent we must build security and peace on this continent.'[58] And as our discussion of policies will show in the next section, both democracy and security-related policies were closely intertwined, yet also contradicting one another.

Democracy Promotion Policies

The American representation of West Africa as a democratically weak region circumscribes the range of policies, of imaginable policies. More specifically, the foundational ideas upon which this representation is based, especially the electoralist and universalist definition of democracy and the increasing concern with security issues, narrowed down the type of policies that decision-makers could imagine.

The State Department and USAID are key actors in the design and implementation of policies dealing with elections, such as election monitoring, training for election staff, democracy-awareness seminars for political parties and journalists. The judicial system is also a key target of US policies, which seek to reform and mold it in ways that will make it similar to those of Western democracies.

---

57   President Bush, Dakar, Senegal, July 8, 2003: <www.whitehouse.gov/news/releases/2003/07/20030708-3.html>.

58   President Bush, Abuja, Nigeria, July 12, 2003. The entire speech can be found at: <www.whitehouse.gov/news/releases/2003/07>.

One can get a sense of this electoralist dimension of democracy promotion in this State Department statement, in which it explains how half of a major account, the Economic Support Fund (ESF), will be used in African countries to 'support democratic development, the rule of law, and respect for human rights through programs that aid legislative and judicial reform, increase transparency and support improved electoral processes, provide training to strengthen governing skills for newly elected officials at the national and local levels, and strengthen civil society'.[59] In West Africa's Burkina Faso, which is governed by an authoritarian regime, ESF money 'would be used to enhance democratization programs following the 2005 presidential election and to prepare for 2006 parliamentary elections'.[60] In another West African authoritarian country, Guinea, US Agency for International Development (USAID) explains that 'If legislative elections take place in 2007 as planned, training workshops on citizen's rights and responsibilities during elections will be organized at the local government level.'[61] And in West Africa's largest regime in transition, Nigeria, the State Department 'will work with ... electoral bodies to provide technical assistance to prepare for future elections. We will support the rehabilitation of governmental institutions critical to democratic stability, including reform of the justice system and work with state and national legislators.'[62]

Critical Analysis

The concept of representation helps the analyst to better grasp the peculiarity and subjectivity upon which political actors found their understanding of a given political reality. It forces us to explain why some elements of a political reality have been emphasized with more insistence while others are being left over. Hence, in the case study analyzed in this chapter, I have shown that the Bush administration, like any other government in the world, holds specific representations of foreign states, which in turn define a range of possible policies. The Bush administration's three representations of West Africa are specific frames which define West Africa's political reality in narrow terms, corresponding to the administration's broad worldview, emphasizing some political elements while excluding others. This final section sets the contrast between these three representations of West Africa and alternative ways to represent West African political reality.

The representation of West Africa as an emerging battlefield in the global war on terror oversimplifies the 'fact' of West Africa's Muslim populations. An alternative representation would rather highlight the heterogeneity of Islam, insisting on the

---

59   *US State Department*, 'FY 2006 Congressional Budget Justification for Foreign Operations', p. 318.

60   *Ibid.*, p. 318.

61   *USAID*, 'Congress Budget Justification FY 06/Guinea Program', p. 14. Available at: <http://www.usaid.gov/policy/budget/cbj2006/afr/pdf/gn_complete05.pdf>.

62   *US State Department*, 'FY 2006 Congressional Budget Justification for Foreign Operations', p. 287.

idea that it is not a homogeneous religion, neither as an ideological belief system nor as a daily social and individual practice. Though Islam is a common religion to many communities in West Africa, it is practiced and imagined in different ways; contrary to the US administration's analogical reasoning highlighted above, a 'madrasa' (Islamic school) in Pakistan cannot be easily compared to a 'madrasa' in Mali; even two Malian 'madrasa' simply cannot be understood as identical 'learning centers of Islamic radicalism', far from it. Similarly, instead of reading West African politics with a special focus on transnational terrorist organizations, one could instead focus on the weak legitimacy of many West African regimes as a critical factor breeding political opposition. Thus, rather than emphasizing these states' 'weaknesses' or 'failures' as enabling factors for global terrorism, analysts could instead consider the weak legitimacy of their regimes. With such alternative representations in mind, one can understand why the policy of providing significant security and military support to West African states of the 'war on terror' front, as illustrated by the Trans-Sahara Counter Terrorism Initiative, could generate outcomes that can produce undesired effects: perpetuating the political power of illegitimate regimes and thus contributing to the radicalization of their opposition.

Similarly, the representation of West Africa as a democratically weak region and in need of US assistance tends to downplay certain elements while overemphasizing others. Surely, elections and judicial reforms are key dimensions of democratic life, but many authoritarian regimes have become 'masters at absorbing' electoralist and judicial reforms without changing their authoritarian foundations.[63] Alternative representations could instead highlight other factors that contribute to the formation of a legitimate regime, without putting an exaggerate focus on electoral engineering. As different authors have shown, a better appreciation of local, culturally informed understandings of the meanings of legitimate governance is needed.[64] Sørensen rightly argues that 'in many cases, perhaps especially in Africa and some parts of Asia, the focus has been on the notion of holding free and fair elections rather than on the broader political, cultural and institutional transformation connected with a process of democratization'.[65]

---

63   Thomas Carothers, 'Is Gradualism Possible? Choosing a Strategy for Promoting Democracy in the Middle East', Middle East Series, *Working Paper* 39, June 2003, Carnegie Endowment for International Peace, p. 11.

64   Christophe Jaffrelot (ed.), *Démocraties d'ailleurs* (Paris: Karthala, 2000); Mikael Karlstrom, 'Imagining Democracy: Political Culture and Democratisation in Buganda', *Africa*, 66/6 (1996): 485–505; Frederic C. Schaffer, *Democracy in Translation: Understanding Politics in an Unfamiliar Culture* (Ithaca: Cornell University Press, 1998); Michael Schatzberg, *Political Legitimacy in Middle Africa: Father, Family Food* (Bloomington: Indiana University Press, 2001).

65   Georg Sørensen, 'The Impasse of Third World Democratization: Africa Revisited', in Michael G. Cox, John Ikenberry, and Takashi Inoguchi (eds), *American Democracy Promotion: Impulses, Strategies, and Impacts* (Oxford: Oxford University Press, 1998), p. 98.

In addition, the representations of West Africa as a weak democratic region and as a significant site for global terrorism increasingly clash one with another. Though he made his observation prior to the 9/11 attacks and the foreign policy shift that followed, Hook correctly points out that the US government 'grew more comfortable with leaders in sub-Saharan Africa who sacrificed democratic principles in the name of maintaining internal and regional stability.'[66] The Bush government's global war on terror has made this remark even more accurate. Hence, alternative representations of West African politics point at consequences that were unexpected by the current American representation of democracy in West Africa. They can show that strong support to any regime which defines itself as an ally in the war on terror, combined with a narrow support for elections, may indeed do more to perpetuate political problems in West Africa than to solve these problems.

Finally, the representation of West Africa as a provider of strategic natural resources, and the policies deriving from this representation, must be set against alternative understandings of the politics of natural resources in West Africa. This representation, and especially the 'national security' discourse upon which it is founded, led the US government to provide security and military support to West African regimes whose democratic credentials were quite weak, thereby trumping the already fragile democracy promotion policies. Meanwhile, the neoliberal paradigm which feeds into this representation, and the policies that derive from such a conception, generates in West African nations social and economic consequences that can eventually undermine, if not contradict, other security and political objectives. As Sandbrook and Romano have shown in the case of Egypt and Mauritius, West African regimes' legitimacy, and even their 'stability', which Western governments revere so much, can be damaged precisely by neoliberal reforms that transfer heavy social and economic costs on West African populations.[67] In addition, instead of representing West African political economy with a narrow focus on energy resources, alternative representations could emphasize less profitable, yet more durable and socially inclusive economic activities, thereby generating less damaging consequences. Finally, this representation of West African natural resources, and the means to access them, also risks undermining the democracy promotion efforts, a consequence that could be avoided with an alternative interpretation of West African political economy. As explained above, states seeking to benefit from the fundamentally neoliberal Africa Growth and Opportunity Act program must meet certain political and social conditions (political pluralism, protection of human rights, protection of workers' rights, etc.). But the actual importance of these social and political conditions in the eyes of the American administration remains unclear as one looks at the list of West African countries deemed 'eligible'. In effect, thirteen

---

66   Steven W. Hook, 'Inconsistent US Efforts to Promote Democracy Abroad', in Peter Schraeder (ed.), *Exporting Democracy: Rhetoric vs. Reality* (Boulder: Lynne Rienner, 2002), p. 213.

67   Richard Sandbrook and David Romano, 'Globalisation, Extremism and Violence in Poor Countries', *Third World Quarterly*, 25/6 (2004): 1007–30.

of West Africa's sixteen states are considered eligible (Côte d'Ivoire, Liberia and Togo are excluded), many of which are authoritarian states in which the rule of law, political pluralism and the protection of human rights are clearly violated on a daily basis, such as Burkina Faso, Guinea and Mauritania.

Conclusion

To sum up, the role of the United States in West Africa in recent years, but more especially under the Bush administration, is predicated upon key representations of West Africa. Echoing a pattern seen in other regions of the world, political events unfolding in West Africa, and responses to deal with these events, are made sense of by the US government through the prism of global terrorism, access to natural resources, and the promotion of an American version of democracy. In turn, US foreign policies towards that region derive from these representations. Though this is too early to get a definite answer, one now needs an in-depth understanding of these policies' consequences in the target countries. How exactly have they affected the local reality of these West African societies? How have local political actors reacted to and responded to these US policies. Answers to these questions should help us understanding the medium and long-term implications of the current American hegemonic/imperial phase in West Africa.

Chapter 10

Contribution or Constraint?
The Role of the North American
Periphery in Redefining US Power

Stephen Clarkson

The voluminous literature on American power naturally focuses on the United States as agent, that is, the international order's *subject*, whose material and material assets are assessed in order to explain its capacity to affect the shape of events almost everywhere outside its borders. Discussions of the United States' recent global position generally start with its massive concrete assets understood in terms of such attributes as the wealth and vitality of its population, the size and dynamism of its domestic economy, the competitiveness and overseas reach of its corporations, the war- and peace-making capacity of its military. Beyond these indicators of its hard power, the United States' clout has also been attributed to the attractiveness of its liberal values, the success of its economic model, and the popularity of its mass cultural products. Such examples of soft power shift more attention to the willingness of other states as *objects* in the international system to bend to Uncle Sam's will. Although US influence is generally understood to be mainly a function of its own hard- and soft-power assets, this chapter makes a further claim: an epistemology which does not also understand American power as a dependent variable is insufficient in an interdependent world.

Surprisingly little attention is paid to the United States as *object* of other state and forces. Yet, the extent to which its present ability to influence the behaviour of other states is itself a function of having gained significant assets through the substantial control it had achieved over them in the past and the continuing use of their resources it can make in the present. This reciprocal aspect of dominant-state power, which is explicitly understood in the concept of 'empire' (when political control and economic exploitation are openly acknowledged and visibly exercised through coercion) is obscured by the fuzzier notion of 'hegemony' (dominance effected through a consensual acceptance of the system-leader's authority) that is generally applied to Washington's dominion in the post–World War II era. This paper posits that, whether imperial or hegemonic, American power cannot be properly calibrated without considering how it is affected – for better or for worse – by its relationships with its international interlocutors in general but, in particular, by its interconnections with its two contiguous neighbours.

Those who study a particular country's US relationship also tend to treat Washington as the independent variable. In North America, Canadianists and Mexicanists overwhelmingly regard the United States in terms of its influence over their two countries, the resulting limitation on their autonomy, and, in turn, their capacity to achieve their own goals in Washington. Few in the continental periphery have considered the problematic of this chapter – whether their country should be considered a constituent element of US power, either buttressing or constraining it. Still, from the beginning of American history, the United States' periphery has played a significant, if under-analyzed, role in constituting and/or constraining both the country's hard, material assets and its softer, psychic power.

The analytical challenge in carrying out this assessment is a good deal more complex than it might first appear. In an attempt to sketch out a methodology for this essay, the first section will provide a conceptual preamble that explains to what extent it makes sense to talk of the United States' peripheries as a component of its own strength. The second section will consider the evolution of the power relationship between the United States and its two peripheries during the two centuries leading up to the attacks on New York and Washington by Al Qaeda. This historical review will provide the context for the third section's attempt to understand the US periphery's role since September 11, 2001 in redefining US power.

Conceptual Preamble: Defining and Redefining US Power

Leaning on the Oxford dictionary's explication of 'definition', ('describes the scope, determines the extent, outlines the essential qualities, specifies with precision, gives its act meaning'), we can distinguish four types of 'redefinition' that have resulted in the aftermath of the Al Qaeda attacks: material power, dynamic power, soft power and interactive power.

Describe the Scope

Let us start from Realist analysts' point of departure, *material power.* Reflecting on the static approach that measures US power by the size of its population, gross domestic product, military might, and natural resources, it is clear that the two peripheral states of North America have added and can add considerably to all these asset types. American power can be 'redefined' if it gains or loses access to one or other of its neighbours' population, markets, or raw materials. New technologies can increase or decrease a country's power: the ability to explore for oil under the ocean bed bolstered Mexico's petroleum reserves considerably and so added to its material power. The capacity to create energy from uranium empowered countries such as Canada which were blessed with that mineral's deposits.

Determine the Extent

When its static power is mobilized to exercise influence abroad, a country's *dynamic power* is a function not just of its own shift in orientation but of the responses of its international partners. When the United States redefined itself by declaring a war on terror after September 11, 2001, its dynamic power was determined by how its interlocutors responded to this initiative. For example, by contributing its troops, Canada buttressed American power in Afghanistan in 2002, whereas Mexico abstained from sending a contingent even of medical orderlies.

Outline the Essential Qualities

Among Internationalist foreign-policy scholars, for whom 'soft power' is a vital corollary of a state's 'hard', material resources, the perceived *legitimacy* of a state's stance plays no less central a role in assessing its international effectiveness. Canada first buttressed the legitimacy of President George W. Bush's Middle-East mission with its support in Afghanistan and then helped delegitimize it by withholding its soldiers from Iraq the next year. Mexico withheld its support for both military engagements and actively blocked US efforts to bend the United Nations to its will by refusing, along with Chile, to support Washington in the Security Council.

Specify with Precision

Beyond a dynamic relationship being redefined through changes in the power transmitter or in the power receptor, a redefinition of a state's *interactive power* can occur following a change in the international political economy context. A change in the global balance of forces will also cause power relations to change. The formation of the Organization of Petroleum Exporting Countries' cartel shifted power from the oil-consuming to the oil-producing states when OPEC was able to double and redouble the price of oil in 1973. Multiplying the value of its oil raised Canada's material power, though whether it was able to mobilize this asset in its relationship with Washington depended not just on who actually owned and controlled its petroleum resources but on whether there was a political will within Canada's governing circles to exercise these assets politically.

Give Exact Meaning

One result of this attempt to see American power as a function of the role played by its periphery should be to help us characterize more accurately the United States' global role. Along a continuum from complete control to total subordination, we may be able to specify whether, in what respect, and when the United States has been or still is an empire, hegemony, commonwealth, or in some cases even a dependency.

US Power Vis-à-Vis Its Continental Peripheries over Two Centuries

Collapsing the development of North America's three coast-to-coast federations into its broadest outlines, we can reduce the double dynamic of resistance and acceptance by the peripheries to the United States' initial expansionism to two facets: ideological-military and economic-cultural.

Manifest Destiny: Ideological-Military Expansionism (Early 19th Century)

Revolutionary America's first imperial mission was to dominate the continent from whose eastern seaboard its self-liberated colonies began their energetic expansion into the hinterland. Through force of arms, US armies secured or seized vast tracts, first from British North America, then from Mexico. After the United States consolidated enormous areas under its flag, the periphery then resisted this expansion through government-driven assertions of autonomy. With the British North America Act (1867), the colonies to the north were cobbled together into a semi-autonomous state whose own defensive expansionist policies (building the transatlantic railroad by 1885) stymied the US push north of the 49th parallel.

Following a disastrous war, Mexico conceded half its territory to the expansionist USA. After it suffered the ignominy of US troops occupying its very capital in 1847, the shattered Mexican Republic consolidated its capacity to maintain its severely amputated territory against a further US expansionism. By the time the United States defeated Spain in Cuba and appropriated what remained of its empire in the Caribbean, Mexico had accommodated itself to Washington's imperial quest while remaining outside its formal domain.

As the cost of overcoming resistance to the north or south exceeded the benefits to be gained by achieving political control of their territory, the geographical limits of the American state stabilized. The dynamics of this first period can be seen as archetypical: the peripheries both contributed to the construction of a rich USA enjoying the largest quota of the continent's best lands with the best weather, while at the same time they denied Manifest Destiny its full continental realization.

Open Door to the Continent: Economic-Cultural Influence (Late 19th Century)

Just as the Canadian and Mexican rhythms were out of sync in the ebb and flow of military-ideational factors in the first part of the 19th century, so did their timing differ when they responded to the United States' government-led trajectory as an industrial giant, whose rapid rise was based both on pirating British technology and protecting its manufacturers from overseas competition.

While trying very hard to maintain its colonial ties with the British imperial market, Canada's second priority was to strengthen its continental economic linkages. It was only when Washington rebuffed several overtures from Canadian politicians to renew the trade-reciprocity treaty it had abrogated in 1866, that Sir John A. Macdonald tried a third option, faute de mieux, in 1879. His National Policy launched a three-pronged import substitution industrialization strategy: railway construction to connect eastern and central Canada with the West, immigration aimed to attract foreigners to settle there, and tariffs to induce foreign entrepreneurs to develop a manufacturing economy in Canada.

Meanwhile, Mexico ended the 19th century embracing export-led economic development powered by foreign capital. British and American investors financed a railroad network to export the natural resources – also developed by foreign investors – that were needed both by Great Britain and the rapidly industrializing economy to the North. This was an informal hegemonic regime into which Mexico willingly inserted itself as a resource periphery connected to the Anglo-American industrial centres. The extent to which Mexican resources buttressed American as well as British economic power was indicated by the two states' powerful, if unsuccessful, reprisals when, after a revolutionary movement ended the authoritarian régime of Porfirio Días, Mexico launched itself on a path of industrial autarchy based on nationalizing foreign-owned enterprises and so divesting the United States and the United Kingdom of their control over its valuable assets.

Changing Context

The second industrial revolution fired by the technologies of the internal combustion engine and electricity turned industry-serving minerals and power-generating rivers into major assets for both the northern and the southern economies. Over the two decades straddling the end of the 19th century, the technological, managerial and strategic environment changed fundamentally with the result that Canada followed an opposite path from Mexico.

Canada's increased material power was largely neutralized as a result of the simultaneous managerial revolution that allowed multi-entity corporations to exercise head-office control over their subsidiary operations – whether mines or mills – in other countries without giving up their ownership rights. When Canada continued to welcome foreign capital, American investors retained control as they increased their share of the country's burgeoning manufacturing and resource economy. Not only did the US economy benefit from secure access to Canada's supply of resources and the increased market available to its mass-produced goods; its investors also pocketed the economic rents that came from owning these subsidiary operations in Canada.

The dramatic shift taking place in the global balance of forces in the wake of Germany's and Japan's rise as competing industrial economies and threatening military powers resulted in the Anglo-American entente of 1906, which allowed Washington finally to lay to rest its fear of Canada as a British imperial threat along its northern border. As articulated to Congress by President Taft in 1911, the United States had a three-point northern strategy: encourage Canada to detach itself completely from the British Empire; discourage its capacity to compete with American enterprise by maintaining high tariffs against its manufactured exports; and encourage its development as a complement to the US economy that supplied it resources, integrated its capital markets, and offered a consumer market in which US firms could get economies of scale.

By the inter-war period, when US investment and trade started to exceed British investment and trade with Canada, the now politically autonomous Dominion could be seen as extending the power of both the old empire across the Atlantic and the young empire to the south. For two brief decades, Canada balanced between a failing formal empire and a rising hegemon, semi-dependent on each, while Mexico remained splendidly safe in its autarchic isolation.

Military Power

This double-fronted role was made dramatically obvious during World War II, when Canada's material power was mobilized by the Mackenzie King government into a formidable war machine that buttressed Britain's defences, helping it to survive in the face of Nazi Germany's massive pressure. Up to Pearl Harbor, Canada also played proxy for the back-stage efforts of President Roosevelt to achieve the same objective, since ways were found to channel US military equipment through Canada to beleaguered Britain. Following the Ogdensburg and Hyde Park agreements signed by King and Roosevelt, the two governments cooperated in strategic planning and military production in order to harness the continent's resources, to defend its shores, and to defeat its common enemies across the Atlantic and Pacific oceans. While the Canadian economy was smaller than the American, it was not subordinate. To this extent the Canadian-American military power relationship approximated a community whose norms were elaborated in solidarity with the British.

Again the contrast with Mexico was stark, since Uncle Sam's southern periphery remained neutral during the second global war. Apart from agreeing to cooperate with the US Navy in its concern about a possible Japanese invasion, Mexico added nothing to American power other than the negative assurance that it would not be used as a military staging area against the United States. Mexican neutrality persisted into the Cold War, a negative presence to the south that Washington could tolerate, given the failure of China and the Soviet Union to establish any significant foothold in the hemisphere beyond Fidel Castro's exceptional bastion in Cuba.

For Canada, the Cold War proved more militarily constraining. Having renounced the development of nuclear weapons, despite its advanced capacity in atomic technology and having let its air force and navy dwindle from their considerable size at the end of the war with Germany, Ottawa found itself becoming a junior partner integrated into the American war machine. Lying as it did under the main bomber and intercontinental-ballistic-missile flight paths between the Soviet Union and the United States, but being enthusiastically committed to containing the communist threat, Canada negotiated a formally bilateral institution – the North American Air Defence Command (NORAD) – into which its air force was integrated under effective US direction. While Ottawa could claim to be in a hegemonic relation with its militarily more powerful partner through its participation in the multilateral, but US-dominated North Atlantic Treaty Organization, it had little choice but behave as an obedient protectorate of the US Strategic Air Command in NORAD. As the 'defence against help' doctrine suggested, Canada had to defend itself against a possible, if improbable, Soviet attack lest the United States do so on its behalf. Although coercive, the near unanimous agreement by Canadians that the Soviet Union constituted an ideological, if not a military, threat to them as well as to the United States made this imperial relationship consensual.

Economic Hegemony

The economic side of the Cold War was a regime comprising the capitalist states and the Third World, whether aligned or non-aligned, that was managed by a number of multilateral financial institutions (International Monetary Fund, World Bank, General Agreement on Tariffs and Trade). Its parallel political order was made up of many international organizations, the United Nations being first among equals. Keynesianism, the globally accepted political-economy paradigm, prescribed that each capitalist state was in charge of managing its own economy. Transborder governance took place formally between governments via their diplomats and informally within the growing ranks of transnational corporations.

Within this post–World War II ideational universe, Ottawa reoriented its hybrid, export-led development model along an almost exclusively North-South axis, privileging US direct investment in its resources and manufacturing sector, which was sheltered by high tariffs to maximize employment in branch-plants and domestically owned enterprises. Building on the foundations established in the first half of the century, Canada provided to the United States not just a rich consumer market for its products plus access to its resources and their rents which US TNCs could capture, but also a flow of human resources trained at public expense in Canada as a kind of farm team supplying talent to the major league, whether John Kenneth Galbraith to Harvard or Mary Pickford to Hollywood.

So overwhelming was US dominance in all the mass cultural media that a nationalist reaction set in during the 1960s, when the legitimacy of US power in Canada was challenged by those who protested Washington's imperial efforts to control Southeast Asia. Disquiet about the US war in Vietnam notwithstanding, Canada's foreign policy from 1945 to 1970 remained focused on playing the role of helpful fixer on the international stage, acting as peacekeeper, participating in international organizations, and muting its disagreements with Washington over its Vietnam, China or Cuba policies. In these ways, Canada provided a major boost both to US hard and soft power, providing its economy raw materials and lending its foreign policy legitimacy.

By contrast, Mexico remained in a resistance mode in the post-war decades, trying to preserve the autarchy of its economy. In actual fact, US investment flowed south of its border, US products sold in Mexican markets, and, in return, Mexico supplied low-cost labour through the bracero program and sold the US larger amounts of oil, albeit from Pemex, the state corporation which kept the economic rents on behalf of the Mexican people.

Transition from Keynesianism to Neoconservatism (1970–1985)

The syncopation between Mexico and Canada's rhythms continued through the 1970s when, coming to the apparently exhausted end of its import-substitution industrialization and facing the need to make some more fundamental rapprochement with the United States, Mexico was preparing to give up its resistance to integration within the American economic machine.

Meanwhile, in response to the United States' imperial excesses in Vietnam and such alarming bouts of system-disturbing unilateralism as President Richard Nixon's unnegotiated delinking of the US dollar from gold in 1971, Canada moved into a half-cocked resistance mode. With Washington rewriting the international economic order's rules as it went, Ottawa contemplated an overt 'third option' that would diversify its economic partners in order to reduce its vulnerability to American actions, reduce its integration in the American economy, and become a more nationally integrated economy.

Based on a rationale developed by a number of government studies – Watkins' Report (1968), Wahn Report (1971) and Gray Report (1972) – that documented the branch-plant economy's chronic inefficiency, low productivity and truncation, the federal government established a series of entities designed to correct some of the economy's worst distortions. The Canada Development Cooperation was to repurchase control of key companies fallen under foreign ownership. The Foreign Investment Review Agency was to negotiate performance requirements with foreign investors to achieve greater benefits for the national economy from their new enterprises. Petro-Canada was to provide a domestic, publicly owned corporate presence in a petroleum sector dominated by US transnational giants. In the fallout from OPEC's second price hike of 1979 and expectations that oil would soon cost $100 a barrel, the high point of Pierre Trudeau's nationalist measures, the National Energy Program, was launched in 1980 to repatriate control over the petroleum industry.

The outrage at FIRA and the NEP expressed in 1981 by the newly elected Reagan administration showed that Washington considered that increased ownership by Canadians of their own oil industry threatened its interests, thus proving it considered not just that Canadian resources were a vital element of its economic base but that, in the unwritten rules of centre-periphery relations, Canada did not have the right to intervene in its own affairs to the prejudice of US corporate interests.

The Triumph of US Economic Hegemony

The Reagan administration's anger at Canada was the by-product of a larger phenomenon – the dismay in the USA about what was seen as its hegemonic decline. It was believed in Washington that other countries were using government measures unfairly to support their companies' competition with US TNCs, whose technology was being pirated and whose scope for expansion abroad was being stymied. While Congress strengthened Washington's unilateral protectionist measures that could be used to punish other states for their offensive, export-promoting measures, the repercussions from taking too tough a stand against individual partners led the US to prefer a more ambitious, multilateral gambit: rewrite the rules of the General Agreement on Tariffs and Trade.

Since the European Community and leading Third-World powers such as Brazil and India were reluctant to accept changes to the global trade regime designed further to empower corporate America, the US developed a third track to its strategy. Negotiating bilaterally with willing interlocutors might establish precedents for the new norms it wanted and so exert pressure on its recalcitrant GATT partners.

Washington started along this track by negotiating with Israel a bilateral trade agreement that proved of little consequence for its grander design. More significant was the Canada–United States Free Trade Agreement (CUFTA, 1989), which broke new ground as far as several key US objectives were concerned:

- *Energy*: Canada guaranteed to maintain its flow of petroleum exports over which it renounced its right to impose a tax. This meant the federal government lost control over the pricing and use of the country's petroleum reserves.
- *Investment*: Canada made the long-resisted concession that the norm of 'national treatment' would apply not just to goods but to foreign investments. This meant the end of industrial-strategy policies designed to promote Canadian enterprise.
- *Services*: the scope of the 'national treatment' norm was also expanded to include services, a radical innovation which threatened the governments' capacity in the long term to prevent the entry of US service corporations into such public sectors as health and education.

Although the world did not take much notice of CUFTA, intense attention was roused when Washington's bilateral strategy extended CUFTA to include its southern neighbour, Mexico, which had changed its economic course in the 1980s by turning its back on economic autarchy, by joining GATT and the OECD, and by starting to disassemble its corporatist state apparatus. When added to APEC, the Asia-Pacific Economic Cooperation in which the United States appeared to be forming another massive economic region in its own image, the prospect that NAFTA would create a second regional trade block discriminating against Europe's interests persuaded the EU to engage more seriously with Washington's trade-policy demands. As a result, NAFTA's negotiation was quickly followed by the World Trade Organization's inauguration (WTO, 1995).

Taken together, these new continental and global regimes represented the post-Cold War apogee of US hegemony. Through a virtual export of its own legal standards, the United States had caused the rules of the now global economic system to be rewritten and, in so doing, presented its continental neighbours with a new external constitution, complete with authoritative norms, rules, rights and institutions that formalized (in a long written document), deepened (making measures more intrusive) and broadened (bringing many new areas of government policy under its disciplines) their semi-autonomous status in the United States' immediate sphere of economic influence.

Norms   Applying the principles of 'national treatment' and 'most favoured nation' to foreign investment required Canada and Mexico to terminate policies previously designed to extract greater benefits both from American- and overseas-based subsidiaries. Within a matter of years, the retail sector in Canada had been overtaken by free-wheeling American corporations, while myriad medium-sized Mexican businesses closed down in the face of massive inflows of cheaper imports often marketed through mega-stores.

Rules   Washington used the trade negotiations to eliminate a number of its neighbours' policies to which it had previously objected. For Canada, this meant the capacity to review foreign takeovers of medium-sized companies.

Rights   Big Pharma made big legal gains by acquiring greatly expanded intellectual property rights with which it could suppress competition by generic drug manufacturers in both Canada and Mexico.

Institutions   Elaborate mechanisms for settling disputes between governments were written into NAFTA. Despite the signatory parties' formal equality, NAFTA's dispute settlement processes actually increased the power asymmetry on the continent. Washington refused to comply with rulings that went against the interests of such powerful economic lobbies as softwood lumber (Canada) and trucking (Mexico), but expected its neighbours to comply when it won panel decisions.

More dramatically, Chapter 11 empowered NAFTA corporations to take direct legal action against government measures that could prejudice their transborder subsidiaries' profitability. Given the overwhelming dominance of US TNCs in the continent's economy, Chapter 11 gave the American private sector a powerful new instrument with which to discipline Mexican and Canadian governments, causing a chill in their efforts to strengthen environmental regulations.

The WTO's dispute settlement system was more symmetrical and more powerful than NAFTA's, giving Canada and Mexico a stronger instrument with which to constrain the protectionism of their common neighbour. Nevertheless, the United States' capacity to shift from consensus- and rights-driven hegemon to force- and might-driven empire can be seen in its unwillingness to comply with the WTO ruling that invalidated the offensive, double-dipping Byrd amendment, which awarded the revenue collected from countervailing and antidumping duties to the very industries that had won this punitive tariff protection from their foreign competition.

Among the continental periphery's business classes, which had supported the cause of trade liberalization and had helped work out its specific rules through close participation in their governments' negotiations, NAFTA and the WTO signified a strengthening and deepening of American *hegemony*. Having helped define the new regime, they participated energetically within it. For those elements of civil society such as the labour and environmental movements or native and cultural organizations, the new economic order's powerful constraints on governmental power signified a dramatic extension of US *imperial* control over their destinies.

Actual resistance to the new economic order varied considerably from country to country. Mexicans developed the most widespread animus against NAFTA, particularly in the countryside where subsidized US corn exports devastated the prospects of small farmers who, in September 2003, congregated by the thousands to protest outside the gates of the WTO ministerial meeting in Cancún. The most dramatic expression of this revolt was the armed rebellion in Chiapas that was symbolically launched on January 1, 1994, the date that NAFTA came into effect. These expressions of resistance revived anti-gringo feeling, limiting popular acceptance of United States' global legitimacy.

Having vented its anxieties in the mid-80s during the first free-trade debate and persuaded by constant media reports of growing trade figures, the Canadian public expressed the least opposition to NAFTA. In counterpoint to Mexican dismay, Canadian approval of NAFTA solidified Canadians' acceptance of the United States' legitimacy, thus extending its soft power.

However articulated in the two peripheral publics' discourses, the new global trade regime represented a substantial redefinition of US power through its deeply intrusive limits on member-state economic policy capacity. It is far less clear how US power was affected following the attacks of September 11, 2001.

The Security State and the War on Terror (2001–)

At first glance, the radical and massive securitization of the American state's domestic political order and the equally massive militarization of its foreign commitments spoke to a reassertion of US power that turned a consensual hegemony into a coercive empire in which other states were labelled as enemies unless they were supporters. Although this picture may be substantially correct for US relations overseas, the complexity of the United States' relationship with its two neighbours requires us to qualify this proposition by distinguishing between security and global defence, whether global or continental.

Continental Security

For Canada and Mexico, the most immediate fallout from the debris of the World Trade Center was the blockade imposed by Washington on its land borders. In its construction of the terrorist threat, the Bush administration was declaring that security trumped trade. But the implications of such a stance were troubling. Pushed to its logical extreme, total security for the United States required economic autarchy, with neither goods nor people crossing its borders.

Clearly, the processes of continental economic, social and cultural integration – which Washington had strengthened and constitutionalized with NAFTA – had created a force that could not be negated from one moment to the next. The US government could easily ignore cries of anguish coming from the other side of its borders. It could not ignore its own auto industry whose sophisticated, just-in-time production processes straddled the three countries, turning any slowdown of commerce at North America's internal borders into instant financial losses. The downside of continental economic hegemony was considerable dependence of the hegemon on unimpeded commercial flows with its peripheries.

Following its refacilitation of border traffic, Washington nevertheless remained determined to enhance its security against future terrorist threats. Even if the nineteen hijackers of September the 11th had not come through Canada – as was originally alleged by New York's junior senator, Hilary Clinton – infiltration across its northern and southern borders by terrorists remained a major concern in Washington. Within a matter of months, 'smart border' agreements had been worked out with Ottawa and Mexico City, committing these capitals to a broad range of new security measures and to the substantial budgetary expense they required.

Taken at face value, these actions suggest a switch from hegemony to empire since Uncle Sam was driving its neighbours to raise their security systems to standards acceptable in Washington. It is true that US officials arriving in Ottawa during the autumn of 2001 to negotiate the strengthening of border measures were suspicious of lax Canadian practices, but they were surprised to find that the Canadians were glad that their interlocutors were finally paying attention to border security. Ottawa was eager to implement various programs and measures, including new high-tech solutions that had been agreed to but then not implemented by the Clinton administration. According to Canadian officials, most of the Smart Border Plan's 30 points announced in December 2001 were made in Ottawa.

At the negotiating table, empire had morphed, but not into community. The coercive pressure that Washington used was access to its market – already exploited as the main bargaining lever to extract economic-policy concessions from its neighbours during the trade-liberalization negotiations but now withdrawn on the grounds of national security in order to extract security-policy concessions. The governments of Canada and Mexico participated in this exercise in empire as interlocutors who also wielded some power. Once the smart-border agreements were signed, Washington depended on its neighbours to implement the agreed-upon policies. Since achieving a continental security perimeter was not possible without Ottawa and Mexico City's active cooperation, the asymmetry in the two capitals' relationship with Washington, for whom the war on terror was the overarching priority, was reduced.

Although the two bilateral relationships remained skewed, the disparity between them diminished. Relations between the Department of Homeland Security's Secretary, Tom Ridge, and his Canadian counterpart, John Manley, were cordial and professional, since the two sides were engaged in what each viewed as a positive-sum game. With Mexico City, tensions were higher once the Bush administration rejected President Vicente Fox's proposals to legalize the status of the millions of undocumented Mexicans working clandestinely and at third-world wages in the American economy. Nevertheless, the large numbers of these 'illegals', whose children born in the United States would become US citizens, along with the many more millions of legally immigrated Mexicans, gave Mexico City soft power in Washington through the Hispanic-American vote. Gulliver's power was constrained by these Spanish-speaking Lilliputians.

Global Defence

The most current and dramatic example of the tension between describing US power as hegemony or empire was presented during the two years following the September 11 attack.

Hegemony When President Bush announced his decision to invade Afghanistan and topple the Taliban government, Secretary of State Colin Powell had little difficulty persuading the rest of the world of the legitimacy of unseating an outcast regime that perpetrated gross violations of human rights and, more important, had harboured and been supported by Osama bin Laden's terrorist organization, Al Qaeda. Although the United States provided the bulk of the military forces for this operation, it had permission to establish bases in neighbouring countries and elicited the active cooperation of many other governments, including that of Canada, which, in February 2002, sent 750 soldiers to fight directly on the ground under American command following the liberation of Kabul.

Empire One year later, the government of Canada refused Washington's request to support the military attack it unleashed on the government of Saddam Hussein. Although Hussein had also tarred himself with human-rights violations, most other governments did not believe the Bush administration's allegation that he had abetted Al Qaeda in its terrorist mission against the United States. Nor was there agreement with the notion that his evident desire for weapons of mass destruction had turned Iraq into such a danger that only pre-emptive attack could forestall its own imminent aggression.

Imposing its own will on the Middle East by force of arms and without the support of the world community, the United States had shifted into imperial mode. Strikingly, despite the peripheries' economic integration and political subordination having been enhanced by NAFTA, Mexico and Canada detracted from US operational legitimacy and refrained from directly buttressing its hard power. Exemplifying its re-entry into the comity of nations, Mexico had won a seat on the UN Security Council where it joined Chile in refusing to concur with Washington's request for the UN to support its invasion.

Canada's dissent was more complex than it generally appeared. At the United Nations, it worked feverishly to broker a deal that could contain the United States. Prime Minister Jean Chrétien even flew to Mexico city to caucus in person with

Vicente Fox and by phone with Eduardo Vargas in order to firm up a coalition of the unwilling in the Security Council. Indirectly, however, Ottawa buttressed the US military effort in Iraq in three substantial ways: it participated in NORAD, which complemented the satellite-based command-and-control system for the United States' war; it sent troops to fight the Taliban in Afghanistan, releasing US soldiers for duty in Iraq; and its navy had units integrated in the US fleet patrolling the Persian Gulf.

Continental Defence

The third dimension of the United States' security reaction to September 11 was its territorial reorganization of continental defence and its renewed push to control planetary defence. The Pentagon's creation of a Northern Command whose remit included Canada, Mexico and the Caribbean reactivated Canada's and Mexico's Cold War responses. Formally prevented by its constitution from any military activity outside its territory, Mexico maintained a disconnection with the new organization, although informal contacts with the Pentagon were quietly nourished.

Caught between public opinion, which disapproved of excessive military cooperation with the Bush administration, and its Department of National Defence, which wanted to take its continental place alongside its senior partners, the Martin government dithered. Making pro-American noises, but deciding against moral or material support for Ballistic Missile Defense, the government maintained a tenuous distinction between rejecting participation in planetary weapons and accepting NORAD's scope being expanded so that it could manage the space-based communications infrastructure for missile defence.

For the general public, the Pentagon's projects smacked of empire. For DND and the Canadian Council of Chief Executives, it was a matter of Canada pulling its weight responsibly within an American hegemony of whose ends they approved and to whose means they felt they made a valuable contribution.

Conclusions

To the extent that US power is a function of (a) hard material resources, (b) soft legitimacy and (c) contextual factors in the global balance of forces, we can see that the North American periphery has played a significant role in (a) boosting or limiting the United States' material resources, (b) supporting or resisting US legitimacy and (c) helping determine the context within which the United States operates. For students of political economy, it is noteworthy that, despite increased levels of continental integration – economic, cultural, demographic – the United States does not appear capable of achieving its Manifest Destiny, a.k.a. imperial control over the whole continent. While business groups continue to support the extension of US hegemony in Mexico and Canada, public perceptions there reject the legitimacy of American imperial projects abroad.

For its part, Washington does not seem intent or able to exert coercive force on Mexico or Canada in order to bend them to its will. Ottawa, for instance, did not pay a severe price for not signing onto the Ballistic Missile Defense program, despite the Bush administration's pressure for it to do so. This suggests that the US potential for empire is quite limited. For their part, Uncle Sam's two peripheral states contribute substantially to a US power whose sway they are on occasion able to restrain, especially when vital world issues are at stake.

Conclusion

Revisiting US Hegemony/Empire

Charles-Philippe David

Little has been resolved in the current profusion of discussion and analysis of empire, and indeed the question of whether the U.S. is, properly speaking, an *empire* or a *hegemon* has barely been broached. Do historic trends suggest that this empire, in its current form, will survive? Can it be compared with the empires of the past? Should the Bush administration be understood as the culmination of a longstanding imperial policy or a passing phase, as a continuation of established U.S. foreign policy or a break with the past?

To analyze the concept of American empire, we must go beyond incidental observation and look at the historic big picture. That is what the contributors to this volume have attempted to do. They approach the question at two levels of analysis: theoretical treatment of the meaning and scope of U.S. hegemony and empirical analysis of concrete aspects of U.S. domination of the international system. Our purpose is not to settle the debate over the nature of American dominance but to explore all its facets and let readers arrive at their own interpretation of the facts.

Empire or Hegemon?

Whether U.S. power can most accurately be described as a case of *empire* or *hegemony* is a question that has given rise to extensive research and lively debate. The idea of American empire, taboo just a few years ago, has become common currency, even within the U.S. intelligentsia,[1] and is now widely used in both academic and political circles. However, the degree to which it is applicable to the role of the U.S. in the world today remains an open question.

The terms in question have specific meanings: *empire* has a territorial dimension and implies control over subjects, while *hegemony* refers to more informal means of persuasion and subjugation of other players in the international arena. Empire is a more realist and military system, while hegemony is more liberal and institutional. The terms are sometimes used interchangeably in contemporary parlance, but despite the semantic confusion there are significant differences between U.S. hegemony as practiced by the Clinton administration and what is often considered Bush's U.S. empire. It is possible, though, that even today the term empire goes too far and we

---

1   See for example Michael Cox, 'The Empire's Back in Town: Or America's Imperial Temptation – Again', *Millennium*, 32/1 (2003): 8.

should speak instead of Michael Cox's 'imperial temptation', or of a new form of empire, an informal empire,[2] a new empire,[3] or an empire by default.[4]

In this respect, the U.S. is a special case: it stands for a specific and distinct idea of empire, which must be understood in context. In the course of its history, it has seized territory, used an arsenal of military, economic and ideological means to reshape the international system, and applied its power of persuasion – its 'soft power' – to influence other states. In short, it has employed all the instruments of domination in every form – so much so that the distinction between empire and hegemony has become blurred, particularly under the Bush administration. It could be argued that the focus on territory and military power in the Bush doctrine signals a return to the traditional idea of empire, propelled by an ideology that pursues imperial designs and espouses direct, unilateral military intervention to control the direction of international events.

But the prophets of doom should bear in mind that the trend is reversible, and indeed the rationale for asserting that a true empire does in fact exist is questionable. It is open to challenge on three grounds. First, the very concept of American empire is now rejected by the majority of Americans, who question the wisdom of trying to exercise direct, territorial control over foreign subjects. Second, U.S. soft power is also limited and in recent years the United States' force of attraction has been coming up against a wall of anti-Americanism in international organizations and in the world in general. Third, supporters of the theory of decline argue that soaring military expenditures are exerting strong pressure on the U.S. economy and could spell trouble for U.S. power in the long term. On this view, the imperial temptation will have a boomerang effect, precipitating the beginning of the end of American might.

Continuity or Rupture?

U.S. hegemony is not a new phenomenon[5] but it seems clear that in abandoning post–Cold War diplomatic practices after September 11,[6] the United States is taking

---

2   John Lewis Gaddis, *We Now Know: Rethinking Cold War History* (Oxford, Oxford University Press, 1997).

3   See the special section edited by Peter Burgess, 'The "New" American Empire' *Security Dialogue*, 35 (June 2004): 227–61.

4   William Odom and Robert Dujarric, *America's Inadvertent Empire* (New Haven, Yale University Press, 2005).

5   See Niall Ferguson, *Empire: How Britain Made the World* (London, Allen Lane, 2003); Andrew Bacevich, *American Empire: The Realities and Consequences of U.S. Diplomacy* (Cambridge, Harvard University Press, 2002); Michael Cox, 'Empire By Denial? Debating US Power', *Security Dialogue*, 35 (June 2004): 228–36; Noam Chomsky, *Hegemony or Survival: America's Quest for Dominance* (New York, Metropolitan Books, 2003).

6   The trend is condemned by Joseph Nye in *The Paradox of American Power: Why the World's Only Superpower Can't Go it Alone* (Oxford, Oxford University Press, 2002); Clyde Prestowitz, *Rogue Nation: American Unilateralism and the Failure of Good Intentions*

a new tack. One school of thought views the new U.S. foreign policy as an extension of the past; another as a break with history. Realists contend that, confronted with an enemy that is forcing it to redeploy and use armed force in order to control the international system, the U.S. has returned to its roots. Post-modern critics suggest that the Bush administration's discourse about 'the enemy' serves as a justification for a military response rooted in appeals to empire and American exceptionalism. In this view, history is linear and the United States' role in the world has developed along lines of continuity. Meanwhile liberals, who believe that spreading democracy and free markets is the cornerstone of U.S. diplomacy, are scrambling to find a logic they can embrace, given the decline of multilateralism under current U.S. policies and the serious rifts in the U.S.–led alliance over Iraq.

The Bush administration's hegemonic policy has been built on three pillars. First, the ideological dimension of the neo-conservative project has exercised considerable influence over the U.S. administration. The 'democratic imperialism' advocated by powerful members of the decision-making circle has impregnated the entire post-September 11 foreign policy-making process, including the decision to invade Iraq, and bent it to neo-conservative objectives. However, the neo-con influence has been in decline in Bush's second term, suggesting that the neo-conservatives were able to take advantage of a combination of circumstances during Bush's first term to so deeply infiltrate the corridors of power. Were it not for September 11 and its unifying effect on right-wing currents within the Republican Party, the neo-con project may well have had less sway over the administration.

Second, the Bush administration has been driven by a determination to act forcefully in the international arena. Its interventionist stance has translated into troops on the ground, first in Afghanistan and then in Iraq, and the doctrinal revolution that led to the adoption of the 'preventive war' strategy. But the pitfalls of waging a lopsided war were neglected. (Typically, empires collapse under the pressure of internal attacks by the 'barbarians'.) Whether it ultimately proves to be a victory or defeat for the U.S., Iraq can be seen as the test case for the current U.S. approach to the exercise of imperial power.

Third, the arrogance of U.S. power reached heights comparable to the early days of the Vietnam War, leading to a build-up of American military capacity, a shunning of public diplomacy, rejection of traditional alliances, contempt for conventional international law and belief in the primacy of American sovereignty. However, during Bush's second term, there has been a real softening of U.S. foreign policy, though it may not have been as dramatic as some critics of the U.S. may have wished.

(New York, Basic Books, 2003); John Newhouse, *Imperial America: The Bush Assault on the World Order* (New York, Vintage Books, 2003); Benjamin Barber, *Fear's Empire: War, Terrorism, and Democracy in an Age of Interdependence* (New York, Norton, 2004).

The Protean Empire

The readiness to apply the word 'empire' to U.S. foreign policy in the recent literature depends on how the term is defined. For example, in *The Imperial Temptation*, Stein Tonnesson argues that the U.S. is not an imperial power in the strict sense of the term and is not likely to become one because empire – a system of formal, territorial control which carries a prohibitive cost – is incompatible with basic American values. However, empire in the broader sense, which is closer to hegemonic influence insofar as it refers more to the capacity to indirectly influence the international system, is more applicable to the U.S., provided it pursues policies that promote the well-being of both Americans and the rest of the international community.[7]

Commentators who presuppose that the U.S. ought to conduct itself as an empire advance different reasons for their view. Members of the realist school such as Ferguson, Kaplan and Boot see it as a matter of historic continuity and argue that the U.S. has a 'duty' to control the international system, taking over from the formal and territorial empires that preceded it.[8] Members of the neo-liberal school such as Ignatieff and Ikenberry support a different type of imperial responsibility, performed more through hegemonic presence.[9] They see it as the function of the empire/hegemon to regulate the international system by using international institutions, salvaging failed states, and securing the cooperation of other nations through persuasion rather than coercion.

Observers who believe the U.S. is in fact an empire disagree about its probable longevity. Lundestad, Gaddis and Ikenberry[10] argue that, given the history of its relationship with Europe, the U.S. is an empire by default or 'by invitation'. On the other hand, Todd,[11] writing from a realist perspective, already foresees the decline of the empire and ultimately its certain death. The empire does not have the necessary resources, economic or military, to maintain itself and continue exporting its social model, while confronting the 'new barbarians'.

---

7   See Stein Tonnesson, 'The Imperial Temptation', *Security Dialogue*, 35/3 (2004): 333.

8   Niall Ferguson, *Colossus: The Price of America's Empire* (New York, Penguin Books, 2004); Robert D. Kaplan, *Warrior Politics: Why Leadership Demands a Pagan Ethos* (New York, Random House, 2002); Max Boot, *The Savage Wars of Peace: Small Wars and the Rise of American Power* (New York, Basic, 2002).

9   Michael Ignatieff, *Empire Lite: Nation-Building in Bosnia, Kosovo and Afghanistan* (London, Vintage, 2003); John Ikenberry, *America Unrivaled: The Future of the Balance of Power* (Ithaca, Cornell University Press, 2002).

10   Geir Lundestad, *The United States and Western Europe Since 1945: From 'Empire' by Invitation to Transatlantic Drift* (Oxford, Oxford University Press, 2003); John Ikenberry, 'Illusions of Empire: Defining the New American Order', *Foreign Affairs*, 83 (September–October 2004): 144–54.

11   Emmanuel Todd, *After the Empire: The Breakdown of the American Order* (New York, Columbia University Press, 2003); Chalmers Johnson, *The Sorrows of Empire: Militarism, Secrecy, and the End of the Republic* (New York, Verso, 2004).

Critics of empire are similarly divided. Michael Mann believes the 'informal' U.S. empire will be incapable of maintaining its hold in the long run since its military power does not rest on firm economic foundations.[12] Therefore, the empire in its current form is not viable and the U.S. will be forced to abandon imperial ambitions. Hardt and Negri make an original post-modern argument to the effect that the U.S. is a global 'de-Americanized' empire, since it dominates international networks of influence without directly controlling territory or other states. They consider the empire to be durable because American imperial policies are gradually being assimilated by other countries, networks and institutions, and imperial discourse is in fact transnational.

Scholars who believe that the U.S. has no imperial vocation likewise disagree about the proper role of the world's most powerful nation. For example, Bacevich castigates the Bush administration for its excesses while Huntington believes the U.S. should concentrate on preserving its cultural identity, which is threatened by the influx of Spanish-speakers.[13] According to Johnson, the bid to conduct an imperial policy that flies in the face of the true aspirations of the American people can only end badly; a nation overcome by the arrogance of power is bound to be brought low by the proliferation of military interventions, the erosion of individual freedoms, the lies told by the political class and, ultimately, economic collapse. Nye, Brzezinski, Kagan and Ikenberry[14] are more optimistic. Their complex analysis concludes that the U.S. is not and should never be an empire, and cannot reasonably go beyond a limited form of hegemony. U.S. foreign policy lacks predictability and cannot be conceived of in terms of imperial 'duty'.

U.S. power has therefore been described in terms of all possible forms of domination, but there is no agreement on its direction or *modus operandi*. The reason for this may be that U.S. foreign policy is not the product of any grand design but rather of fluctuating interactions between political and bureaucratic factors.

Empire and Decision-Making

U.S. power is, first and foremost, the outcome of the interplay between political and bureaucratic perceptions and forces. The constellation of bureaucratic atoms and political electrons is constantly shifting.[15] Consequently, it is difficult to find an overarching purpose in U.S. foreign policy, for it is the result of the combination

---

12   Michael Mann, *Incoherent Empire* (New York, Verso, 2003).

13   Samuel Huntington, *Who Are We? The Challenges to America's National Identity* (New York, Simon and Schuster, 2004).

14   Joseph Nye, *Soft Power: The Means to Success in World Politics* (New York, Public Affairs, 2004); Zbigniew Brzezinski, *The Choice: Global Domination or Global Leadership* (New York, Basic Books, 2004); Robert Kagan, *Paradise and Power: America Versus Europe in the Twenty-first Century* (London, Atlantic Books, 2003).

15   See Valerie Hudson, 'Foreign Policy Analysis: Actor-Specific Theory and the Ground of International Relations,' *Foreign Policy Analysis*, 1 (March 2005): 1–30.

of unpredictable, immediate interests. This is why American foreign policy seems to be riddled with contradictions, constantly swinging back and forth between the 'imperial temptation' and the 'refusal of empire.'

Analyses of the foreign policy-making process point towards two general conclusions. First, the future course of U.S. foreign policy is impossible to predict, just as the nature of American power can hardly be assessed with objectivity. Too many considerations must be factored in (such as the President's character and leadership style, the ideology and perceptions of decision-makers and advisors, organizational factors and bureaucratic infighting, relations between the White House and Congress, the influence of the media, and unpredictable international and domestic events, which can quickly alter the course of foreign policy.) Secondly and consequently, analysis of U.S. foreign policy demands careful observation of the players, the institutions and the decision-making process (which are often neglected by international relations theories).

Whether the current state of unipolar domination is called American empire or U.S. hegemony, it is the outcome of a decision-making *process* more than of objective facts. Regardless of the form of U.S. domination, whether it operates as a traditional or new-type hegemon, whether it develops into a formal empire or not, whether the imperial drive is considered accident or design, each characteristic of U.S. foreign policy and each decision is produced by the intersection of the multiple interests and influences that operate on the closed circle of White House policy-makers and advisors. There, in the inner sanctum of power, where differing perceptions clash with or complement each other, the process is played out and the decisions are made.

So the question of what direction the American empire will take in the future is one that no one can answer, for it is at the juncture of the various currents that run through American society that foreign policy is shaped by the President's advisers. It is not surprising, then, that some observers foresee the empire's decline and some its resurgence. The American empire is shot through by perpetual contradictions defined by the specific features and complexity of the institutions, forces and actors that shape U.S. foreign policy. There can be no single rational, objective explanation for the hegemon's motives and actions. It is at the centre of the decision-making process, shrouded in complexity, that researchers must seek the reasons and ferret out the shifts and constants in American diplomacy.

Index

Bender, Thomas 24
Benin 191, 194
Beschloss, Michael 91
Betts, Richard 78
Beylerian, Onnig 117–34
Biden, Joe 106, 110
bilateral agreements
  Asia 165, 166, 167, 173, 177, 179
  energy policy 192
  trade 67, 211
Bin Laden, Osama 34, 46–7, 58, 90, 119,
    121–2, 215
Biological Weapons Convention 70, 83
Blair, Tony 128n41, 149, 151
Bolton, John 59, 88, 92, 106, 108, 111
Boot, Max 73, 222
Bosnia 38, 60, 90, 157
Boxer, Barbara 110
Bremer, L. Paul III 125
British Empire 5n14, 48, 206, 207
  see also United Kingdom
Brzezinski, Zbigniew 223
Burkina Faso 198, 201
Burma (Myanmar) 170, 177
Burnham, Walter Dean 21
Bush doctrine 12, 13, 33–5, 42–9, 220
Bush, George H.W. 35, 96
Bush, George W. 2, 11, 21, 48
  Afghanistan invasion 205, 215
  Africa 181, 183, 189, 191, 197, 198
  anti-Americanism 138
  approval ratings 89, 92, 101–2, 103,
    108, 109, 111
  Arab-Islamic world 129, 133
  Asia 161
  Congressional resistance to 88, 89,
    105–11
  Congressional support for 87–9, 91, 94,
    95–105, 111–12, 113
  democracy promotion 196
  economic downturn 58–9
  empire 219, 220, 221
  energy policy 192
  Europe-US relations 141, 144, 145, 147,
    153, 160
  homeland security 51–3
  international law 67–8, 70–6, 77–9,
    81–3, 84
  Iraq War 98–9

Millennium Challenge Account 195
Mount Rushmore speech 51–3, 54, 55
national security state 60
neoconservatives 12, 221
preemption doctrine 97–8
reality shaped by Administration 61–3,
    64, 65
religious conception of freedom 197
rhetoric of 81–3
Saudi Arabia relationship 30
strategy 33–4
as threat to benign liberal order 23
war on terror 45–6, 47, 117–18
Buzan, Barry 163, 164
Byrd, Robert C. 98, 99, 101, 102, 113–14

Cambodia 177
Canada 5n14, 204, 205, 217
  CUFTA 211
  economic development 206–8, 209, 210
  military power 208–9
  NAFTA 212, 213
  RIMPAC exercises 166
  security and the war on terror 213–16
  US expansionism 206
Canada-United States Free Trade Agreement
    (CUFTA) 211
capitalism 8, 9, 209
Carter, Jimmy 136
Carter, Ralph G. 93, 95, 102
Castro, Fidel 208
Catley, Bob 79n51
censorship 58
Central Asia 159, 187
Central Intelligence Agency (CIA) 53, 63,
    77, 136
Chad 184, 188
Chaplin, Joyce 5n14
Cheney, Dick 34, 35, 39, 81–2, 95, 108, 190
Chile 166, 205, 215
China 8, 25n12, 30, 151, 165
  acceptance of US hegemony 162
  democracy 129
  economic growth 161, 164, 168, 179
  Japan relations with 170, 172, 173, 174,
    179
  Kyoto Protocol 82
  Northeast Asian security complex 163
  rise of 164, 168–73, 178, 179

Djibouti 189
Dodd, Lawrence C. 104
Dominican Republic 73
Doty, Roxanne 24
al-Douri, Izzat Ibrahim 125
Dowd, Maureen 55
Doyle, Michael 23, 26–7, 28
DPRK *see* Democratic People's Republic
    of Korea
Dratel, Joshua 76
Dueck, Colin 33
Durbin, Dick 107
Duroselle, Jean-Baptiste 141

East Africa Counter-Terrorism Initiative
    (EACTI) 188–9
economic issues
    Bush doctrine 44
    Chinese growth 161, 168, 169, 179
    economic downturn 58–9
    European Union 149
    Greater Middle East Initiative 130
    ignored by PNAC report 41
    Indian growth 161, 164, 168, 178
    North America 206–8, 209–10
    Northeast Asia 163
    South Asia 163–4
    Southeast Asia 164
    US-EU trade 143, 159
    see also neoliberalism; trade
Economic Support Fund (ESF) 189, 198
Edwards, John 11, 77, 101
Egypt 75, 121, 184, 200
empire 6, 53, 203, 219–20, 222–4
    analytical errors 22, 25
    concept of 1, 2
    exceptionalism 22, 221
    Hardt and Negri 60–1
    hegemony distinction 27–8
    Ikenberry 29–30
    lesson of 49
    liberalism 10
    'of liberty' 10, 17
    neoconservatism 12–13
    neoliberal hegemony 15
    North America 214, 215, 217
    race 23
    'of security' 17
    study of 7–9

US political science 23–4
    see also imperialism
energy resources 190–2, 193–4, 195, 204,
    210
    see also oil
entertainment industry 54, 56–7
Eritrea 189
ESF *see* Economic Support Fund
Ethiopia 189
ethnocentrism 45
EUCOM *see* US European Command
Europe 30, 37, 135–60
    anti-Americanism 138–40, 141–2
    decline of US image 136
    differences within 146–7, 148, 149
    diplomatic tensions 144–6
    Greater Middle East Initiative 131
    Iraq War 128
    perception of US hegemony 136, 142–3,
        146–7
    PNAC report 39, 40
    role of the EU 150–1
    trade interests 211
Evans, C. Lawrence 104–5
exceptionalism 2, 5, 10, 22–4, 45, 221
    fractured discourses of 17
    liberal tradition 15
    nationalism 12
    US colonial policy 7
exemplarism 196

'failed states' 31, 177, 197, 199
Feingold, Russ 97, 106, 107, 110–11
Ferguson, Kennan 4
Ferguson, Niall 222
Finland 141
Foreign Military Financing (FMF) program
    189
foreign policy
    Africa 191
    analogical reasoning 186
    Bush doctrine 12, 13, 33–5, 42–9, 220
    coercion 2
    Congress 87–9, 91–5, 101, 102, 109–10,
        112–13
    grand strategy 33
    imperialist turn 1
    international law 67–85

World Trade Organization (WTO) 169, 211, 212–13
Wright, Luke 7
WTO *see* World Trade Organization

Young, Bill 100
Yugoslavia, former 48, 70

al-Zarqawi, Abu Musab 121, 125, 127
al-Zawahiri, Ayman 121
Zegart, Amy 92n19
Zhao Ziyang 169
Zheng Bijian 168
Žižek, Slavoj 58n21